THE ORIGINS OF ATTACHMENT

The Origins of Attachment: Infant Research and Adult Treatment addresses the origins of attachment in mother–infant face-to-face communication. New patterns of relational disturbance in infancy are described. These aspects of communication are out of conscious awareness. They provide clinicians with new ways of thinking about infancy, and about nonverbal communication in adult treatment.

Utilizing an extraordinarily detailed microanalysis of videotaped mother–infant interactions at 4 months, Beatrice Beebe, Frank M. Lachmann, and their research collaborators provide a more fine-grained and precise description of the process of attachment formation. Second-by-second microanalysis operates like a social microscope and reveals more than can be grasped by the naked eye.

The book explores how, alongside linguistic content, the bodily aspect of communication is an essential component of the capacity to communicate and understand emotion. The moment-to-moment self- and interactive processes of relatedness documented in infant research form the bedrock of adult face-to-face communication and provide the background fabric for the verbal narrative in the foreground.

The Origins of Attachment is illustrated throughout with several case vignettes of adult treatment. Discussions by Carolyn S. Clement, Malcolm Owen Slavin, E. Joyce Klein, Estelle Shane, Alexandra Harrison, and Stephen Seligman show how the research can be used by practicing clinicians. This book details aspects of bodily communication between mothers and infants that will provide useful analogies for therapists of adults. It will be essential reading for psychoanalysts, psychotherapists, and graduate students.

Beatrice Beebe is Clinical Professor of Medical Psychology (in Psychiatry), College of Physicians and Surgeons, Columbia University, New York State Psychiatric Institute; faculty at the Columbia Psychoanalytic Center, the Institute for the Psychoanalytic Study of Subjectivity, and the New York University Postdoctoral Program in Psychotherapy and Psychoanalysis.

Frank M. Lachmann is a teacher, supervisor, and a member of the Founding Faculty of the Institute for the Psychoanalytic Study of Subjectivity, New York; and a Clinical Assistant Professor, New York University Postdoctoral Program in Psychotherapy and Psychoanalysis.

THE ORIGINS OF ATTACHMENT

Infant Research and Adult Treatment

Beatrice Beebe and Frank M. Lachmann

Collaborators:
Joseph Jaffe, Sara Markese, Karen A. Buck,
Henian Chen, Patricia Cohen, Lorraine Bahrick,
Howard Andrews, and Stanley Feldstein

Discussants:
Carolyn S. Clement, Malcolm Owen Slavin,
E. Joyce Klein, Estelle Shane, Alexandra Harrison,
and Stephen Seligman

Routledge
Taylor & Francis Group

NEW YORK AND LONDON

First published 2014
by Routledge
711 Third Avenue, New York, NY 10017

and by Routledge
27 Church Road, Hove, East Sussex BN3 2FA

Routledge is an imprint of the Taylor & Francis Group, an informa business

© 2014 Taylor & Francis

Library of Congress Cataloging in Publication Data
Beebe, Beatrice, 1946–
    The origins of attachment : infant research and adult treatment /
    Beatrice Beebe and Frank M. Lachmann.
    pages cm
    1. Attachment behavior in children.
    2. Infants—Care—Psychological aspects.
    3. Mother and infant—Psychological aspects.
    4. Nonverbal communication in infants. I. Lachmann, Frank M. II. Title.
    RJ507.A77B433 2014
    618.92'8588—dc23
    2013022801

ISBN: 978-0-415-89817-1 (hbk)
ISBN: 978-0-415-89818-8 (pbk)
ISBN: 978-1-315-85806-7 (ebk)

Typeset in Times New Roman
by Swales & Willis Ltd, Exeter, Devon, UK

TO JOSEPH JAFFE AND DANIEL STERN,
IN MEMORIAM

TO ANNETTE, SUZANNE, AND
PETER LACHMANN

CONTENTS

CONTENTS

FIGURES

ABOUT THE AUTHORS

Beatrice Beebe, Ph.D., is Clinical Professor of Medical Psychology (in Psychiatry), College of Physicians and Surgeons, Columbia University; Communication Sciences Laboratory, Department of Child and Adolescent Psychiatry, New York State Psychiatric Institute; faculty, Columbia Psychoanalytic Center, Institute for the Psychoanalytic Study of Subjectivity, and New York University Postdoctoral Program in Psychotherapy and Psychoanalysis.

Frank M. Lachmann, Ph.D., is a member of the Founding Faculty of the Institute for the Psychoanalytic Study of Subjectivity, New York, teacher and supervisor; Clinical Assistant Professor, New York University Postdoctoral Program in Psychotherapy and Psychoanalysis.

Howard Andrews, Ph.D., is Associate Clinical Professor of Neuroscience (in Biostatistics), Mailman School of Public Health, Columbia University; Associate Clinical Professor of Neuroscience (in Psychiatry), College of Physicians and Surgeons, Columbia University.

Lorraine Bahrick, Ph.D., is Professor, Department of Psychology, Florida International University; Director, Infant Development Laboratory.

Karen A. Buck, M.A., is a statistician collaborating with Dr. Beebe, Communication Sciences Lab, Department of Child and Adolescent Psychiatry, New York State Psychiatric Institute.

Henian Chen, M.D., Ph.D., is Associate Professor of Biostatistics, Department of Epidemiology and Biostatistics, and the Director of the Biostatistics Core at the Clinical and Translational Science Institute, University of South Florida, College of Public Health.

Carolyn S. Clement, Ph.D., is faculty and supervisor, NYU Postdoctoral Program in Psychoanalysis and Psychotherapy, formerly Co-Chair of the Relational Track of the NYU Postdoctoral Program, and Associate Editor of *Psychoanalytic Dialogues*.

Patricia Cohen, Ph.D., is Professor of Epidemiology in Psychiatry, College of Physicians and Surgeons, Columbia University; Senior Research Scientist, New York State Psychiatric Institute.

Stanley Feldstein, Ph.D., is a collaborator with the Communication Sciences Lab, New York State Psychiatric Institute; Professor Emeritus of Psychology, University of Maryland, Baltimore County.

Alexandra Harrison, M.D., is a training and supervising analyst in Adult, Child and Adolescent Psychoanalysis, Boston Psychoanalytic Society and Institute; Assistant Clinical Professor in Psychiatry at the Harvard Medical School, Cambridge Health Alliance; and Core Faculty of the Parent–Infant Mental Health Certificate Program, University of Massachusetts, Boston.

Joseph Jaffe, M.D. (deceased), was Professor of Clinical Psychiatry (in Neurological Surgery), Columbia University; Communication Sciences Lab, Department of Child and Adolescent Psychiatry, New York State Psychiatric Institute.

E. Joyce Klein, LICSW, is a graduate of the Massachusetts Institute of Psychoanalysis and of the Advanced Training Program in Psychoanalytic Psychotherapy, Boston Psychoanalytic Society and Institute. She is in private practice in Cambridge, MA.

Sara Markese, Ph.D., is a clinical psychologist specializing in early childhood psychotherapy, in her private practice in Fairfax, Virginia (Therapy at the Square), and in a group practice in Reston, Virginia (Family Compass). She is a research collaborator with Dr. Beebe, Department of Child and Adolescent Psychiatry, New York State Psychiatric Institute, Columbia University.

Stephen Seligman, Ph.D., is Clinical Professor of Psychiatry at the Infant–Parent Program, University of California, San Francisco; Training and Supervising Analyst, San Francisco Center for Psychoanalysis and Psychoanalytic Institute of Northern California; and Joint Editor-in-Chief of *Psychoanalytic Dialogues*.

Estelle Shane, Ph.D., is a founding member, past president, training and supervising analyst and faculty at the Institute of Contemporary Psychoanalysis, Los Angeles. She is training and supervising analyst and faculty at the New Center for Psychoanalysis. She is on the faculty of the University of California at Los Angeles Department of Psychiatry and is on the editorial boards of several psychoanalytic publications.

Malcolm Owen Slavin, Ph.D., is a founder and past president of the Massachusetts Institute for Psychoanalysis. He teaches and supervises at many psychoanalytic institutes worldwide and is an editor for *Psychoanalytic Dialogues, Contemporary Psychoanalysis* and the *International Journal of Psychoanalytic Self Psychology*.

PREFACE

This book addresses the origins of attachment in mother–infant face-to-face communication and its implications for adult treatment. Mother–infant communication provides the foundation for emotional development from infancy through young adulthood. In this book we use microanalysis of videotaped interactions to show how mothers and infants co-create subtle and complex patterns of relatedness during face-to-face communication at 4 months. We document how these patterns lead to styles of secure, resistant, and disorganized attachment when the infant is one year old. Remarkably, several research teams have documented that styles of attachment at one year predict the organization of experience in young adulthood. Thus face-to-face communication between mother and infant at 4 months is a foundational process with a trajectory into adulthood.

Our research provides clinicians with a new look into the origins of relatedness in infancy and the nature of mother–infant communication disturbances. The new relational configurations in infancy that we discovered are relevant not only to infant attachment at 12 months, but also to the trajectory into adulthood. Moreover, patterns of relatedness that we document between mother and infant provide parallels and analogies for patient–therapist face-to-face interactions in the adult treatment setting.

We use the term communication in two senses. One refers to the linguistic content of messages, including wishes and fantasies, which is directly relevant to adult treatment. The second refers to the way communication has most often been studied in infant social interactions, "...a framing of the interaction—a 'getting into sync'—that involves a process in which persons act in ways that are responsive to the actions of those with whom they are in communication" (Bloom, 1993, p. 84). This aspect of communication is usually out of awareness. It conveys the affective quality of the relationship through such patterns as eye contact, body and head orientation, facial expression, vocal rhythm coordination of speech sounds and silences, hand gestures and touch. We refer to this aspect of communication as implicit and procedural.

Although psychoanalysis tends to focus on the linguistic content of communication, it is now increasingly understood that the bodily or implicit aspect of communication is not only necessary for communication with language (Bloom,

1983), but it is an essential component of the very capacity to communicate and understand emotion (Bucci, 2011; Hennelenlotter et al., 2008; Oberman, Winkielman, & Ramachandran, 2007). Moreover, as Trevarthen (1998) argues, communicative competence is prelinguistic and begins at birth. Linguistic forms of communication and intersubjectivity have their foundation in prelinguistic forms.

Part I introduces the research to clinicians interested in development, face-to-face communication, and attachment. We provide a frame that will facilitate the reading of the research. We also address the relevance of our findings for adult treatment with several clinical vignettes. Part II presents the research findings in a narrative and accessible format. Our goal is to make our research available to clinicians. Part II concludes with a general discussion of the relevance of our research to adult treatment. In Part III we invite several psychoanalysts to comment on ways that our infant research findings on the origins of disorganized attachment are informative to practicing child and adult clinicians: Carolyn S. Clement, Malcolm Owen Slavin, E. Joyce Klein, Estelle Shane, Alexandra Harrison, and Stephen Seligman.

Research on mother–infant communication might seem very far from the clinician's day-to-day concerns in the practice of adult treatment. But in fact, the moment-to-moment self- and interactive processes of relatedness documented in infant research are the bedrock of adult face-to-face communication as well. They provide the background fabric for the verbal narrative that is in the foreground.

These moment-to-moment processes are rapid, subtle, co-constructed, and generally out of awareness. And yet they profoundly affect moment-to-moment communication and the affective climate in adult treatment, organizing modes of relating. The collaborative participation of the analyst in this process is an essential, but little-explored arena. As Lyons-Ruth (1999) argues, critical aspects of therapeutic action occur in this implicit, procedural mode which may never be verbalized, and yet powerfully organize the treatment.

ACKNOWLEDGEMENTS

As we, Beatrice Beebe and Frank Lachmann, attempt to integrate our research on the origins of attachment with its relevance for adult treatment, we are poised between two worlds. We are grateful to our colleagues and students in both infant research and psychoanalysis.

In the course of the two decades since this research was initiated in 1992, we have many people to thank. First we are grateful to the mothers and infants who so generously participated in this research. Beatrice Beebe thanks New York State Psychiatric Institute (NYSPI), where the Communication Sciences Laboratory is housed; Bradley Peterson of NYSPI for his inspirational leadership and support of this project; Michael Myers of NYSPI for his support of our research program; and Eric Marcus of the Columbia Psychoanalytic Center for his support of our research for almost four decades.

As this book goes to press we mourn the passing of Joseph Jaffe, August, 2012, and Daniel Stern, November, 2012. Joe Jaffe and Beatrice Beebe were close research colleagues from 1969 to 2012; they ran the Communication Sciences Lab together from 1992 to 2012. Jaffe's thinking inspired the "dyadic systems view." Daniel Stern inspired Beatrice Beebe with a love for the intricate process of mother–infant moment-to-moment communication. Beatrice Beebe worked with Dan Stern at NYSPI from 1969 to 1975, which included her Ph.D. dissertation and postdoctoral fellowship.

We thank the psychoanalytic communities who have encouraged our work on the relevance of infant research for adult treatment: for both of us, the New York University Postdoctoral Program in Psychotherapy and Psychoanalysis and the Institute for the Psychoanalytic Study of Subjectivity. We thank for Beatrice Beebe the Columbia Psychoanalytic Center, and for Frank Lachmann the Postgraduate Center.

Beatrice Beebe thanks her research colleagues who have contributed so much to this research program: Stanley Feldstein, Jeffrey Cohn, Daniel Messinger, Edward Tronick, Amie Hane, Amy Margolis, Cynthia Crown, and Michael Jasnow.

We are very grateful to John Kerr, our in-house editor and an extraordinary colleague, friend and mentor during this journey. We thank Kristopher Spring, our first editor for this book, and Kate Hawes, our editor at Routledge, for her generosity and patience.

We thank Aviva Irwin for her thoughtful, careful shepherding of this manuscript; Hope Igleheart for her continuous involvement in the research and her support and careful reading of the manuscript; Estelle Shane, who helped translate the original research findings into experience-near concepts; and Lin Reicher for her inspiration, her ability to translate the research into the treatment situation, and her extensive consultations on the manuscript. We thank Howard Steele for his generous collaboration on this project in the original publication of this research in his journal, *Attachment and Human Development,* 2010. We thank John Burke and William Hohauser of ESPY TV for their video expertise and their dedication to our filming lab and our research over the past three decades.

We thank Elizabeth Carlson who coded the Ainsworth Strange Situation videotapes and made an important contribution to the study; Mary Sue Moore, who taught us the most about what attachment means; Karlen Lyons-Ruth, Jude Cassidy, and Mary Sue Moore for their extensive work on the interpretation of results; George Downing, Alexandra Harrison, Dan Siegel, Doris Silverman, Anni Bergman, Steven Knoblauch, Jean Knox and Carol Munter, for their consultations on the manuscript. We thank Dolores, for her generosity and collaboration in this work. We thank Larry Sandberg, "Dr. S," for his extraordinary collaboration in the work with Sandra, and we thank Sandra.

We thank our discussants in this book who generously worked with the implications of our findings on the origins of disorganized attachment for adult and child treatment: Carolyn S. Clement, Mal Slavin, Joyce Klein, Estelle Shane, Alexandra Harrison, and Stephen Seligman.

This research could never have happened without the remarkable dedication of the students who filmed and coded these mother–infant interactions. We thank Lisa Marquette, Caroline Flaster, Patricia Goodman, Jill Putterman, Limor Kaufman-Balamuth, Elizabeth Helbraun and Shanee Stepakoff, who filmed the mothers and infants from 1992 to 1997. We thank Lisa Marquette, Elizabeth Helbraun, Michaela Hager-Budny, Shanee Stepakoff, Jane Roth, Donna Demetri-Friedman, Sandra Triggs-Kano, Greg Kushnick, Helen Demetriades, Allyson Hentel, Tammy Kaminer and Lauren Ellman, who coded the mother–infant interactions, second-by-second, over a 10-year period, 1993–2003.

This research could not have flowered without the dedication of a brilliant statistical team: Patricia Cohen, Karen Buck, Henian Chen, Howard Andrews, Sanghan Lee, and Don Ross. This generous group translated our 19,800 seconds of data of mother–infant behaviors at 4 months into our measures of behavioral qualities, and self- and interactive contingency, which predicted attachment outcomes.

We tried to understand our findings by creating short video demos and frame-by-frame analyses which illustrated the results. We thank Kari Gray and Jennifer Lyne, former film-makers turning psychologists, for creating these illustrations. We thank J.T. Yost who created "cartoon" illustrations based on these frame by frame analyses, which protected the confidentiality of the mothers.

As the research went to press in its original publication in *Attachment and Human Development*, many lab assistants participated. We thank Alla Chavarga,

Alina Pavlakos, Julia Reuben, and Robbie Ross, who finalized the manuscript; Nidhi Parashar, our research coordinator; Kate Lieberman and Brianna Hailey, our lab coordinators; Kara Levin, Adrianne Lange, Joseph McGowan, Sarah Miller, and Lauren Cooper who participated in editing; and Matthew Kirkpatrick, Max Malitzky, and Helen Weng.

We thank our students and colleagues who contributed in many ways over the two decades as this work was generated: Michael Ritter, Anni Bergman, Sara Hahn-Burke, Nancy Freeman, Donna Demetri Friedman, Rachel Altstein, Jennifer Lyne, Glenn Bromley, Robert Gallagher, Naomi Cohen, Alan Phelan, Danielle Phelan, Paulette Landesman, Tina Lupi, Irena Milentevic, Marina Koulomzin, Jeri Kronen, Jillian Miller, Rhonda Davis, Victoria Garel, Leslie Michael, Stephen Ruffins, Jessica Silverman, Kristen Kelly, Sarah Temech, Priscilla Caldwell, Elizabeth White, Yana Kuchirko, Greer Raggio, Jessica Latack, Sara Schilling, Michael Klein, Annee Ackerman, Sam Marcus, Iskra Smiljanic, Jenny Lotterman, Gena Bresgi, Ali Pivar, Christy Meyer, Emily Brodie, Sandy Seal, Claudia Andrei, Nina Finkel, Adrienne Lapidous, Nicholas Seivert, Linda Rindlaub, Abby Herzig, Sonya Sonpal, Imran Khan, Julia Disenko, Michelle Lee, Hwe Sze Lim, Marina Tasopoulous, Emlyn Capili, Jessica Sarnicola, Nancy Richardson, Nicole Selzer, Heather Chan, Eunice Lee, and Catherine Man.

For their thoughtful contributions on the treatment implications of this work, we thank the members of The Eastern Division, International Association of Psychoanalytic Self Psychology; the 8-Lecture A study group, Galit Atlas-Koch, Elizabeth Cramer, Gloria Demby, Leslie Gibson, Ruth Graver, Hope Igleheart, Jane Kupersmidt, Carol Munter, Sonia Orenstein, Lisa Piazza, Andrea Remez, Luz Towns-Miranda; and the members of the Monday afternoon study group: Francoise Jaffe, Priscilla Lincoln, Thomas Wagner, Tamar Erez, Abby Hertzig, Kristin Long, Stephanie Vanden Bos, Susan Richenthal, Alice Rosenman, Hillary Mayers, Marie Sacco, Lynn Stoller, Mark Sturgeon, Pamela Allon.

We thank the members of Dr. Beebe's Ph.D. seminar: Michael Ritter, Adrianne Lange, Jennifer Lyne, Robert Galligan, Glen Bromley, Naomi Cohen, Amy Reale, Liliya Endres, Yelena Bromberg, Robin Herbst.

As this book goes to press, we thank the research assistants who currently make everything possible: Claire Jaffe, Dan Friedman, Aviva Irwin, Mirella Brusanni, Sara Van Hoose, Meghan Loeser, Dan Vigliano, Kristin Schutz, Kaitlin Walsh, Maeva Schlienger, Daisy Bear, Zachary Neumann, Jane Roth, Caroline Kazlow. We mourn the passing of Ella Bandes, talented at mathematics, dance, painting, and life.

In our previous publication, *Rhythms of Dialogue in Infancy* (Jaffe, Beebe, Feldstein, Crown, & Jasnow, 2001), Mary Sue Moore and Rebecca Warner were regretfully inadvertently omitted from the acknowledgements.

This work was funded by grants from NIMH RO1 MH56130, the Koehler Foundation, the American Psychoanalytic Association, the Edward Aldwell Fund, the Bernard and Esther Besner Infant Research Fund, the Los Angeles Fund for Infant Research and Psychoanalysis (Beatrice Beebe); and in part by grants from the National Science Foundation (SBE 0350201) and the National Institute of Child

Health and Human Development (RO1 HD 053776) (Lorraine Bahrick).

Permissions

Portions of Chapters 5 to 7 and the Appendix were originally published by Beebe, Jaffe, Markese, Buck, Chen, Cohen, Bahrick, Andrews and Feldsten (2010), *Attachment & Human Development, 12* (1–2), 3–141, entitled, "The origins of 12-month attachment: A microanalysis of 4-month mother–infant interaction." Sections of this work are reprinted with permission from the Journal (http://www.tandfonline.com/doi/full/10.1080/14616730903338985).

Part I

MOTHER–INFANT COMMUNICATION AND ADULT TREATMENT

1

THE ORIGINS OF RELATEDNESS
Film Illustrations

In this chapter we invite you into our mother–infant filming lab to "watch" several films of mother–infant face-to-face interaction at 4 months. We describe two mother–infant dyads who will be classified as securely attached at 1 year. One illustrates a pattern of "facial mirroring," and one a pattern of "disruption and repair." We then present a pair at 4 months who will be classified as exhibiting disorganized attachment at 1 year. Based on these films and our findings, we infer what mothers and infants might come to expect in their interactions. The expectancies of dyads on the way to secure attachment, compared to disorganized attachment, are strikingly different. In the following chapter we discuss how infants come to represent their social experiences at this early age.

Microanalysis reveals subtle, split-second events that are often not visible with the naked eye in real time. It is this "subterranean" level of communication that our research reveals. This level of detail generated new findings on the origins of communication disturbances in infancy. And it is this split-second level of communication which may powerfully inform adult treatment. These moment-to-moment processes are rapid, subtle, co-created by both mother and infant, and generally out of awareness. Nevertheless they continue to influence how we act and feel, from infancy to adulthood. They profoundly affect moment-to-moment communication and the affective climate, organizing different modes of relating.

The mother–infant "action–dialogue" generates infant and maternal expectancies of how action and interaction sequences unfold from moment-to-moment, within the self, within the partner, and between the self and the partner. The films that we describe illustrate how strikingly different expectancies are created, as these patterns repeat over time and form generalized action-sequence (procedural) memories. These expectancies involve anticipation of what will happen, as well as memories of what has generally happened in the past (Haith, Hazan, & Goodman, 1988). Expectancies refer to the same process that Stern (1985) terms RIGs: representations of interactions generalized, or Bucci (2011) terms emotion schemas.

In our descriptions below we attempt to translate the action–dialogue language into words in an effort to facilitate our understanding of these action sequences. However, we do not imply that as infants develop, these patterns are actually translated into a linguistic format. We assume that early infant expectancies are encoded in a nonverbal, imagistic, acoustic, visceral, or temporal mode of information, and that they may not necessarily be translated into linguistic form (see Bucci, 1985, 1997).

Four-Month Face-to-Face Communication and 12-Month Attachment

In the section below we describe the interactions of two "future" secure dyads and one "future" disorganized attachment dyad. We term them "future" because the 4-month infant cannot be classified for attachment until 12 months. In the Ainsworth separation–reunion paradigm used to assess attachment, infants must be old enough to crawl or walk toward and away from the mother as she leaves and returns (Ainsworth, Blehar, Waters, & Wall, 1978). As we look at these dyads at 4 months, we know what the 12-month attachment outcome will be, but that is still in their future.

To understand these films, we first review how we film 4-month face-to-face play, and how the 12-month Ainsworth attachment assessment is conducted. Based on this assessment, infants are classified as secure or insecure (avoidant, resistant, and disorganized). In this chapter we illustrate dyads at 4 months who are on the way to secure, and to disorganized, attachment.

Four-Month Face-to-Face Communication

When infants are 4 months old we invite mothers and infants to our laboratory. We film them as they interact face-to-face. The infant is in an infant seat, and the mother is seated opposite. The mother is instructed to play with her infant as she would at home, but without toys. One camera is focused on the mother's face and hands, and one camera on the infant's face and hands. The two cameras generate a split-screen view, so that both partners can be seen at the same time. The mother and the infant are left alone in the filming chamber to play for 5–10 minutes.

We then painstakingly code 2½ minutes of each mother–infant film second-by-second, a "microanalysis." It took 10 years to obtain the data we used in the research in this book. Twelve devoted doctoral students coded the films across this period (see Acknowledgements).

Face-to-face communication in the early months of life sets the trajectory for patterns of relatedness as they develop over the lifetime. Face-to-face communication elicits the infant's most advanced communication capacities. Its importance for social and cognitive development is widely recognized (Beebe & Lachmann, 2002; Feldman, 2007; Field, 1995; Jaffe, Beebe, Feldstein, Crown, & Jasnow, 2001; Stern, 1985; Malatesta, Culver, Tesman, & Shepard, 1989; Messinger, 2002; Fogel, 1992; Tronick 1989).

This research has documented that mother–infant interaction is a continuous, reciprocally coordinated process, co-created moment-to-moment by both partners. Each partner affects the behavior of the other, often in split-seconds (Beebe, 1982; Beebe & Stern, 1977; Stern, 1971), but not necessarily in similar, symmetrical, or equal ways. We have termed our approach to mother–infant face-to-face communication a "dyadic systems" approach (Beebe, Jaffe, & Lachmann, 1992; Jaffe et al., 2001; Beebe & Lachmann, 2003; Beebe, Knoblauch, Rustin, & Sorter, 2005).

The dyadic system is defined by the ways that both mother and infant co-create their face-to-face communication. The infant is an active contributor, having a remarkable range of engagement as well as disengagement behaviors (Beebe & Stern, 1977; Brazelton, Koslowski, & Main, 1974; Stern, 1971, 1985; Murray & Trevarthen, 1985). Processes of self-regulation and interactive regulation go on simultaneously within each partner. Each person monitors and coordinates with the partner, and at the same time regulates his or her own inner state. In this view all interactions are a simultaneous product of self- and interactive processes (Gianino & Tronick, 1988; Sander, 1977; Thomas & Martin, 1976; Tronick, 1989). In the process each partner develops expectancies of "how I affect you," and "how you affect me." Each also develops expectancies of how one's own self-regulation processes unfold.

The 4-month face-to-face paradigm is organized around play, with no other goal than mutual enjoyment (Stern, 1985). In contrast, the attachment paradigm taps fear by assessing how the infant manages the threat of separation and the process of reunion (Cassidy, 1994; Sroufe, Egeland, Carlson, & Collins, 2005; Steele & Steele, 2008). Thus we bring together two different research paradigms which assess different motivational systems. Ainsworth herself believed, as do we, that the two research paradigms are likely to inform one another (Blehar, Lieberman, & Ainsworth, 1977).

Attachment Assessed at 12 Months

In our laboratory, at 12 months mothers and infants take part in the Ainsworth separation–reunion paradigm, termed the Strange Situation (Ainsworth et al., 1978). The extent to which the infant uses the parent as a secure base from which to explore, and as a safe haven when distressed, is central to the coding of attachment types.

Mother and infant participate in 3-minute periods of play, separation, and reunion. The sequence is then repeated a second time. In the first separation the infant remains with a "stranger," a trained graduate student; in the second the infant is alone. These 3-minute separations are cut short if the infant becomes too distressed. Infants are classified as having a secure or insecure (avoidant, resistant, or disorganized) attachment style based on the infant's reactions in the reunion episodes.

In the reunion episodes the *secure* infant can easily be comforted, using the mother as a secure base, and then return to play. The insecure-*avoidant* infant shows little distress at separation, avoids the mother at reunion, and continues to play on his own. The insecure-*resistant* infant is very distressed at separation, but cannot be comforted by the mother's return and does not easily return to play.

In the reunion episodes, the *disorganized* infant simultaneously approaches and avoids the mother. For example the infant may open the door for her but then sharply ignore her. Disorganized infants may show incomplete movements and expressions, simultaneous displays of contradictory approach and avoidance patterns, confusion and apprehension, and momentary behavioral stilling. For example, these infants may reach their hands out toward the mother as she enters, but at the same time back up. Or the infant may cling to the mother, but cry with face averted.

These behaviors of infant disorganized attachment reflect a breakdown in behavioral organization under the stress of the heightened activation of the attachment system following separation (Main & Solomon, 1990; Solomon & George, 1999). The child does not have a coherent strategy for dealing with the stress of the separation. Threat and distress do not subside once the mother returns. Unlike the secure infant, the disorganized infant does not return to exploring the environment and the toys. Studies of the mothers of disorganized infants have revealed that these mothers usually have a history of unresolved loss, mourning, or abuse (Lyons-Ruth, Bronfman, & Parsons, 1999; Main & Hesse, 1990). Thus, in the film description below of the 4-month "future" disorganized attachment dyad, although it is easier to feel for the infant, it is important to have empathy for the mother as well.

Using global assessments and clinical ratings, over 60 studies have shown that the security of the child's attachment to the parent is dependent on maternal emotional sensitivity (De Wolff & van Ijzendoorn, 1997). Sensitivity involves alertness to infant signals, appropriateness and promptness of response, and capacity to negotiate conflicting goals (Ainsworth et al., 1978). Such maternal sensitivity tends to promote a secure relationship in which the infant can use the mother as a base both for protection and nurturance as well as for exploration of the environment. The insecurely attached infant, on the other hand, spends either too much or too little time in proximity to the mother or in exploring the environment. The balance between attachment and exploration is thereby upset.

However, as important as parental sensitivity is, it does not robustly predict disorganized attachment. Our detailed second-by-second microanalysis of mother–infant communication at four months reported in this book contributes to filling this gap. Far fewer studies have examined the origins of attachment with microanalytic methods (see Beebe et al., 2010, for a review).

Descriptions of Films of 4-Month Mother–Infant Interactions: "Future" Secure and "Future" Disorganized Dyads

We now turn to descriptions of several mother–infant interactions at 4 months. The microanalyses enable us to see the subtle and rapid details of these interactions. As you "view" the films, keep in mind that the infant is developing "expectancies" of these action and interaction sequences (see Chapter 2). As these microprocesses are repeated over and over, the infant develops an *anticipation* of how the pattern will proceed. The examples of two future secure attachment dyads, compared to a future disorganized attachment dyad, illustrate how strikingly different patterns of infant expectancies are created.

The recurrent nature of the infant's experiences generates expectancies of how each individual's behaviors affect the partner's behaviors, as well as affect his or her own behaviors, across time. This procedural dimension of face-to-face communication is also known as "implicit relational knowing" (Lyons-Ruth, 1999), "emotion schemas" (Bucci, 1997, 2011), and "working models" by attachment researchers. These self- and interactive processes generate patterns that the infant comes to recognize, remember, and expect. They organize procedural, presymbolic representations of self and others that influence the trajectory of the infant's emotional experiences throughout development (see Chapter 2).

Attachment researchers argue that these representations or models provide one process by which patterns of intimate relating and attachment are constructed. Lyons-Ruth (1999, 2008) proposes that patterns of knowing the partner, and being known by the partner, are constructed through expectancies of how these early interactions go. As we will see in Chapter 4, for infants on the way to disorganized attachment, these expectancies of how early interactions go generate a trajectory in development that predicts young adult outcomes including dissociation. In the adult treatment situation, these expectancies may be in the background as "shadows" of early communication disturbances.

However, we still do not understand the details of these representations in infancy, how they are mutually constructed by mother and infant, and how they predict attachment outcomes. Despite many studies of maternal "sensitivity," very little work has attempted detailed second-by-second study of these early patterns. That is, what are the interactive details of "maternal sensitivity"? And what is the infant's role? This was a key motivation for our study.

In our descriptions of the films below, we first provide a description of a section of the film based on viewing it in real time. This description might fit what you, as the viewer, would see while watching the film with the naked eye.

We then provide a second-by-second microanalysis of this same section of the film. This process slows down the communication into Stern's "split-second world" (1971, 1977; Beebe, 1982; Beebe & Stern, 1977). This level of viewing reveals what is lost to the naked eye in real time. It reveals the moment-by-moment negotiation of attention, emotion, orientation, and touch. It reveals the subtle "mis-steps" in the dance, momentary expressions of sadness or disappointment in the mother's face, or a subtle infant grimace. It also reveals moments of mother and infant simultaneously rising into joyous smiles, or repair moments when the hands of both mother and infant reach for the other in the same instant. The microanalysis generates the data of our study. Because of this microanalysis, we are seeing aspects of interactions that have not been documented before. This is one of the key new features of our study.

Microanalysis is performed by shifting back and forth across 2 seconds. Thus it becomes possible to see the movement and change from one second to the next. In the microanalysis sections we annotate the second by a change from one second to the next. For example, "second 33 to 34," indicates that we are describing any changes that begin in second 33, that are now visible in second 34. We note that the vocal channel is lost when examining the film second-by-second.

7

BEATRICE BEEBE AND FRANK M. LACHMANN

"Facial Mirroring:" Film Illustration of a Future Secure Dyad at 4 Months

To illustrate examples of secure attachment, we describe brief sections of two films of 4-month mother–infant interactions where the infants were classified as securely attached at 12 months: "facial mirroring" and "disruption and repair."

Real-Time Video Description of Facial Mirroring: 18 seconds

This film illustrates a sensitive mutual "facial mirroring" process. Because we describe the minute details of the interaction, this description will take some time.

The film section opens with the mother and her infant gazing at each other, as the mother swings her infant's right-hand fingers with her left hand, and says enthusiastically, "We're going to sing, right?" The infant holds mother's swinging finger with his right hand, while his left hand moves slightly in rhythm with his mother's finger. As the mother begins to sing, the infant smiles and briefly vocalizes. The infant continues to smile as mother sings; the infant's feet move slightly. Mother moves her head forward and back, and then forward at the end of the song.

At this moment the infant's smile sobers to a closed mouth, his head moves down, and he looks down, breaking eye-contact with mother. (The infant's gaze away is a form of self-regulation which facilitates infant down-regulation of arousal; Field, 1981). These infant movements are synchronized with the rhythm of mother's final words of her song: "You, you, you, you, you." The mother looks down at the infant's belly and pokes it gently. The infant then looks back at his mother and both make eye-contact.

The mother now gently takes her infant's hands and puts them together as she leans in; simultaneously the infant's open mouth turns into a smile. Mother then raises her infant's arms and moves them out wide as she says: "Sooooooo big!" The infant wiggles his feet and opens his mouth, as the mother's mouth also widens. Both then move their heads up and open their mouths fully, emerging into big open-mouth "gape" smiles. A gape smile indicates the height of the smile display, with a fully opened mouth accompanying the smile.

Second-by-Second Microanalysis Description of Facial Mirroring

We describe a 5-second section, followed by a 10-second break in the film, and then an 11-second section. This description will take some time; there is a great deal happening once the film is slowed down.

Second 33: Mother and infant gaze at each other. They approximately match facial expressions. Each has a partially open mouth, with a hint of widening. As the infant holds his mother's finger with his right hand, the mother swings this hand. The infant's free left hand moves, synchronized with his mother's finger movement.

8

Second 33 to 34: Mutual gaze continues. The mother's mouth opens wide, corners partially widened, in a partial gape smile. Mother and infant match each other's facial expressions. The infant's left hand moves in synchrony with his mother's finger, which moves the infant's right hand.

Second 34 to 35: Both mother and infant heighten their smiles: increased mouth opening and increased mouth widening.

Second 35 to 37: Both mother and infant decrease their levels of smile. The infant has a moderately open mouth, with a hint of a smile. The mother begins a mock surprise facial expression with partially pursed lips. Her head moves up slightly. As she moves her infant's right hand, the infant's free left hand moves down slightly.

[Break in sequence; then "closing down" sequence begins.]

Second 48: As we re-enter, mutual gaze continues, and the infant curls his right fingers around his mother's finger on her left hand. Both mother and infant have similar facial expressions of partially open mouths, with a hint of positiveness, but not quite an actual smile. The infant's free left hand moves outward.

Second 48 to 49: As the infant looks down and breaks eye-contact for the first time, the mother closes her teeth together with a tightened quality, with her mouth slightly parted, continuing to gaze at the infant's face.

Second 49 to 50: The infant moves his head down, closes his eyes more, and moves his free left hand and left foot slightly down. Simultaneously the mother moves her head down and forward toward the infant, with a more tense mouth, still gazing at the infant. She moves her free right hand in, about to poke the infant gently on the belly.

Second 50 to 52: As the infant moves his head down further, fully closing his eyes and mouth, the mother lightly pokes his belly.

Second 52 [change within second]: The infant looks at his mother, with his mouth closed, sober-faced, as he raises his free left hand. The mother's smile decreases slightly, and her lips are more closed.

Second 52 to 53: The mother begins a "mock surprise" facial expression as the infant moves his head up slightly and continues to look at his mother. As the mother begins to reach for the infant's left hand, his left hand and his feet move in synchrony with her hand movement.

[Mother is ready to go back up into positive play.]

Second 53 (change within second): The infant looks down, breaking eye contact. The mother's mouth closes and tenses (she seems surprised). She continues to reach for the infant's left hand.

Second 53 [another change within this second]: The infant looks up at his mother's face, with a hint of positive mouth widening ("positive attention"), mouth closed. The mother relaxes her mouth, parting her lips slightly. As she reaches for her infant's free left hand, he moves his feet.

[Mother and infant begin to move incrementally back up into positive engagement; mutual gaze continues from here on.]

Second 53 to 54: The mother's mouth begins to curl into a smile; the infant remains in positive attention. As the mother grasps the infant's left hand and brings both his hands in toward the center, the infant's head and hands move upward.

9

Second 54 to 55: Both mother and infant simultaneously move their heads up and open their mouths. The mother smiles, and the infant's face show a hint of positiveness, not yet a smile. The mother brings both of the infant's hands down and into the center.

Figure 1.1 illustrates the remaining frames in the sequence during which they maintain mutual gaze.

Second 55 to 56: see Figure 1.1, frames 1 to 2. Both mother and infant open their mouths further and move their heads up higher. Mother's smile increases, as she raises both the infant's hands up.

Second 56 to 57: see Figure 1.1, frame 2 to 3. As the mother pulls her infant's arms up and out wide, in unison they open their mouths into full gape smiles and move their heads further up, as if reaching for each other. A "gape" indicates a full display of mouth opening. The infant's right leg lifts and his toes curl up.

Second 57 to 58: see Figure 1.1, frame 3 to 4. The mother pulls the infant's arms still wider, slightly tilts her head, opens her eyes further and widens her smile with a flirtatious quality. The infant continues in a gape smile. This is the apex of the mutual positive sequence.

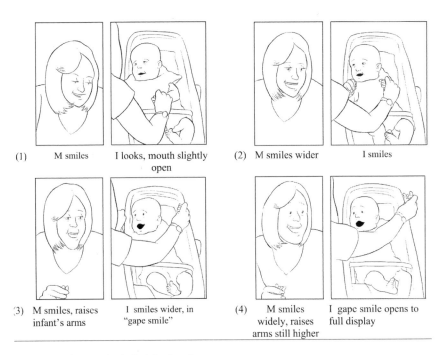

| (1) | M smiles | I looks, mouth slightly open | (2) | M smiles wider | I smiles |
| (3) | M smiles, raises infant's arms | I smiles wider, in "gape smile" | (4) | M smiles widely, raises arms still higher | I gape smile opens to full display |

Figure 1.1 Secure dyad: facial mirroring

Note. Although the mother and infant are shown as if side by side, they are filmed facing each other. Each labeled frame—(1), (2) etc.—is one frame of a split-screen view of a single moment; one camera is on the mother's face, and one camera is on the infant's face. M = mother; I = infant.

Comment on Microanalysis of Facial Mirroring

The microanalysis reveals aspects of the interaction that cannot be discerned in real time. The extraordinary synchronization of movements of head up and mouth opening, as the pair moves incrementally into increasing levels of display of positive affect, are visible only in the microanalysis. The combination of head up and mouth opening has a reaching quality. Similarly, the pair "closes down" together, moving their heads down and closing their mouths roughly in unison.

The complex interaction that occurs around the infant looking down also cannot be discerned in real time. It is a moment of a very slight "misstep in the dance." Watching in real time, my students often insist that the infant looked down because the mother moved her finger in toward the infant's belly, about to poke. But the microanalysis reveals the opposite order: the infant looked down first, the mother reacted with some facial tensing, and then she lightly poked the infant's belly.

There is another slight "misstep" as the infant looks back and seems to be ready to return to the mutual gaze engagement, and the mother is poised to "go back up." But the infant looks down very quickly one more time before fully returning to the engagement (see second 53, change within the second). With the microanalysis one sees the mother react to this. Her mouth closes and tenses, and she seems surprised. Nevertheless they quickly regain their step. As the infant looks back for the second time, mother stays very close to the infant's shifts, and does not "move ahead" of him by beginning to rise into smiles before he is quite ready. This is an important moment as she gives him time to readjust, and she follows his lead.

They then both move incrementally back up to the peak positive shared gape smiles, illustrated in Figure 1.1. In this process they are both learning the sequences that lead to intense moments of positive mutual engagement. They are also learning how to gently increment down and disengage from such heights, allowing the infant a moment of re-regulation, a visual "time-out," as he looks down for a moment. Infants use such moments of looking away to re-regulate their arousal, dampening their heart rate down into a more comfortable range, and then they can look back (Field, 1981). Mother and infant then both rejoin and build back up to the height of positive affect, with fully opened smiles. Expectancies of comfortably matching the direction of affective change, moment-by-moment, are thus created in both partners. This expectancy includes the room for moments of looking away and re-regulation of arousal.

Although this sequence describes a mother and an infant, we might imagine a similar sequence played out by adult lovers. Eibl-Eibesfeldt (1971) performed frame-by-frame analyses of lovers flirting on park benches and showed similar sequences of synchronized smiling, mouth opening, and movement of the head up. He was able to obtain such intimate footage by altering his camera to disguise its focus. Whereas the focus of the camera seemed to be straight ahead, in fact the camera was shooting from the side, where the lovers were. Thus the lovers had no idea that they were being filmed, and they continued to flirt.

"Disruption and Repair": Illustration of a "Future" Secure Mother–Infant Interaction at 4 Months

Whereas the previous interaction had a tiny "misstep" in the dance, the dyad illustrating "disruption and repair" has a slightly larger misstep. The mother caught it and helped to repair it immediately. All dyads, mother and infant, therapist and patient, lovers, have missteps in the dance and must learn to repair them. Usually this process occurs seamlessly, out of awareness. But sometimes we have to bring this process into awareness to repair it.

Real-Time Video Description of Secure Disruption and Repair: 20 seconds

The film begins with the mother and infant looking at each other. The mother says a drawn-out "Hiii" as she leans in and smiles widely. The infant vocalizes with a slightly positive tone and smiles. His hands play with the blanket on the seat as his head moves a bit forward, while he continues to look at mother. Mother repeats "Hiii" while moving in closer to the infant with a partial "loom," and she laughs. ("Loom" movements are ones in which the mother's head and face move in very close to the infant's face, within a few inches.) The infant quickly becomes distressed, frowns, and moves his head back as he raises his arms. He seems to have reacted to the loom. He looks away from his mother and whimpers. The mother immediately moves back into an upright position and sobers.

The mother offers her hands to the infant, "Here, take my hands," with a lilting prosody. The infant takes her fingers, while the mother sings, "That's my fingers." The infant's eyes follow the mother's hand movements until she begins to raise his hands. The infant then looks at his mother. Mother smiles and sings in rhythm with the movements of their hands while the infant gazes at her, with a slight positive expression.

The mother moves her hands down onto the infant's lap, and the infant still holds on to his mother's fingers. The mother now has a broad, highly positive smile. The infant smiles too, almost as broadly as his mother. The mother's smile slightly decreases as she says, "Can you say "ahhh," as she slowly leans in close to the infant, another partial loom. The infant giggles and lowers his head, and then moves his head back up, meanwhile continuing to gaze at his mother. Both infant and mother match the rhythm of their mouth and head movements.

Second-by-Second Microanalysis Description of Secure Disruption and Repair

Once again we must slow down the process and examine it second-by-second to really see what is happening. We selected eight moments across the 20 second sequence to illustrate this interaction, presented in Figure 1.2. Thus the illustrations are not in an exact second-by-second sequence; some seconds are skipped.

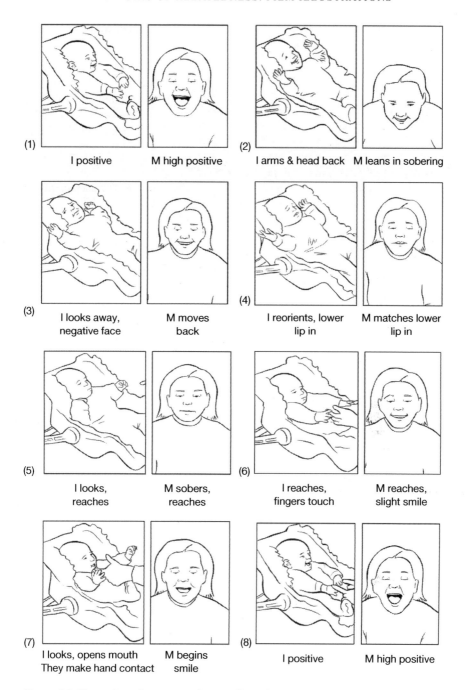

Figure 1.2 Illustration of secure attachment: disruption and repair

Note. Frames (1) to (8) are selected frames from a 20-second sequence.

Figure 1.2, moment 1: They both begin with positive facial expressions while looking at each other.

Figure 1.2, moment 1 to 2: As mother leans in, sobering, the infant moves his head back and his arms up and back.

Figure 1.2, moment 2 to 3: The infant turns his head away slightly, breaks eye-contact, frowns and grimaces. The mother simultaneously moves back toward upright.

Figure 1.2, moment 3 to 4: The infant reorients to his mother, but gazes down, with his lower lip drawn in, an "uh oh" expression. Remarkably, the mother exactly matches this expression in the same moment, exquisitely entering the infant's state. This is a magical moment, not visible in real time.

Figure 1.2, moment 4 to 5: The infant looks at his mother who has a sober face; both reach their hands out toward the other in the same moment.

Figure 1.2, moment 5 to 6: The infant reaches with both hands, and his mother reaches to join him with a slight smile.

Figure 1.2, moment 6 to 7: The infant looks at his mother and opens his mouth as mother begins to smile; they both make hand contact.

Figure 1.2, moment 7 to 8: Both smile at the other. Mother's smile reaches a full gape smile.

Comment on Disruption and Repair

This sequence illustrates maternal management of infant distress by "joining the infant's distress." The mother exactly matches her infant's "uh-oh" expression of the bottom lip pulled in. The infant's eyes are closed during this moment. But we can see that the mother joins the exact quality of the infant's distress, exquisitely sensing the infant's state. This moment is not visible in the real-time video, but it is the key to this interaction. Then both participate in the repair, reaching for each other. From the real-time video it is not easy to see that they reach their hands out to each other in the exact same moment. They then gradually build back up to the original positive engagement.

Digressing briefly into a parallel for adult treatment, the therapist might do something similar with a patient, out of awareness. That is, the patient may be distressed and the therapist might "enter" the patient's state for a moment by matching or echoing the patient's distressed facial expression with a similar one of her own. Most likely neither partner will be quite aware of this. But it will play an important role in the empathic climate. We return to this topic in Chapters 4 and 8.

A "Future" Disorganized Mother–Infant Interaction at 4 Months

To anticipate Chapter 4, disorganized attachment at one year predicts adulthood psychopathology. Here we describe a 4-month interaction of a dyad on the way to infant disorganized attachment at one year. We ask ourselves, what might be the consequences of this kind of interaction, as it repeats over and over? What kind of expectancies might this infant be generating? What might this infant be like as a young adult? We are seeing the process of disturbance as it is being formed.

It is important to hold in mind that the mothers of disorganized infants are suffering from unresolved loss, abuse, or trauma, and are thought to be in a continuing state of fear (Lyons-Ruth et al., 1999; Main & Hesse, 1990). We discuss this further below (see Chapter 7).

Real-Time Video Description of Future Disorganized Dyad: 23 seconds

As the section opens, both the mother and the infant are looking at each other. The infant smiles and whimpers simultaneously (an instance of infant "discrepant affect," positive and negative affect in the same second, which predicts disorganized attachment in our data). The mother smiles (an instance of maternal smile to infant distress, which predicts disorganized attachment in our data.) The mother tickles the infant's stomach and asks: "Are you happy?" (an example of mother not acknowledging the infant's distress).

The infant whimpers and clenches his fists and fingers the strap of his seat. The mother looks away and says: "Oh no. No, don't cry." [It seems to be so difficult for this mother to acknowledge and accept her infant's distress.] The infant whimpers, looks away, and arches away. Mother touches the infant roughly, saying, "What's wrong?" (Mother's words and tone acknowledge the infant's distress, but the rough touch is discrepant with her tone and words.)

The mother then displays a "mock surprise" expression to the infant's distress (an instance of maternal surprise to infant distress, which predicts disorganized attachment in our data.) The infant then simultaneously smiles and whimpers (another example of infant discrepant affect). The infant then immediately brings his hands up to his face, obscuring it with his hands while whimpering.

Second-by-Second Microanalysis Description of a Future Disorganized Dyad

This description will take some time. There is a great deal going on here.

Second 04: As this section begins, both mother and infant are smiling at each other. The mother looks at her infant, but the infant now looks slightly down, perhaps at the lower part of the mother's face. (From the real-time video we know that the infant also whimpers here while he smiles.)

Second 04 to 05: The infant looks further down, his head moves down, and he sobers partially to "positive attention," looking at mother with slightly open mouth, no smile. The mother continues to smile and moves her head slightly forward. As her hand reaches the infant's left hand, the infant lightly rests his fingers on top of her hand. (This is a complex moment. The mother does not seem to acknowledge her infant's mild distress. The infant reaches for the mother's hand, possibly an attempt to soothe.)

Second 05 to 06: The infant sobers further, and juts out his bottom lip with a partially open-mouthed "pout expression." The mother moves her head back and her smile decreases to just a hint of a smile. She moves her hand to the infant's left hand. (Here the mother begins to respond to the infant's mild distress with a reciprocal sobering of her own.)

15

Second 06 to 07: The infant's face sobers to neutral. The mother pulls her head back, with tight compressed lips. (This looks like a disappointment reaction, with a hint of sadness.) As she pulls the infant's hand toward her, the infant's head moves down and his body moves forward slightly with the pull. (Here mother's pulling does not work to re-engage her infant; instead, he moves his head and body further down into a greater disengagement.)

Seconds 07 to 09: The infant now becomes overtly distressed; his eyes are almost closed, his head moves back as his mouth opens into a cry face, and he frowns. The mother's lips become partially compressed, a complex expression with a hint of a smile, with both negative and positive qualities. (Her face looks ambivalent with a slight mischievous quality.) As her hand touches the infant's right hand, her head and body move forward toward the infant.

Second 09 to 10: The mother's face shows the largest change so far, a full display of a tight, compressed lips expression, with sadness. (This looks like a strong disappointment reaction.) The infant looks down, with a partially open, neutral mouth, and his head moves back and slightly to his left. His hands relax as mother moves her hand away from his chest.

Seconds 10 to 12: The infant now looks directly at his mother as she suddenly becomes slightly threatening. Her body moves sharply forward toward her infant, with an asymmetrical head slant to the right. As she moves forward and to her right, the infant turns away slightly to his left, with a distinctly negative frown, as he continues looking at her. His right hand moves slightly back and up, away from her; his left hand fists. As his feet move, his mother grabs his foot.

Seven seconds later we re-enter.

Second 19: The infant is looking down, with strong facial distress, a frown and pre-cry face. The mother has a closed, neutral mouth. (She does not acknowledge or mirror her infant's distress; she looks detached.)

Second 19 (change within second): The infant is more upset, whimpering, and his frown deepens, while his fist is still clenched. The mother grimaces, with a hint of disgust, and moves her head back. (This is a very difficult moment to observe; the level of mismatch is disturbing.)

Seconds 19 to 21: The mother touches the infant's right hand as she moves her head down, and her grimace softens to interest. The infant calms down, his frown softens, and his facial expression shifts to interest, while he continues to look down. Both soften their faces and move into the interest range together. (This is an important moment of mutual repair; however it is difficult to sustain.)

Second 21 to 22: The infant becomes more distressed, his mouth opens more, with a hint of a grimace. The mother has a "woe-face," a sympathetic distress expression. Her head moves slightly forward. The infant curls his hand down beside her hand, but he does not soothe on her hand. (In the mother's woe-face we see her capacity to empathize with her infant.)

Second 22 to 23: The infant's hint of a grimace continues. His fingers open over (but not on) his mother's hand. The mother's face is in the interest range.

Second 23 (change within second): The infant looks at his mother as he frowns with a surprised, alarmed expression with eyebrows raised, eyes widened. His limbs stiffen, and his right hand pulls back. Mother pulls her head back and grimaces, with a disgust expression, a slight pout of her lower lip, narrowed eyes. Her hand moves to cover the infant's left hand. (Her face registers the infant's distress. However, her response is disgust, rather than empathic woe-face.)

Second 23 to 24: As the infant becomes intensely facially distressed, pulling his head back, with eyebrows still raised in alarm, his mother shows a sudden fully open-mouthed mock surprise face, showing the whites of her eyes. (Showing the whites of one's eyes is frightening, as noted by Main & Hesse, 1990. Again the mother registers the infant's distress, but she reacts with a frightening expression, rather than an empathic one.) She pulls her hands back from the infant. (Infant distress followed by maternal surprise predicts disorganized attachment in our data.)

Seconds 24 to 27: As the infant abruptly turns his head and body away from his mother, partially covering his face with his right hand, with a negative facial expression just barely visible, and pulling at the seat cover with his left hand, his mother smiles and laughs. (From the real-time video we know that the infant whimpers here as well.) (Again the mother registers the infant's distress, but she reacts with laughter, not with an empathic expression. Infant distress followed by maternal smile predicts disorganized attachment in our data.)

Comment on Illustration of Future Disorganized Attachment

This mother is perceiving and responding to the infant's changes of behavior, noting every change. Thus, the difficulty is not a sheer absence of responsiveness. There is a complex dance here, but it is an extremely uncomfortable and mismatched one.

The mother does not seem to be able to respond empathically to the infant's distress. Often she over-rides the infant's distress, trying to distract him, or to "ride negative into positive." She is very aware of her infant's behavior, but what does it mean to her? It is important to retain empathy for the mother. Her face shows sadness and disappointment and she moves back from the baby, disengaging from him.

In Chapter 7 we develop the argument that the mother's own prior history of unresolved distress is triggered by the infant's distress, disturbing her ability to respond empathically. We conjecture that the mother's "stonewalling" the infant when he is distressed, or smiling or being surprised at his distress, may be dissociative efforts to regulate her own unresolved distress by emotional withdrawal and unresponsiveness to her infant. This future disorganized dyad is a good exemplar of the 4-month patterns of communication difficulties of dyads on the way to disorganized, compared to secure, attachment (see Chapter 7).

Frame Illustrations of Difficult Moments in Future Disorganized Attachment Dyads

Figure 1.3 illustrates difficult moments, in various dyads, which illustrate some of our findings on the origins of disorganized attachment at 4 months. Figure 1.3a illustrates infant distress, and the difficulties that mothers had in showing empathy for infant distress. Figure 1.3b illustrates two maternal "loom" sequences and the infant's difficulties with the loom; looming movements come very close in toward the infant's face.

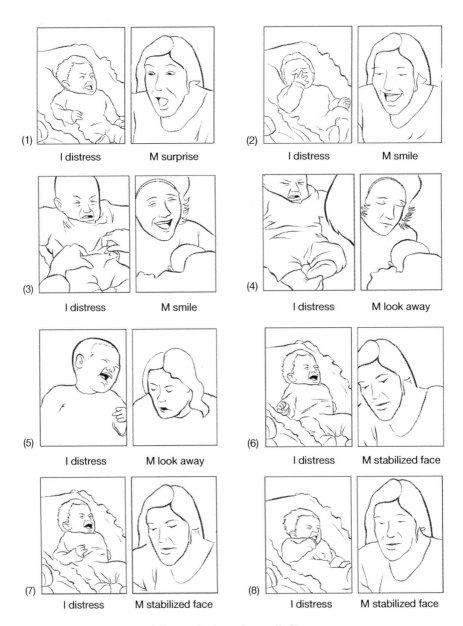

Figure 1.3a Illustrations of disorganized attachment (1–8)

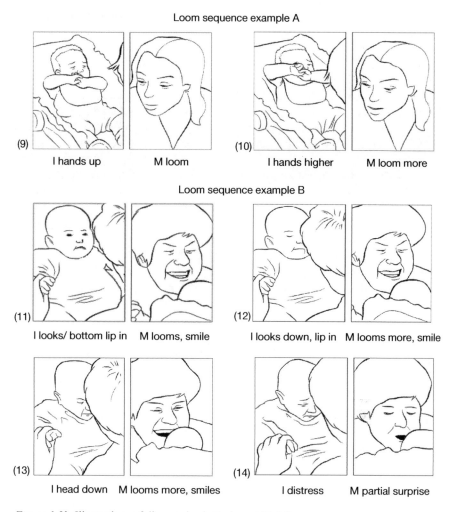

Figure 1.3b Illustrations of disorganized attachment (9–14)

Note. Although the mother and infant are shown as if side by side, they are filmed facing each other. Each labeled frame—(1), (2) etc.—is one frame of a split screen view of a single moment; one camera is on the mother's face, and one camera is on the infant's face. Frames (1) and (2) comprise a sequence, 3 seconds apart. Frames (3) and (4) are taken from separate sections of the interaction. Frames (6)–(8) comprise a 4 second sequence illustrating high mother face self-contingency, "stabilized face." Frames (9) and (10) comprise a 2 second maternal loom sequence. Frames (11)–(14) illustrate a second maternal loom sequence across 3 seconds.

Figure 1.3a (1–8) presents visual illustrations of infant facial distress. Infants on the way to disorganized attachment showed more vocal distress, and more combined facial and vocal distress.

Figure 1.3a (1) to (2) illustrates a sequence of maternal surprise to infant distress, frame (1), followed by maternal smile to infant distress, frame (2), in the same dyad described above (see Second 23 to 24 above). First the mother shows a surprise face in which she shows the whites of her eyes, which may be threatening. Then the mother smiles broadly as the infant strikingly looks away and partially covers his face, so that he does not see her smile.

Figure 1.3a (3) is another example of maternal smile to infant distress.

Figure 1.3a (4) and (5) illustrate maternal looking away from the infant's face, despite the greater facial and vocal distress of infants on the way to disorganized attachment.

Figure 1.3a (6) to (8) illustrate the mother "closing up" her face as the infant becomes more and more distressed, across a 4-second sequence within one dyad. As the distressed infant opens his eyes, frames (6) to (7), the mother's closed-up face remains stabilized, although her head angle shifts; likewise as the infant's distress increases, frames (7) to (8), the mother's facial affect remains stabilized. This is an example of high maternal facial affect self-contingency, an over-stabilized, "frozen" face, like a brief moment of a "still-face." In the still-face experiment, mother and infant play naturally face-to-face. The mother is then instructed to hold a perfectly still face. Infants typically react with distress and averted gaze. Mother and infant then resume natural play (Tronick, 2007).

Figure 1.3b illustrates two maternal loom sequences, example A (frames 9–10) and example B (11–14). In example A, in frame (9) the infant puts his hands up in front of his face (a defensive gesture available from the beginning of life) as the mother looms; in frame (10) the infant raises his hands still more as his mother looms in further.

In the second loom sequence example B, in frame (11) the infant looks at his mother with his bottom lip pulled in (a gesture of "uh-oh"), giving a wary impression, as his mother looms in while smiling. In frame 12, as the mother looms further, the infant closes his eyes and pulls his lips into a full "compressed lips" expression, conveying visual avoidance and a feeling of tightness. In frame 13, as the mother looms in further with a still bigger smile, the infant dips his head down, with a negative expression, conveying distress. In frame 14, the infant shows an unhappy grimace, even further distressed; only now does the mother's partial surprise face show that she senses something is wrong. At each point the infant signals discomfort, but the mother over-rides that signal until the final frame.

Comment: These frames vividly illustrate the degree of mismatch between the infant and the mother in dyads where the infant is on the way to disorganized attachment. Maternal surprise or smile faces to infant distress seem to be an emotional "denial" of infant distress. They seem to be an active maternal emotional inability or refusal to "go with" her infant, to join her infant's distress, disturbing her infant's ability to feel sensed. The over-stabilized face of the mother may protect her from feeling her infant's distress, and her own. Maternal "closed up" faces often occurred at moments of infant distress, as if the mother is "going blank," possibly dissociating. To remain empathic to her infant's distress might re-evoke the mother's own original traumatized state. Both maternal looking away, and maternal looming in, disturb the potential for mutual gaze. Looming in is too close, and looking away is too far away, revealing a discordance within the mother.

Illustrations of Expectancies

We now turn to the question of what the infant comes to expect from his or her interactive encounters. How are infant expectancies of social interactions created? We use the video descriptions above to illustrate how the action sequences of the exchange develop into expectancies. For each pattern we attempt to translate the "action–dialogue" into language, as if the infant or mother could put the experience into words.

In the facial mirroring description above of a dyad on the way to secure infant attachment, if the action dialogue could be translated into language, we infer that mother and infant create the following expectancies of their interaction: "We follow each other's moves as we look at each other and look away. We follow each other's faces up and down, as we become more and less positive. We can go bit by bit all the way up to the top together, to sunbursts of joyous open smiles. We each can anticipate how the other's gaze, face and engagement will go. What we feel, and what we do, shows up in the other in a resonant way: we do not have to be vigilant; we do not have to withdraw." The infant might feel, "I feel secure because I am with you. I feel sensed and joined by you."

In the disruption and repair description above of a dyad on the way to secure infant attachment, if the action dialogue could be translated into language, we infer that the infant creates the following expectancies of their interaction: "You sense how I feel. If I become distressed, I can expect you to honor my distress, to join me in my moment of hesitation or worry. I know that you will wait for a moment while I re-regulate myself at my own pace. You are right there, ready to join me bit by bit, as I gradually come back to engage with you. Then I can anticipate that we will together find each other's faces, and move incrementally bit by bit back up into mutually joyous smiles."

We infer that the mother comes to expect: "If you look away, and become distressed, I know how to help you. I can slow down, and wait for you to come back. I can find you again by reaching for your hands, making contact through our hands, and I can trust that gradually you will come back to me. We can find each other's faces again, and we can return to our mutually joyous smiles."

In the future disorganized attachment dyad description above, if the action sequences could be translated into language, we infer that the infant creates the following expectancies of their interaction: "I feel so upset and you're not helping me. I feel confused about what you feel and what I feel. You seem happy or surprised when I am upset. I don't understand you. You don't get me. You stonewall me in my distress. I feel helpless to influence you. I feel frantic. "

We infer that the mother might feel: "Your distress makes me feel anxious and inadequate. I can't let myself be too affected by you; I'm not going to let myself be controlled by you or your moods. I just need you to smile and be happy; I won't hear of anything else."

In the frame illustrations of difficult moments in future disorganized attachment dyads (Figure 1.3a), if the action sequences could be translated into language, we infer that the infant creates the following expectancies of their interactions:

- *Figure 1.3a (1):* "I am feeling distressed, and yet my mother is surprised. What can I make of that? I feel confused about what I feel."
- *Figure 1.3a (2)* and *(3):* "My mother is smiling while I'm distressed. I don't want to look at her. She does not recognize my distress or sympathize with me. I am lonely in my distress."
- *Figure 1.3a (4)* and *(5):* "I'm feeling distressed, and yet my mother looks away from me. Where is she? I feel so alone."
- *Figure 1.3a (6)* to *(8):* "I'm feeling distressed, and my mother is looking at me, but she does not seem to really see me. Her face doesn't move. And I'm getting more and more upset. But her face doesn't move. I don't know where she is. She really doesn't get me. There's something wrong."

Loom Sequence A, Figure 1.3b (9–10):

- *Figure 1.3b (9)* "My mother is moving in too close to my face. I feel a little threatened. I put my hands up to protect my face. I feel a little trapped."
- *Figure 1.3b (10)* "My mother is moving in even closer to my face. I feel a little more threatened. Doesn't she see how I'm trying to protect my face? But it's not working. I put my hands up even further. I want her to stop. I'm worried she won't. It's scary."

Loom Sequence B, Figure 1.3b (11–14)

- *Figure 1.3b (11)* "My mother is moving in close to my face, and she's really smiling. I feel wary. She is holding my hands; I can't even move them. I can't get away."
- *Figure 1.3b (12)* "My mother is moving in even closer to my face. I look down. Uh-oh. Nowhere to go."
- *Figure 1.3b (13)* "She's coming in even closer! I feel upset. I can't get away from her. I feel cornered."
- *Figure 1.3b (14)* "Now I'm even more upset. She's backing up. Good. But I never know whether she will or she won't come in on me like that."

Conclusion

In this chapter we invited you into our laboratory. We described in detail several films of mother–infant interactions at 4 months in which infants were classified secure attachment, and disorganized attachment, at one year. By describing the films first in real-time and then, second-by-second, we illustrated how microanalysis reveals more than can be grasped with the naked eye. The films vividly illustrate striking differences in the experiences of infants on the way to secure, compared to disorganized, attachment. To anticipate later chapters, this second-by-second process generates the ways in which, in adult treatment, each partner comes to feel sensed, known, and recognized by the other, as well as the ways in which this process may falter, be repaired, or become derailed.

2

THE ORGANIZATION OF
RELATIONAL EXPERIENCE IN
EARLY INFANCY

We now turn to the question of how infant relational experience at 4 months is organized. In the descriptions of interactions in the previous chapter, we inferred different forms of procedural expectancies of action sequences, such as facial mirroring and disruption and repair. In the origins of disorganized attachment, we inferred infant expectancies of being unable to obtain empathy and comfort when distressed, and disturbances in experiences of being sensed, known and recognized. For the infant, we construe knowing and being known as expectancies of procedurally organized action sequences. We also inferred maternal expectancies of being unable to get the positive responses from their infants that they so need, and maternal tendencies to withdraw emotionally from their infants in distress.

Now that we have immersed ourselves in the moment-by-moment experiences of several dyads, we step back from the films to consider a number of broader themes in the organization of infant relational experience. What does the infant come to represent from these experiences? How is it possible that these early procedural expectancies set a trajectory in development, such that interactions at 4 months predict attachment outcomes at one year?

First we offer a note of definition. In the world of adult treatment, we most generally consider the verbalized narrative and declarative memory. Declarative memory (also known as semantic memory) refers to symbolically organized recall for information and events.

In contrast, in what follows we are concerned with the 4-month infant's preverbal modes of processing information and events, often termed implicit processing. The aspect of implicit processing that we are concerned with here is termed "procedural," which we use to refer to action sequences. These include attention processes, facial and vocal emotion (such as prosody, intensity, pitch), spatial orientation toward and away from the partner, and touch. This is Bucci's (1997) realm of the subsymbolic. Procedural memory refers to skills or action sequences that are encoded nonsymbolically, become quasi-automatic with repeated practice, and influence the organizational processes which guide behavior (Emde, Birengen, Clyman, & Oppenheim, 1991; Grigsby & Hartlaub, 1994; Squire & Cohen, 1985).

What does the infant come to represent from her experiences by 4 months? To address this question, we consider the following themes in the organization of infant relational experience:

- the representational newborn;
- the dialogic newborn, and the dialogic origin of mind;
- contingency detection at birth and the generation of expectancies;
- self- and interactive processes as organized through expectancies;
- presymbolic representation;
- representation and internalization prior to language;
- three principles of salience in the organization of infant experience.

The Representational Newborn

We begin with the nature of the infant's information processing at birth. We assume an information-processing model in which the infant's perceptual abilities ensure a capacity for seeking out, perceiving and interacting with social partners from birth (Brazelton et al., 1974; Berlyne, 1966; Haith et al., 1988).

Meltzoff has documented a rudimentary form of presymbolic representational intelligence in the early weeks and months of life. He showed that infants have the capacity to detect correspondences between their own actions and those of a model. As early as 42 minutes after birth, infants can imitate gestures of the experimenter (Meltzoff, 1985, 2007; Meltzoff & Moore, 1998; see Beebe et al., 2005 for a review). In Meltzoff's view, imitation is a process by which something of the other is taken on by the self. The infant is very active in this process. At this early age, in the first hour of life, the infant watches the experimenter. The infant sucks on a pacifier, so he could not possibly imitate while he watches. The experimenter poses a gesture, such as opening the mouth or sticking out the tongue. The pacifier is now taken out of the infant's mouth. Over the next 2.5 minutes the infant progressively makes gestures increasingly similar to that of the facial gesture demonstrated by the experimenter. It is an active state of intentionally trying to match the gestures.

Meltzoff holds that the infant is comparing his own action, such as mouth opening, against an internal memory, schema, or representation of the action of mouth opening that he saw the experimenter make. The imitation is intentional, goal-corrected, and mediated by memory. By 6 weeks, the infant can observe the model one day, return 24 hours later, and imitate the action. Upon the infant's return, the experimenter sits in front of the infant with a neutral face. The infant first stares at the experimenter, but gradually begins to make successive efforts to make the same facial display seen the day before. "These studies suggested that imitation can be mediated by a representation of the now-absent acts" (Meltzoff & Moore, 1998, p. 56). The representation constitutes a model against which the infant can match his own performance and guide his behavior.

How is this possible? The mechanism is cross-modal matching: the infant maps what he sees (mouth opening gesture) onto what he feels proprioceptively with his face (facial movements that are sensed as progressively similar to what he saw). The infant can translate between environmental stimuli and inner states, detecting matches or correspondences, from the beginning of life. Through the perception of cross-modal correspondences, both infant and partner sense the state of the other, and sense whether the state is shared. In Meltzoff's view, the infant's perception of these correspondences provides the infant with a fundamental relatedness between self and other. Meltzoff (1985), Trevarthen (1998), and Stern (1985), all key theorists of infant forms of intersubjectivity, agree that infant capacity to recognize cross-modal correspondences is a central mechanism allowing the infant to capture the quality of another's inner feeling state.

Meltzoff's work offers a radical change in the way we conceptualize the origin of mind in psychoanalysis (see Beebe et al., 2005). Far earlier than we thought, there is a rudimentary capacity to represent, and to match, the behavior of another person. In Meltzoff's view, the origin of mind begins at birth with the perception, "You are like me." The key mechanism is the perception and production of similarity. The sense of self derives from one's own movements as seen in the actions of the other, and actions of the other experienced proprioceptively as similar to one's own movements. Others have states similar to one's own. Meltzoff's imitation experiments powerfully present a case for the point of view that the infant in the first months of life has a presymbolic, representational intelligence (see also Bornstein, 1985). This capacity may be based in part on "mirror neurons" (Rizzolatti, Fadiga, Fogassi, & Gallese, 1996; Wolf, Gales, Shane, & Shane, 2001).

We construe "mind" here from the point of view of the infant, that is, expectancies of procedurally organized action sequences. We do not mean to imply that infants reflect on their expectancies.

Meltzoff's work is relevant to psychoanalysis in a second way. Seeing oneself in the actions of the other, or recreating the other's actions in the self, is one reason why mirroring experiences are so powerful. The capacity to detect that "you are like me," or to reproduce the other's behavior, so that "I am like you," contribute to feeling "known" or "on the same wavelength" (see Beebe & Lachmann, 2002). These processes later in development may contribute to the formation of identifications, as Benjamin (1995) argues. Moreover, the implications for a psychoanalytic theory of development are profound. These experiments show that infants do not begin life unaware of the partner. On the contrary, they are inherently social from birth.

In the psychoanalytic dyad, correspondences (which can be cross-modal or within the same modality) allow either patient or analyst to bring internal process and behavior into a correspondence with that of the partner. Correspondences are one process through which each partner can feel sensed and known by the other. Correspondences are created largely out of awareness and are subject to the multiple vicissitudes of transferences of both analyst and patient (see Beebe, 2004). In the case vignettes from adult treatment that we present at the end of Chapter 4, experiences of feeling known early in development are strikingly absent.

Dialogic Origin of Mind

The philosopher Charles Taylor (1991, p. 34–35) has argued for the dialogic origin of mind:

> The general feature of human life that I want to evoke is its fundamentally dialogical character. We become full human agents . . . through our acquisition of rich human languages of expression . . . I want to take 'language' in a broad sense, covering not only the words we speak but also other modes of expression . . . including the languages of art, of gesture . . . But we are inducted into these . . . through exchanges with others who matter to us . . . The genesis of the human mind is in this sense not 'monological,', . . . but 'dialogical' . . . the making and sustaining of our identity . . . remains dialogical throughout our lives.

Infant research in the last few decades has confirmed Taylor's dialogic origin of mind. Reviewing three key theorists of infancy, Meltzoff, Trevarthen, and Stern, we find that they all conceptualize the origins of a theory of mind in infancy (Beebe et al., 2005). For each, mind begins as a shared mind, and the central question is, how could the infant sense the state of the other? Despite differences in their theories, they posit that the infant's perception of correspondence is the most central means for sensing and creating shared states, and that the infant's capacity for cross-modal perception is key in detecting correspondences. All conceptualize a highly complex, presymbolic infant representational intelligence.

Based on an experimental paradigm, Meltzoff conceptualized a representational newborn who processes social information from birth. Based on the study of the face-to-face exchange, Trevarthen (1998) conceptualized a dialogic newborn in a reciprocally communicative dyad. From birth, the infant has an inherently emotional and communicative brain, a dyadic "conversational" mind. Trevarthen's description of the emotional newborn, participating in proto-conversation, takes us to an inherently dyadic, dialogic mind.

Trevarthen (1998) argued that human sympathetic consciousness is an innate ability. It allows both infants and caretakers to be in immediate sympathetic contact, aware of the other's feelings and purposes without words and language. This sympathetic contact occurs through approximate "matches" or "correspondences" in communicative expressions. Trevarthen (1977, 1998) as well as Stern (1985, 1995) argued that infants are sensitive to correspondences not only of form, but also of time and intensity, across modalities. Trevarthen described mother and infant behaviors as contingently coupled in time, imitated in form, and brought into register in intensity range. The particular patterns formed by the dyad will guide action, and will be learned and remembered. This contingent inter-coordination enables each to resonate with or reflect the other. Correspondences regulate both interpersonal contact and inner state.

Trevarthen's position is consistent with, but deepens, the contemporary view that adult mind is dyadic and organized in interaction (see for example Aron, 1996; Mitchell, 2000; Stolorow and Atwood, 1992; Beebe et al., 1992, 2005). Moreover, Trevarthen (1998) holds that linguistic forms of correspondence and intersubjectivity have their foundation in prelinguistic forms, and that intersubjectivity is initially preverbal and dialogic.

Stern (1985, 1995) also sees the origins of mind in the interactive process itself. Like Trevarthen, Stern is interested in correspondences as a reciprocal dyadic process across time: each partner is changing with the other. This bi-directional influence process is emphasized by both Stern and Trevarthen. Stern is interested in the *how* of behavior, the dynamic, shifting patterns of rhythms, shapes, and activation. "Dynamic micro-momentary shifts in intensity over time that are perceived as patterned changes within ourselves and others" allow us, rather automatically and without awareness, to "change with" the other, to "feel-what-has-been-perceived-in-the-other" (Stern, Hofer, Haft, & Dore, 1985, p. 263).

This process underlies the concept of "affect attunement," one of Stern's central contributions. Affect attunement is defined by Stern as cross-modal correspondences in intensity, timing, and "shape" of behavior. By "shape" Stern means the contour of behavior, such as rising or falling tones. These correspondences are based on dynamic micro-momentary shifts over time, perceived as patterns of change that are similar in self and other. Stern gives as an example a baby who bangs a toy in a particular rhythm. His mother does a shimmy, wiggling her body in the exact rhythm of the infant's banging.

Each partner potentially changes with the slight shifts of the other. The infant perceives the state of the other based on the intensity, timing, and shape of the partner's behavior. The infant's capacity to recognize cross-modal correspondences is the perceptual underpinning of affect attunement. This process enables the infant to capture the quality of another's inner feeling state, and to discriminate whether it is shared. Affect attunements are "automatic," with relative lack of awareness, an aspect of implicit, procedural processing. Stern argues that processes of affect attunement are so powerful because they contribute to attachment security and the capacity for intimacy. The individual learns that some subjective states are shareable, and some are not. As we discuss in Chapters 4 and 8, this process is ubiquitous in adult treatment as well. Usually out of awareness, it provides each partner with a way of knowing whether one's feeling state is acknowledged by the other.

The meaning of correspondences is elaborated by Sander's (1977) concept of "matched specificities," defined as a "resonance between two systems attuned to each other by corresponding properties" (Weiss, 1970, p. 162). An example might be similar vocal rhythms in mother and infant. The presence of matched specificities yields awareness in each partner of the state of the other. This concept underlies Sander's "moment of meeting," a match between two partners such that the way one is known by oneself is matched by the way one is known by the other. This match facilitates the development of agency, identity, and coherence in the child's experience of inner and outer (Sander, 1995). Sander's moment of meeting became central to the thinking of the Boston Study Group (see for example, Stern et al., 1998).

Sander (1977), Trevarthen (1977), Stern (1971), and Tronick (1989), among others, have been influential in formulating a mutual, bi-directional regulation model of communication. Mutual regulation is based on each partner's ability to detect that the partner's behavior is contingent on, that is, predictable from, his own actions, and vice versa. Mutual regulation is also based on each partner's perception of micro-momentary shifts over time, and whether these shifts generate correspondences. Mutual regulation includes not only the coordination of affect, but also of attention, orientation, and touch. It includes the coordination of turn-taking, vocal rhythms, and timing of all kinds.

Trevarthen and Sander suggest that the capacity for the mutual regulation of joint action is available from birth. Positioning mutual regulation as a capacity available from the beginning of life is an essential corollary of Trevarthen's dyadic, dialogic mind at birth. Although mutual regulation is endorsed in varying ways by many streams of psychoanalysis (see for example Aron, 1996; Benjamin, 1995; Stolorow & Atwood, 1992), the position that mutual regulation is central to communication from birth deepens and extends current psychoanalytic views. Mutual regulation becomes a primary organizing principle of all communication and development.

One implication for adult treatment is that dialogic communication and mutual regulation are inherent in the infant's capacity, and thus remain a lifelong resource. All linguistic forms of intersubjectivity continue to depend on pre-linguistic forms (Trevarthen, 1998). Thus all adult psychoanalytic treatments are dependent on pre-linguistic forms of communicative competence and intersubjectivity, not just those of more disturbed patients. However, pre-linguistic forms of communication can come to the fore when later aspects of development falter (see Beebe, 2004).

The dyadic, dialogic origin of mind has much in common with Balint's (1992) primary object love, Bowlby's (1969) theory of attachment, and Sullivan's (1953) view of affect contagion in infancy. It is consistent with the position of relational theorists (Aron, 1996; Mitchell, 2000) that the adult mind is dyadic and inter-actional, with Kohut's (1971) concept of the self-object and with Stolorow and Atwood's (1992) critique of the "myth of the isolated mind." However, the focus of these adult theorists is not on the origin of mind, but rather on the organization of adult mind. Infant research adds to these psychoanalytic theorists in its description of the complexity of the dyadic exchange from birth. Infant research has revealed a far more sophisticated and communicative mind than was ever imagined.

We add one caveat. Whereas most forms of correspondence accrue to experiences of being known, and shared mind, some forms of correspondence are not optimal. One striking example of a non-optimal form of correspondence is the pattern of mutually escalating over-arousal (see Beebe et al., 2005). In this pattern, each partner escalates the ante, as the infant builds to a frantic distress, and the mother makes increasingly frantic efforts to engage the infant. In one example of this pattern in a future disorganized infant, the infant finally threw up.

29

"Contingency Detection" from Birth and the Generation of Expectancies

How do infants create expectancies of their dyadic action–dialogue world? Infants have intrinsic motivation to detect pattern and order in events occurring across time. The infant is a "contingency detector" from birth (DeCasper & Carstens, 1980; Papousek, 1992), detecting predictable consequences of his own actions, by estimating probabilities of "if-then" sequences (Saffran, Aslin, & Newport, 1996; Tarabulsy, Tessier, & Kappas, 1996).

Contingencies are defined as temporal relations between the infant's own behaviors and consequences in the environment (interactive contingency), or consequences in his own behaviors (self-contingency). For an event to be perceived as contingent by the infant, it must occur rather rapidly, and it must be predictable, that is, occurring with greater than chance probability, following the infant's behavior. In fact, contingencies tend to be extremely rapid. Stern (1971, 1977, 1985) coined the phrase the "split-second world" in characterizing the ways in which mothers and infants respond to each other during face-to-face interactions. Research since that time has confirmed this concept (see Beebe et al., 2010, for a review).

Infants are highly sensitive to ways that their behaviors are contingently responded to (DeCasper & Carstens, 1980; Hains & Muir, 1996; Haith et al., 1988; Jaffe et al., 2001; Murray & Trevarthen, 1985; Stern, 1971, 1985; Watson, 1985). The infant's perception of contingencies, in conjunction with a good-enough environment, organizes the infant's expectation that he can affect, and be affected by, the partner. This is one crucial origin of the experience of effectance (White, 1959) or agency (see Sander, 1977; Rustin, 1997). Gergely and Watson (1996) have suggested that the infant's capacity to interpret stimulation as contingent (or not) may well be the most fundamental of the infant's capacities for interpreting sensory information. A similar position is held by Fagen and Rovee-Collier, who have used the infant's capacity to perceive contingencies to document a remarkable array of early abilities to create expectancies of anticipated events, and to remember them across days and weeks (Fagen, Morrongiello, Rovee-Collier & Gekoski, 1984; Shields & Rovee-Collier, 1992). Thus infant learning of contingencies involves cognitive processes of expectation and anticipation (Tarabulsy et al., 1996). This process of anticipation helps explain why the procedural world of action sequences is split-second.

Infants predict when events will occur and recur, generate procedural expectances of action sequences, and act on these expectancies (Haith et al., 1988; Mandler, 1988). To demonstrate experimentally the existence of infant expectancies, Haith et al. (1988) showed infants a series of slides of checkerboards, bull's eyes, and schematic faces. The researchers videotaped one of the infant's eyes. They showed the infants two series, one regularly alternating to the left and the right of visual center, and the other appearing randomly in left or right position. The infants detected the spatiotemporal rule that governed the regularly alternating series and developed expectancies for the impending event. They showed antici-patory eye movements, such that that their eyes focused on the slide a fraction of a second before it appeared. Haith and colleagues concluded that, "as early as 3.5 months of age, the baby can create an action-based perceptual model of the situ-ation he or she confronts, can generate short-term expectations from this model, and can support action . . . This modeling, expectation and action sequence serves to maintain continuity in an ever-changing perceptual world . . ." (Haith et al., 1988, p. 477).

The nature of each partner's contingent coordination with the other affects the infant's ability to attend, process information, and modulate behavior and emo-tional state, moment-by-moment. These reciprocal contingency processes are essential to the creation of infant and maternal social expectancies and interac-tive efficacy, and to infant cognitive development (Hay, 1997; Lewis & Gold-berg, 1969; Murray, Fiori-Cowley, Hooper, & Cooper, 1996; Sander, 1995; Stern, 1985; Trevarthen, 1977; Tronick, 1989). To anticipate Chapters 4 and 8, this same process operates in adult treatment. However, in adult treatment it is largely in the background, and the verbal narrative is in the foreground.

The fact that expectancies operate so pervasively, so early, accounts for the enormous influence they have in organizing experience (Fagen et al., 1984). Neu-rophysiological evidence also suggests that familiarity, repetition, and expectancy provide the most powerful organizing principle of neural functioning (Gazzaniga & LeDoux, 1978; Pally, 2005).

The creation of expectancies is a central theme in Stern's work (1977, 1985, 1995). In one study, Stern (1977) was interested in how fast a person could execute an arm movement. He analyzed a film of Muhammad Ali boxing in the first round of the Ali–Mildenberger world heavyweight title in 1966. In Stern's (1977) microanalysis of 16 mm film (24 frames per second), 53% of Ali's left jabs, and 36% of Mildenberger's left jabs, were faster than visual reaction time (180 milliseconds).

Stern goes on to argue that although at least 53% of Ali's jabs should have con-nected, in fact very few did. Why? He suggests that a punch in boxing is not the actual stimulus to which the response is a dodge or block. Instead, we must look at larger sequences of patterned events (expectancies):

> It is more reasonable to consider a punch or a dodge as a hypothesis-probing or generating attempt on each fighter's part to understand and predict the other man's behavioral sequences . . . Viewed this way, the successful punch reflects one fighter's ability to decode the other fight-er's ongoing behavioral sequence, so that the other fighter's next move is correctly anticipated in time and in space. What is truly amazing is how expert humans are at rapidly acquiring temporal and spatial 'maps' of another person's behavioral sequences, even when a major point of an activity such as boxing is to keep the behavioral sequences in constant flux and as unpredictable as possible (Stern, 1977, p. 87–88).

31

Stern's analysis points out that it is necessary to predict the opponent's next move in order to have time to "get there" at the same time as the opponent is also moving. Anticipation is a key aspect of expectancies. In more usual social situations we are not trying to hide this information about our movements; we display our behavioral schemas very openly. Stern's "maps" fit our concept of expectancies. We form temporal-spatial-affective anticipatory expectancies of another person's behavioral flow in relation to our own. Stern terms this expectancy, or procedural representation, a "mini-plot" of the coordination of the two partners' behaviors (1977, 1985; Beebe & Stern, 1977). We have also referred to it in this chapter as an "action–dialogue."

Self- and Interactive Regulation as Patterns of Expectancy

Predictability and contingent relations in social behavior reduce uncertainty about what likely happens next and generates interactive agency (Warner, 1992). Both partners generate patterns of expectation, constructed through self and interactive processes. Both come to anticipate the sequence of one's own actions over time, and the sequence of one's own actions in relation to those of the partner.

Although rarely studied together, both self- and interactive processes are essential to communication and the creation of procedural expectancies. To give an example of self-processes, as an individual speaks, her hands often gesture at moments in a rhythm synchronized with her speech rhythm. This rhythm is organized within the individual, with a distinctive degree of predictability of the durations of sounds and silences. However, this rhythm is also organized in part by interactive processes, here the partner's responsiveness. If the partner occasionally nods his head in rhythm with the individual's speech and hand rhythm, the individual will most likely feel understood and keep going in a characteristic way. But if the partner shows no rhythms which synchronize and thus acknowledge the individual, most likely the individual will change her rhythm of speaking as well as the nature of her verbal content, in an effort to be better understood or received. The process of moment-to-moment variation, such as variations in the durations of the sounds and silences in speech rhythms, or the rhythms of head nods, provides an essential means of sensing oneself and one's partner.

Presymbolic Representation

An early presymbolic, procedural representational world is being organized as early as 4 months. Infant procedural expectancies of self- and interactive processes during social interactions constitute a presymbolic form of representation. Symbolic forms of representation do not begin to emerge until the end of the first year.

This presymbolic world is organized by the procedural action–dialogue of the dyad, and by the ensuing expectancies of how action and "inter-action" sequences unfold in space and time, from moment-to-moment, with accompanying arousal

32

patterns. These self- and interactive processes generate patterns that the infant comes to recognize, remember, and expect (Beebe & Lachmann, 2002; Stern, 1985; Tronick, 1989). This is the world that Lyons-Ruth (1998b, 1999) and Stern and colleagues (Stern et al., 1998; Boston Change Process Study Group, 2005, 2007) refer to as "implicit relational knowing."

Infant procedural representational capacities in the first 3 to 4 months are extensive (see Beebe & Lachmann, 2002; Bornstein, 1985; Haith et al., 1988; Lewkowicz, 2000; Mandler, 1988; Stern, 1985). Not only do infants perceive contingencies, they can estimate durations of events lasting seconds or fractions of seconds. They detect features of stimuli, such as facial shapes, temporal patterns, and spatial trajectories. They translate cross-modally, for example between visual and auditory channels, facilitating abstraction of pattern from different modalities. Moreover, infants remember the details of stimuli in learning experiments for at least 24 hours, and sometimes up to 2 weeks (Shields & Rovee-Collier, 1992).

These processes can be described as "schema" or "model" formation, the generation of procedural models of features of stimuli, events, and action sequences, allowing the infant to recognize what is new, and to compare it with the familiar. Such model formation is an index of fundamental representational processes. Using these capacities, infants generate generalized expectancies, procedural representations, or "internal working models" (terms which we use as synonyms) of recurrent and characteristic interaction patterns.

These representations are relatively persistent, organized classifications of information about expected interactive sequences. They are formed by the active process of constructing incoming information. The infant's active construction of presymbolic representations provides a key organizational feature of the system, linking 4-month patterns of interaction to 12-month attachment outcomes, which are then linked in recent studies to young adult outcomes, as we review in Chapter 4.

Nevertheless, representations can be reorganized and transformed as incoming information is reinterpreted and reordered, based on past experiences and current expectations. In this transformational model, development proceeds through a process of regular restructurings of the relations within and between the person and the environment (Sameroff, 1983). Thus, although interactions in infancy set an important trajectory in development, they can be modified by later experiences, if these later experiences are importantly different from earlier ones.

Summary of Presymbolic, Procedural Forms of Representation

To describe the organization of procedurally organized presymbolic representations, we suggest that infants will store models of how interactions unfold, in the dimensions of time, space, affect and arousal (Beebe & Lachmann, 2002; Beebe et al., 2010).

- In time, infants will store the rate, rhythm, sequence, and tightness of contingency of the behaviors, as well as the durations of events.

- In space, infants will store patterns of mutual approach–approach or approach–avoid.
- In affect, infants will store the positive and negative tones and intensities of faces and voices, their patterns of moving in the same affective direction or not, and whether these are shared.
- In arousal, infants will also store an associated arousal pattern, and a proprioceptive experience of their movements over time.

Based on these dimensions of time, space, affect, and arousal, below we describe salient interaction patterns of infant procedural social representations. These interaction patterns will guide our description of the origins of secure vs. insecure attachment in the following chapters.

- Facial and vocal "mirroring" generates an expectation of matching and being matched in the direction of affective change. Such mirroring provides each partner with a behavioral basis for entering into the other's feeling state. It generates experiences which contribute to feeling "known," attuned to, or "on the same wavelength."
- "State transforming" generates the expectation of being able to transform an arousal state through the contribution of the partner (see Stern, 1985).
- "Disruption and repair" generates the expectation of interactive repair following facial-visual mismatches.
- "Chase and dodge" generates the expectation of misregulation of spatial-orientation patterns, without repair, such that "As you move in, I move away; as I move away, you move in" (Beebe & Lachmann, 1988, p. 114).
- "Self- and interactive contingency" generate expectancies of particular degrees of contingent coordination in one's own rhythms of behavior, in those of the partner, and the degree of coordination between the two partners' rhythms of behavior. Self-contingencies generate expectancies of the degree of stability in the self's and in the partner's own rhythms. Degree of self-contingency generates the degree to which the person can anticipate her own next move, accruing to temporal coherence over time. Interactive contingencies generate expectancies of the degree to which each partner responds to the other (see Chapter 3 for further definitions).

Presymbolic Representation and Infant Internal Working Models of Attachment

The literature on "internal working models" of attachment, based on procedural expectancies of actual infant experiences (see Main, Kaplan, & Cassidy, 1985), and a parallel literature on the origins of procedural forms of infant "self and object representations," have proceeded largely separately. In our work we integrate them. The concept of an internal working model is consistent with the experimental literature on infant contingency detection and procedural representation reviewed above.

Bowlby and subsequent attachment researchers have suggested that the recurrent nature of the infant's experiences leads to the development of procedural representations or "internal working models" of self and others. These working models are generalized representations of events experienced that influence the infant's emotional experiences and expectations throughout development (Bowlby, 1973; Bretherton & Munholland, 1999). Consistent with this view, a large empirical literature documents that variations in social interactions in the first months of life predict later social and cognitive outcomes (see Beebe & Lachmann, 2002, for a review).

Main et al. (1985) define internal working models as "a set of conscious or unconscious rules for the organization of information relevant to attachment . . . which lead to individual differences in the mental representation of the self in relation to attachment . . . [and which] direct not only feelings and behavior, but also attention, memory, and cognition" (p. 67). These working models lead to differences in nonverbal behavior and ultimately to differences in patterns of language and structures of mind. Although attachment researchers argue that internal working models provide one process by which patterns of intimate relating and attachment security are constructed, understanding of the details of these models remains rudimentary. Explication of these details is necessary to further understand the origins of internal working models of attachment in the first half year of life, one key motivation for our study.

Knowing and Being Known

Lyons-Ruth (1999, 2008) argues that the organization of intimate relating is at stake as the infant develops early procedural representations. Intimate relating entails the fundamental issue of how the infant comes to know, and be known by, another's mind. We reiterate that knowing refers to infant procedural expectancies. Similarly, Stern argues that processes of affect attunement are so powerful because the individual learns that some subjective states are shareable, and some are not. This learning powerfully affects attachment security and the capacity for intimacy. Learning which states are shareable, and which are not, defines the arenas in which one can, and cannot, know and be known by another's mind.

Lyons-Ruth (1999, 2008) proposes that the outcome of this process of coming to know and be known by another's mind is dependent on whether the partner is capable of a collaborative dialogue. Collaborative dialogue involves close attention to the other's initiatives, openness to the other's state across the entire range of positive to negative emotions, attempts to comprehend the state or subjective reality of the other, the attempt to respond in a way that acknowledges or elaborates on that state, ability to negotiate similarity and difference, and efforts to repair disruptions. Collaborative dialogues generate internal models in which both partners are represented as open to the experience of the other; each can know and be known by the partner's mind. Lyons-Ruth's position is similar to those of Meltzoff, Trevarthen, and Stern.

Lyons-Ruth (1999) suggests that incoherent or contradictory dialogues involve a collapse of intersubjective space in which only one person's subjective reality is recognized. The partner's initiatives are ignored, over-ridden, or not acknowledged. Lyons-Ruth (1999, 2008) argues that such failures of collaborative dialogue generate contradictory internal models, in which the partner represents both roles, such as, "I should accept your control; I should attempt to control you."

To understand contradictory dialogues, Lyons-Ruth (1999) describes how complex "control systems" for skilled actions, such as communicating, are developed by coordinating single relational procedures, such as facial affect, with other procedures, such as vocal affect. Flexible integration of these procedures is essential to higher-order coordinations. However, when procedures conflict, the lack of integration can disturb the development of flexible control systems. An example is the contradictory pattern of simultaneous positive facial affect but negative vocal affect that we documented in the origins of disorganized attachment. This description of conflicting or unintegrated domains of knowledge is consistent with the concept of intermodal discordances, described in Chapters 3 and 7, in which contradictory procedures are organized in different communication modalities at the same time. Discordant information is difficult to integrate into a coherent percept, and may remain unintegrated (Shackman & Pollak, 2005). These concepts set the stage for our understanding of the origins of dissociative processes, taken up in later chapters.

Representation and Internalization

We have described the organization of presymbolic representation in the first year. This description can simultaneously illuminate processes of "internalization." Although it has been argued that internalization is different from processes that establish the original representations of the internal and external world, we have argued (Beebe & Lachmann, 1994, 2002) that these two processes are not distinct in the first year. Whether they are ever distinct is an important issue, which is nevertheless beyond the scope of this discussion. Both Loewald (1962) and Schafer (1968) pointed out the intimate connection between the first representations and the earliest forms of internalization. We confine our discussion to the presymbolic origins of internalization and Schafer's (1968) definitions of internalization.

Schafer (1968) created an interactive model of internalization. Internalization is based on what both the organism and the environment, infant and mother, co-create. However, Schafer's model includes various one-way influence concepts in which the organism receives the influence of the environment. For example, the environment provides the regulations of soothing, restraint, guidance, and mastery. In clinical practice and much theorizing, the latter version of internalization has dominated our thinking.

But only a fully bi-directional interactive model can take into account the complexity of early interactive organization and the origins of internalization processes. For example, in the facial mirroring sequence described above we suggested that expectancies of comfortably matching the direction of affective change, moment-by-moment, were co-created by both mother and infant. This expectancy included room for moments of infant looking away and re-regulation of arousal. We suggested that both were learning the sequences that lead to moments of high positive mutual engagement, and both were learning how to gently increment down from such heights. In describing the slight misstep in the dance, we noted an important moment as the mother gave the infant time to readjust, and she followed his lead. They were then both able to move incrementally back up to the peak positive shared "gape" smiles. As these sequences recur, the infant develops a generalized expectancy or procedural representation of this process.

Moreover, in Schafer's definition, inner regulations are assumed to result from the subject's transformation of regulatory interactions with the environment. In contrast, our position is that all regulatory interactions with the environment have simultaneous self-regulatory consequences, and all self-regulatory efforts have simultaneous interactive consequences, from the beginning of life. Thus, regulatory interaction with the environment does not become "inner" regulation in any linear fashion.

Instead regulatory interactions and self-regulation proceed hand in hand, and shape each other, from birth. Rather than viewing interactive regulations as transformed into self-regulations, existing self-regulations are altered by, as well as alter, interactive regulations. Both infant and caregiver continuously co-create, elaborate and represent the regulations, which are simultaneously interactive and self-regulatory.

In our view, internalization is not an optimal metaphor (see also Goldberg, 1983). It inevitably carries the implications of transporting the outer to the inner and the suggestion that the internal increasingly supplants the external. Likewise, the idea of "taking in the functions of the other" has no place in our model, because regulatory functions are always jointly co-created (see also Benjamin, 1995).

We thus suggest a view of the organization of infant experience in the first year in which both partners bring to the interaction organized behavior and mutually construct self- and interactive modes of regulating their joint activity. The expectation and representation of the self- and interactive modes of regulation constitute the "inner" organization (Beebe & Lachmann, 1994). This model puts the bi-directional nature of the regulation center stage. It further articulates the role of the subject in the regulation process, and it emphasizes the dyadic nature of the co-creation of experience. We use the concept of procedurally organized representation rather than internalization.

Three Principles of Salience Organize Early Representation

Further, we have proposed three "principles of salience," criteria by which expectancies of social interactions are categorized and procedurally represented (Beebe & Lachmann, 1994). The principle of ongoing regulation captures the characteristic modes of self- and interactive regulation. For example, Stern's (1985) theory of "representations of interactions generalized" (RIGs) implicitly uses the principle of ongoing regulations to explain how early infant procedural representations are organized. That is, the representation ("RIG") is based on a generalized abstraction of a typical sequence.

The principle of disruption and repair describes a specific sequence broken out of the broad pattern. For example, in the second secure dyad we illustrated, we selected a specific disruption and repair sequence. This dyad may come to represent such sequences as an expectation of the likelihood of repair, and an expectation of how the process of repair will proceed.

To the degree that the ongoing regulations are in the positive range, such as various matching interactions, experience is organized by what is predictable, expectable, coherent, and coordinated. In contrast, the principle of disruption and repair points toward experience as organized by disjunction and difference, but also the possibility of repair. The expectation is created that the disjunctive moments may be followed by moments of reconnection and positive engagement. Disruption and repair organize experiences of coping, effectance, re-righting, and hope (Tronick, 1989). We consider these counterpoints to be simultaneously constituted.

Single experiences can also be organizing. In the principle of heightened affective moments, one dramatic moment, positive or negative, stands out in time. Heightened moments are formative in their effect far out of proportion to their mere temporal duration (see Pine, 1981). Although affective experience is also organized in the principles of ongoing regulation and disruption and repair, intense affect is a sufficiently unique dimension in the creation of expectancies to justify its consideration as a third organizing principle. For example, in the illustration of the disorganized dyad we described, moments of infant distress, followed by mother's smile or surprise face, are relatively infrequent. However, they are salient, powerfully disturbing, heightened affective moments. In contrast, positive heightened affective moments are akin to Tronick's (1998) concept of dyadic expression.

After the first year, as representations become increasingly symbolic, using the principle of ongoing regulations the eventual representation, if ever translated into verbal form, may be something like, "I can expect that things will usually go like this." Using the principle of disruption and repair, the representation may be, "This is what happens when things are off. I can expect that they will get fixed, and this is how we fix them." Using the principle of heightened affect the representation may be, "What a wonderful (or terrible, or awesome) moment."

Over the course of the first year and beyond, these three principles constitute criteria by which interactions will be categorized and procedurally represented. Using the three principles, the expectation and representation of the dyadic modes of self- and interactive regulation, as organized by the three principles of salience, are fundamental aspects of inner organization.

The Origins of Working Models of Attachment at 4 Months

The following concepts will guide our understanding of variations in internal working models in the origins of attachment at 4 months:

38

- In the social sphere, a procedural, presymbolic representational world is being organized, formed in the interactive process of self-in-relation-to-other, and thus inherently dyadic.
- Through the perception of correspondences between one's own behavior and that of the partner, which are organized via form, time, and intensity across modalities, both infant and partner can sense the state of the other, and can sense whether the state is shared or not.
- Infant procedural representations of face-to-face interactions include a variety of patterns, such as facial mirroring; disruption and repair; state-transforming; mutual approach or approach–avoid spatial orientation, including spatial patterns of intrusion; and degrees of self- and interactive contingency.
- The three principles of salience are descriptions of fundamental dyadic processes which determine the centrality of social events for the infant: ongoing regulation, disruption and repair, and heightened affective moments.
- When contradictory procedures are organized in different communication modalities, unintegrated, conflicting procedural representations are likely to develop.
- Collaborative vs. contradictory dialogues generate coherent vs. unintegrated infant internal working models of attachment.
- What is at stake in these procedural representations is the organization of intimate relating. This entails the fundamental issue of how the infant comes to know, and to be known by, another's mind, as well as how he comes to know his own mind. Mind is construed as procedural expectancies.

In summary, this chapter considered what the infant comes to represent from his experiences. In Chapter 3 we turn to the headlines of our new findings on the origins of disorganized attachment, and a review of the new approach that generated these findings.

3

THE ORIGINS OF RELATEDNESS
IN DISORGANIZED ATTACHMENT
Our Approach

This chapter presents the headlines, so to speak, of our new findings on the origins of disorganized attachment. Four-month infants on the way to disorganized attachment show discrepant, contradictory, and conflicted patterns of communication, in the context of intense distress. Maternal emotional withdrawal from distressed infants compromises infant interactive agency and emotional coherence. Based on our findings we propose that these infants come to experience and represent *not being sensed, known or recognized* by their mothers, and difficulty *knowing themselves,* particularly in states of distress. We propose that they come to expect and represent experiences of confusion about their own basic emotional organization, about their mothers' emotional organization, and about their mothers' response to their distress. These experiences set a trajectory in development which may disturb the fundamental integration of the person.

These far-reaching conclusions about the origins of disorganized attachment emerged from a new approach, based on an extraordinarily detailed microanalysis of videotaped mother–infant interactions at 4 months. Our approach allowed us to investigate the process of attachment transmission in a more fine-grained and precise way, and to discover new patterns of relational disturbance in infancy.

In this chapter we first review the new approach we used to generate our findings. We describe the ways in which we coded our films for mother and infant behavior second-by-second, breaking down the modalities of communication into attention, affect, orientation, and touch.

We explain how we measured the concepts of self- and interactive regulation, which we now define more narrowly as self- and interactive contingency. Although the term regulation is somewhat broader in meaning than contingency, for our purposes these terms can be used interchangeably. In our work they refer to predictability over time.

Self- and interactive contingency measure the *process* of relatedness across time. In contrast, most studies of mother–infant interaction measure rates of specific behavioral qualities, such as looking away, or intrusive touch. We documented that both the *process of relatedness* and rates of specific *behavioral qualities* are important in understanding the origins of attachment formation at 4 months.

Understanding the details of our new approach will be important in understanding our new findings and our later chapters.

The second part of this chapter briefly reviews our findings on the origins of disorganized attachment generated by this approach. Our findings provide new ways of thinking about the dynamics of relational configurations in infancy that are relevant not only to 12-month outcomes, but also to adulthood. This brief review will set the stage for our translation of each of our findings on the origins of disorganized attachment into analogies and parallels for adult treatment in Chapter 4.

Our Approach to Measuring Mother–Infant Communication at 4 Months

New Features of Our Approach

- Whereas most research has focused on maternal antecedents of infant attachment, particularly "sensitivity," we examine the dyad, analyzing both infant and mother. The infant's experience will be shaped not only by the parent's patterns of behavior, but also by his own.
- Whereas most prior research has used global measures of maternal sensitivity, we use measures based on microanalysis, coding behavior second-by-second from split-screen videotapes of 4-month mother–infant face-to-face interaction.
- Whereas most prior research has measured qualitative features of behavior (such as maternal intrusive touch) rather than the *temporal process of relating*, we integrate both.
- Whereas research on mother–infant face-to-face interaction has focused on interactive contingency (often termed "interactive regulation" or "mutual regulation"), we examine contingencies which define both self- and interactive processes. Thus we ask whether antecedents of attachment are found in contingent processes *within* mothers and *within* infants as they interact (*self-contingency), between* the partners (*interactive contingency),*or *both.*
- Whereas parental regulation of infant distress has been seen as central to attachment security, we broaden the focus to an examination of regulation through multiple communication modalities: visual attention, facial and vocal affect, spatial orientation, and touch, defined below. Infants are sensitive to all modalities and are capable of coordinating them to apprehend affective states (Murray et al., 1996; Stern, 1985; Trevarthen, 1977; Tronick, 1989; Beebe et al., 2010).

Within the face-to-face exchange, gaze and facial affect are central modalities of communication (Stern, 1985; Tronick, 1989; Weinberg & Tronick, 1994). Infant vocal affect is an important means of communication of emotion, particularly of distress. Infant-initiated touch is a salient but not well-studied behavior (but see Weinberg & Tronick, 1994). Affectionate to intrusive patterns of maternal touch are central but less studied (but see Field, 1995; Stack, 2001). Maternal spatial orientation and infant head orientation are not well-studied (but see Beebe & Gerstman, 1980; Beebe & Stern, 1977; Stern, 1971).

The assessment of multiple communication modalities accomplishes two central goals. First, we gain greater specificity in describing communication disturbances in infancy. It allows us to describe all the dimensions of face-to-face relating, not just affect. As we hypothesized, disturbances in attachment formation were identified in all the communication modalities we measured. This finding is very important. For example, vis-à-vis orientation and mutual gaze create the setting "frame" for affective exchanges (Stern, 1985; George Downing, personal communication, April 7, 2008). And touch was salient in the origins of insecure attachment.

Second, face-to-face communication generates multiple simultaneous emotional signals, all of which qualify the meaning of one another (Watzlawick, Beavin, & Jackson, 1967). These signals are typically congruent. Redundancy and congruence facilitate selective attention, learning, and memory (Bahrick & Lickliter, 2002; Lickliter & Bahrick, 2001). However, these simultaneous signals may also convey conflicting or discordant information in the context of disturbance (Shackman & Pollak, 2005). Discordances among communication modalities generate confusing communication patterns. Only by examining multiple channels of communication, each coded separately, can we identify such conflicting or discordant signals. We documented that conflicting, discordant communications are central to communication disturbances in the origins of disorganized as well as resistant attachment.

Modalities of Mother–Infant Face-to-Face Communication

We code mother and infant behaviors during face-to-face communication. The mother is instructed to play with her infant as she would at home, but without toys. There are no instructions to refrain from picking the infant up. The infant is in an infant seat, and the mother is seated opposite, in the same plane.

Our coding is based on what mothers and infants actually do in this face-to-face play. The camera captures the head, upper torso, and hands of both partners. Some of the behaviors are completely symmetrical. For example, each partner can look at and away from the other's face; each partner has the full possible range of positive to negative facial affect.

But the mother's range of movement of her bodily orientation, from sitting upright, to moving forward, to looming in, is different from that of the infant, who is loosely strapped into the seat. However, the infant has a large range of head movements, from oriented vis-à-vis, to minor and major head aversions, to a full 90° aversion in which his head is tucked into his shoulder, to arching his torso back and partially turning away from the mother.

Touch behavior is also not symmetrical. The mother has a far greater repertoire of different kinds of touches than does the infant. For the mother we coded different types of touch in an effort to capture nuances and qualities of maternal touch (affectionate, such as stroke or caress; static, such as hold hand or finger; playful, such as tap, tickle, rub; jiggle-bounce; touch the infant through an object, such as piece of the infant's clothing; and rough, intrusive touch).

When we code the communication modalities of attention, affect, orientation, and touch, each second receives a separate code in each modality, separately for each partner. In this way we were able to test a very large range of possible dysregulations, as well as discrepancies between communication modalities, that might be associated with insecure attachment.

We code in the following way (for details please see Appendices A–E):

- *attention* (looking at and away from the partner's face);
- *affect* (*facial affect*: degrees of positive to negative facial expressions; *vocal affect*: degrees of positive to negative tones);
- *orientation* (mother's orientation from sitting upright to leaning forward to "looming" in; infant's head orientation from vis-à-vis to arch away); and
- *touch* (*mother touching infant*, from affectionate to intrusive forms of touch; *infant touching* his/her own skin, touching an object [such as chair or clothing], touching mother).

Only examination of separate modalities can identify potentially discordant communication, as well as specify exactly which modalities of communication may be involved in the development of insecure attachment. On the other hand, only a composite measure, such as facial-visual engagement, provides a holistic, gestalt approach to capturing the quality of the interaction. In this study both separate modalities and the composite measure of facial-visual engagement were important in identifying the origins of insecure attachment.

Measures of Mother and Infant Behavioral Qualities

From these second-by-second codes we first created rates of specific mother and infant "behavioral qualities." For example, we assessed the percent of time in gazing away, positive and negative facial affect, and infant orientational aversions such as 90° head aversion or arch. We assessed the likelihood of maternal orientational intrusions, such as loom, and the mother-approach–infant-withdraw pattern of "chase and dodge." We assessed the likelihood of infant touch, and of maternal intrusive touch. We also assessed the likelihood of specific discrepant patterns, such as moments of infant discrepant smile and whimper. We assessed interpersonally discrepant patterns, such as infant distress greeted by maternal smile or surprise.

Measures of "Process" of Relating: Contingency

From these second-by-second codes we then created contingency measures of the self- and interactive *process of relating across time.* In creating an average rate of

43

a behavioral quality, the moment-by-moment temporal process is lost. In contrast, contingency measures preserve the moment-by-moment process. Both kinds of measures were important in the origins of insecure attachment.

Self- and interactive contingency assess the process of predictability across time. We use the term "contingency" interchangeably with the terms "predictability," "coordination," and "regulation." Whereas our prior work (Beebe & Lachmann, 2002) used the terms self- and interactive "regulation," these concepts are now more narrowly defined as self- and interactive *"contingency."* Below we review our rationale for preferring "contingency." Note that the term *interactive contingency* is used in the same way as we have formerly used the term *interactive regulation.* However, *self-contingency* is a far more narrow term than *self-regulation.* Self-contingency refers to the process of self-predictability across time, the stability of one's own behavioral rhythms.

For example, the rate of gazing away addresses the overall percentage of time of looking away. In contrast, interactive contingency of gaze examines the degree to which each partner follows the direction of the other's gaze at and away from the partner's face, moment-by-moment. Self-contingency of gaze addresses the individual's own predictability of looking at and looking away from the partner.

Contingency Processes

Contingency processes are the foundation of social communication. The nature of each partner's contingent coordination with the other affects the infant's ability to attend, process information, and modulate behavior and emotional state (Hay, 1997). Contingency processes are essential to the creation of infant and maternal social expectancies. These procedural expectancies of action sequences generate presymbolic, procedural representations or models of "how interactions go" (Stern, 1985; Beebe & Lachmann, 2002).

In our approach, contingency is a neutral concept. It acquires a clinical meaning only when used in relation to a clinical construct, such as maternal depression, or infant attachment.

The Optimum Midrange Model of Interpersonal Contingency in the Prediction of Attachment

The role of interpersonal contingent coordination in infant development has been unclear. It is often assumed that *more* "contingency," "attunement," "synchrony," or "coordination" is optimal for communication. In contrast, high contingency may be an index of stress. More contingency is not necessarily "better."

We favor an optimal midrange model of interactive contingency. Jaffe et al. (2001) documented that midrange interactive contingency was optimal for secure attachment; higher and lower degrees of contingency predicted different types of insecure attachment. A number of studies now converge on this model, in which both higher and lower degrees of contingent coordination are problematic.

44

Maternal overstimulation, intrusiveness, inconsistency, and particularly high or low levels of infant or mother responsiveness are associated with insecure outcomes (see Beebe et al., 2010, for a review).

Higher contingent coordination increases the predictability of the interaction. High coordination is seen as excessive monitoring, or "vigilance," a dyadic effort to create more moment-to-moment predictability. It can be seen as a coping strategy elicited by novelty, interactive challenge, or threat. Low coordination is seen as inhibition of monitoring, or withdrawal. Midrange coordination leaves more "space," more room for uncertainty, initiative, and flexibility within the experience of correspondence and contingency—and is optimal for secure attachment (Beebe et al., 2000; Jaffe et al., 2001).

In predicting attachment from self and interactive contingency at 4 months, our central hypothesis is that insecurity biases the communication system toward contingency which is both heightened (in some modalities) and lowered (in others), compared to values of secure dyads. This hypothesis was largely confirmed in the results we present in later chapters. That is, self- and interactive contingencies of dyads on the way to insecure attachment were both higher and lower than those of dyads on the way to secure attachment.

Assessing Contingency Allows Us to Determine that Mother and Infant are Actually Communicating

How do we know that mother and infant are actually communicating? How do we know that each partner's behavior actually affects, or alters that of the other? How do we know whether each individual is actually "adjusting" his own behavior based on what the partner just did? The answer depends on the analysis of interactive contingency.

The usual correlational methods can show only that the two streams of behavior of the two partners vary together, go up and down together, but not who affects whom. Two streams of behavior which look highly correlated may be similar only as an artifact of strong self-predictability in both people (Gottman & Ringland, 1981). For example, if both have a strong and similar rhythm, so that their tempo and beat is roughly the same, they will seem highly correlated whether or not they are actually affecting one another.

The statistical strategy for assessing whether each partner's behavior affects that of the other, time-series analysis (a form of lagged correlation), circumvents this problem. This approach is probabilistic, not causal. This method distinguishes influences that operate intra-individually from those that operate between individuals. It identifies how each person's behavioral stream unfolds in time (self-contingency), and whether and to what degree each person's stream influences that of the partner as they progress through time (interactive contingency).

Time-series analysis is consistent with a theory of interaction which takes into account both how the person is affected by his own behavior, as well as by that of the partner (Thomas & Martin, 1976). It is essential to integrate self- and interactive contingency, since each person must *both* monitor the partner *and* regulate inner state. Self and interactive processes are concurrent and reciprocal, each affecting the success of the other. As important as this theory is for infant social development, it has remained relatively unexplored empirically. Indeed, studies of interactive- and self-regulation have tended to exclude each other (but see Gianino & Tronick, 1988; Sander, 1977). Our own empirical studies of the past decade have integrated self- and interactive contingency in the examination of mother–infant communication disturbances (Beebe et al., 2007, 2008, 2010, 2011).

This integration of self- and interactive processes is important in the study of disordered interactions. There has been a tendency to locate the source of difficulty in one partner or the other (for example, in early infant self-regulatory difficulties, or in maternal intrusion or insensitivity). In contrast, by understanding how the relative salience of self- vs. interactive difficulties in each partner varies with different kinds of difficulties, such as disorganized attachment, or maternal depression, clinical intervention can be more finely focused.

Time-series analysis first requires that a series of behaviors be carefully recorded in sequence, in actual time, for each partner separately. For example, imagine movements of the mouth, eyes, and head in the facial mirroring analysis described in Chapter 1. They include mouth openings, eyebrow raises, shifts of head orientation, shifts in direction of gaze, smiles and so on. When timed for precise onsets and offsets, these behaviors last on average one-quarter to one-third of a second (Beebe, 1982; Beebe & Stern, 1977; Stern, 1985). In the data presented in this book, we coded mother and infant behaviors to a one-second precision (see Appendices A–E). It took 12 dedicated Ph.D. students 10 years to code the data in this book (see Acknowledgments).

Next the analysis determines the predictability of each partner's own behavior, self-contingency; and the predictability of each individual's behavior from the prior behavior of the partner, interactive contingency.

Interactive Contingency Defined

Interactive contingency picks up consistently occurring moment-to-moment adjustments that each individual makes to changes in the partner's behavior. This process is usually out of awareness. The term interactive contingency is used interchangeably with contingent coordination when it increases clarity. Interactive contingency can be translated into the metaphor of expectancies of "how I affect you," and "how you affect me." When each partner is contingently coordinated with the other, we prefer the term "bi-directional" to "mutual" coordination to avoid any implication of positive mutuality, since bidirectional coordination can occur in aversive as well as positive interactions.

Interactive contingency measures interpersonal coordination across the entire session analyzed. We analyze the first 2½ minutes of each mother–infant play session. For example, the degree of contingent facial coordination, metaphorically "facial mirroring," measures the degree to which the partner follows the affective direction of the individual's facial changes, across the whole 2½ minutes

46

analyzed. As the individual becomes more positive, so does the partner; as the individual dampens her face, so does the partner. Interactive contingency does not refer to a particular one-step sequence, such as the likelihood that the infant's vocalization is followed by the mother's smile.

Self-Contingency Defined

The time-series model addresses the dyad as they interact. It does not assess an individual as if he or she were in isolation. Self-contingency addresses the predictability of an individual's behavior *within* the dyadic context.

Self-contingency is defined as adjustments of an individual's behavior that are correlated with her own prior behavior. It refers to the degree of predictability, that is stability or variability, within the individual's own rhythms of activity, as she interacts with a particular partner. Degree of self-contingency provides the individual with continuous information about the likelihood of staying in the same state. It generates an expectancy (out of awareness) of the degree to which one can anticipate one's own next move.

Degree of self-contingency addresses the range from over-stabilized, to mid-range degree of predictability balanced with variability, to agitated loss of predictability. Degree of self-contingency of one's own behavioral rhythms is an ongoing ubiquitous process, but it is very much in the background, like breathing.

When one's ongoing behavioral stream is less predictable, we infer lowered ability to anticipate one's next move, a "destabilization." In contrast, heightened self-contingency indicates behavior tending toward an overly steady, non-varying process, translated into the metaphor of "self-stabilization." It may indicate wariness. At the extreme of self-stabilization, the person becomes "frozen."

To illustrate heightened facial self-contingency, people may hold their faces in a partially frozen posture, holding in distress after a traumatic experience, such as September 11, 2001 (Beebe, Cohen, Sossin, & Markese, 2012). One has the impression that if the person's face moved more normally, it might "break" into unbearable distress.

As another example, in our findings on the origins of disorganized attachment, we found that mothers of future disorganized infants "over-stabilized" their faces. That is, from moment-to moment their faces tended to be too stable, like a temporary "still-face," lacking the degree of variability in expression that characterized mothers of future secure infants. In the "still-face" experiment, following natural face-to-face play, the mother is instructed to hold a perfectly still face (Tronick, 2007). Infants typically react with distress.

To illustrate lowered self-contingency, in our findings, mothers of future disorganized infants showed lowered gaze self-contingency. That is, they were less predictable than mothers of future secure infants in their patterns of looking and looking away from the infant. This lowered predictability disturbs the infant's ability to expect when mutual gaze may occur. This disturbance is very important, because mutual gaze is a key foundation of the face-to-face encounter.

Illustrating Time-Series Analysis

Time-series analyses provide separate assessments of the infant's self-contingency, the mother's self-contingency, the infant's interactive contingency, and the mother's interactive contingency. Figure 3.1 illustrates *infant* self- and interactive contingencies defined by time-series analysis. A parallel drawing would illustrate mother self- and interactive contingencies. In Figure 3.1 the infant's current behavior (t_0), as it is correlated with the infant's own just prior behavior, is used to generate infant self-contingency. The same infant current behavior, as it is correlated with the mother's just prior behavior, is used to generate infant interactive contingency.

Figure 3.1 shows our analysis which uses a moving 4-second "window." We predict the behavior of each partner at a particular second in time (t_0) from the 3 prior seconds. We can illustrate this, for example, with infant looking and looking away from the mother's face. To calculate *infant gaze self-contingency*, second 4 in the infant's stream of behavior identifies t_0, the predicted moment. At each predicted moment the infant's gaze could be at or away from the mother's face. The prior 1 second back (t_{-1}), 2 seconds back (t_{-2}), and 3 seconds back (t_{-3}) in the infant's behavioral stream identify the 3 prior seconds. At each of these

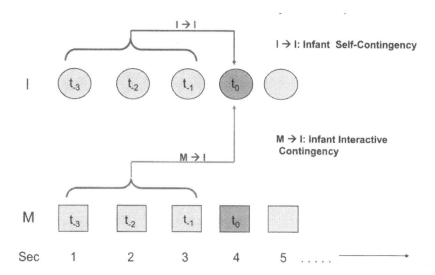

Figure 3.1 Illustrations of infant self- and interactive contingencies defined by time-series analysis

Note. To calculate infant self-contingency, second 4 in the infant's stream of behavior identifies t_0, the predicted second. A weighted average of seconds t_{-1}, t_{-2}, and t_{-3} in the infant's behavioral stream identify the "weighted lag," which is used to predict t_0. To calculate infant interactive contingency, a weighted average of seconds t_{-1}, t_{-2}, and t_{-3} in the mother's behavioral stream is used to predict t_0 in the infant's behavioral stream. For both self- and interactive contingency, this is an iterative process in which second 5 will then identify the new t_0, and seconds 2, 3, and 4 will identify the new "weighted lag." A parallel diagram would depict mother self- and interactive contingency.

prior moments the infant could be looking at or away from the mother's face. A weighted average of the prior 3 seconds is used to predict the current moment. This is an iterative process in which second 5 will then identify the new predicted moment (t_0), and seconds 2, 3, and 4 will be used to create a new weighted average. This is the next "window." This process continues across all the seconds coded, generating one overall assessment of infant self-contingency. Given that the infant is looking at, or away, from the mother's face at a particular moment, self-contingency estimates the likelihood that he was also looking at, or away in the prior 1, 2, and 3 seconds. That is, infant gaze self-contingency assesses the infant's own self-predictability within the interactive encounter: the likelihood that the infant continues to gaze at, or away, from the partner.

We calculate *infant gaze interactive contingency* similarly. A weighted average of the prior 3 seconds of the *mother's* looking at and away from the infant's face is used to predict the current moment of the *infant's* looking at or away from the mother. This process continues across all the seconds coded, generating one overall assessment of infant interactive contingency. This measure estimates the likelihood that the infant is looking at (or away from) mother's face in a particular moment, given that the mother was looking at (or away from) the infant's face 1, 2, and 3 seconds prior. This measure thus estimates the likelihood that the infant adjusts his looking (or looking away) based on whether the mother just looked (or looked away) in the prior 3 seconds.

In calculating in an individual's interactive contingency, his own self-contingency is statistically removed. Thus the analysis asks whether, over and above the predictability in the individual's behavior, there is any further variation in the individual's behavior that is predicted by the prior behavior of the partner. Similarly, in calculating the infant self-contingency, the infant's interactive contingency is removed (see Beebe et al., 2010, for details of method).

A Contingency Approach to Regulation

We adopt the terms self- and interactive *contingency* to avoid confusion over the many different meanings of the term "regulation" and "self-regulation." We nevertheless construe our self- and interactive contingency measures as forms of self- and interactive regulation.

In our prior work, through the publication of Beebe and Lachmann, *Infant research and adult treatment* (2002), we used the terms self- and interactive *regulation*. Through 2002, the research of Beebe, Jaffe, and colleagues did not include a specific measure of self-regulation. But since 2002 we introduced our new measure of self-contingency into our data analyses (Beebe et al., 2007, 2008, 2010, 2011). We were initially tempted to call it "self-regulation."

But self-contingency is only one dimension of self-regulation. Self-regulation itself is a complex and multi-faceted concept with many definitions. For example, self-regulation has been defined as down-regulation of arousal (Field, 1981), affect tolerance of positive states as well as the management of distress (Kopp,

1989), and an infant's tendency to be fearful, or to approach, when confronted with a novel situation (Hane, Fox, Henderson, & Marshall, 2008). In our prior writing, we used the term self-regulation to cover all these definitions.

Self-contingency is a narrower concept than self-regulation. Self-contingency addresses the degree to which a person's current action is influenced by his or her prior actions. We thus decided to change our term to self-contingency to avoid confusion. Our change in terms represents our effort to be more precise. However, our term interactive "contingency" is used by us in exactly the way we have used interactive "regulation" in prior work.

Self-contingency, the degree of predictability of an individual's behavioral rhythm across time, is a narrow but nevertheless important *dimension of self-regulation* (Thomas & Malone, 1979; Warner, 1992). Behavioral forms of self-regulation are originally grounded in basic biological rhythms, such as those of breathing (Feldman, 2007). The rhythms of human behavior are loose and irregular, or "nonperiodic" (Jaffe et al., 2001). Variations in the predictability of behavioral rhythms affect the individual's ability to anticipate, out of awareness, her own next move. Such variations also affect the partner's ability to anticipate the individual's behaviors.

As Messinger and colleagues argue self-predictability is fundamental to our understanding of infant social competence (Messinger, Ruvolo, Ekas, & Fogel, 2010). And we suggest in the next chapter that it is important in adult treatment as well. Moreover, predictability of behavior is the most general of the concepts of self-regulation. It is a fundamental principle of brain and behavior organization. The brain continuously anticipates changes in the environment and within the organism (Llinas, 2001; Pally, 2000).

Among the modalities coded, many possible pairings of infant–mother modalities could be made. We chose to generate eight mother–infant "modality-pairings" for examination of self- and interactive contingency at 4 months in relation to attachment at 12 month. Figure 3.2 depicts these pairings. Wherever possible we paired mother and infant in the same modality.

We now turn to a description of self- and interactive contingency across the communication modalities we assess.

Self- and Interactive Contingency Assessments in Our Data

Interactive contingency of gaze examines the degree to which each partner follows the direction of the other's gaze on and off the partner's face. For example, in our prior work, when mothers reported higher (vs. lower) levels of depressive symptoms at 6 weeks post-partum, by 4 months both mothers and infants were *less likely* to follow the other's gaze direction (Beebe et al., 2008).

Self-contingency of gaze refers to how predictably an individual looks and looks away from the partner's face. For example, mothers of 4-month infants who are on the way to 12-month disorganized attachment show a lowered self-contingency of gaze. This finding indicates that the mother is less predictable in her gaze patterns. It will be harder for the infant to anticipate when the mother will look, when she

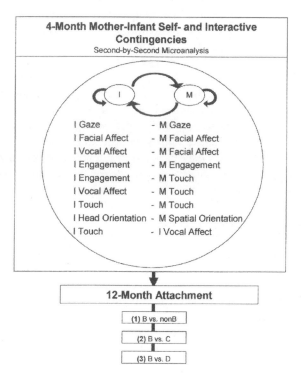

Figure 3.2 Design of the study: 4-month mother–infant self- and interactive contingencies (second-by-second microanalysis) were analysed for each of the modality pairings listed above (eg I Gaze–M Gaze). We report differences between
b (secure) vs. non B (all insecure), vs. C (insecure/resistant) and vs. D
(insecure/disorganized).

will look away, and for how long.

Interactive contingency of affect is examined as two patterns of affective
"mirroring," the likelihood that partners share direction of affective change: (1)
mother–infant facial affect mirroring and (2) maternal facial affect–infant *vocal*
affect mirroring.

For example, in our prior work, depressed mothers and their infants both followed the other's affective direction *more,* but followed the other's gaze direction
less (Beebe et al., 2008; Beebe, Lachmann, Jaffe et al., 2012). These findings are
a good example of inter-modal discrepancy. Whereas attention and affect usually
operate together as a "package," the depression group showed a peculiar split: lowered contingent coordination of attention, but heightened coordination of affect.
Both mothers and infants in the depression group did not pay as much attention
to whether the partner was available for social engagement. But, they heightened
their facial coordination with the partner's affective direction, brightening and
sobering with the other's similar shifts. The mother may be overly "thrilled" when

51

the infant is positive, and overly disappointed when the infant is negative. This example also illustrates our concept that interactive contingency can be "excessive" (vigilant) or "insufficient" (withdrawn).

Self-contingency of affect is examined as the degree to which the individual is predictable, or stable, moment-to-moment in (1) facial affect from positive to negative and (2) vocal affect from positive to negative. The most predictable pattern is one in which the individual continues to be in the same state from moment-to-moment, thus entirely "stable." The least predictable pattern in one in which the individual continues to change from moment-to-moment, which we dubbed "destabilized."

Interactive contingency of touch examines the degree to which, as infants touch more, mothers touch more affectionately (and vice versa); and whether the more affectionate the mother's quality of touch, the greater likelihood of infant touch (and vice versa).

Self-contingency of maternal touch refers to how predictably mothers shift across the continuum from affectionate to intrusive touch. In a highly predictable touch pattern the mother is changing types of touch more slowly; she is more likely to stay in a particular type of touch.

Self-contingency of infant touch refers to how predictably infants shift across the continuum from "none" to one, to two or more types of touch per second. Infant touch is coded as touching one's own skin, touching mother, or touching an object.

Interactive contingency of maternal spatial orientation and infant head orientation measures mutual approach and mutual withdrawal, or one partner approaching and one withdrawing. For example, as the infant orients away from the mother, what is the mother's likelihood of sitting back in an upright posture, vs. leaning forward or "looming" in close to the infant's face? Reciprocally, as mothers move forward, from upright to forward to loom, what is the likelihood that infants move away, from en face (oriented directly vis-à-vis mother) toward arch? This latter pattern is one of "mother chase–infant dodge" (Beebe & Stern, 1977; Beebe et al., 2010).

Self-contingency of maternal spatial orientation refers to how predictably mothers shift across the continuum from sitting upright, to leaning forward, to looming in.

Self-contingency of infant head orientation refers to how predictably infants shift across the continuum from en face to degrees of orienting away, toward 90° aversion, to the extreme of arching away.

We also created a composite variable of *facial-visual engagement* (see Appendix A). Engagement levels represent modes of interpersonal relatedness across a continuum from high positive engagement to negative affect and visual disengagement. This variable provides a holistic, *gestalt* approach to capturing the quality of the interaction. It integrates how the individual coordinates both looking and affect at the same time. Infant engagement is a composite of gaze on/off mother's face, head orientation from en face to arch, and facial affect and vocal affect (from positive to negative), ordered from a high score of "high positive engagement"' to a low of "cry." Mother engagement is a composite of gaze and facial affect, ordered from a high score of "mock surprise" to a low of "neutral/negative face" with gaze off.

Interactive contingency of facial-visual engagement examines the degree to which each partner follows the direction of the other's visual attention as well as affective direction.

Self-contingency of facial-visual engagement examines the stability of the individual's tendency to look at the partner as well as to show positive affect; or to look away from the partner and show dampened or negative affect.

The Meaning of Heightened and Lowered Contingency

We interpret heightened interactive contingency as an effort to create more predictability in contexts of novelty, challenge, or threat, translated into "activation" or "vigilance." Vigilance for social signals is an important aspect of social intelligence, likely an evolutionary advantage with uncertainty or threat (Ohman, 2002). Clinically this picture might translate into a mother who is "trying too hard," or "following too closely."

We interpret lowered interactive contingency as "inhibition" or "withdrawal," where metaphorically each partner is relatively more "alone" in the presence of the other (Beebe et al., 2000; Jaffe et al., 2001). The partner's lowered interactive contingency compromises the individual's ability to anticipate consequences of his own actions for the partner, lowering the individual's interactive agency.

Hay (1997) suggests that social experiences that force the infant to pay too much attention to the partner, *a heightened interactive coordination*, or reciprocally to pay too little attention, *a lowered interactive coordination*, are likely to interfere with the infant's developing ability to attend to the environment, disturbing social and cognitive development. Either heightened or lowered infant contingent coordination may disturb the infant's ability to modulate his own emotional state while processing information.

Our Approach to Mother–Infant Communication Predicted Attachment Outcomes

Self- and interactive contingency, and rates of behavioral qualities, across the modalities of attention, affect, orientation, and touch, constitute the methods of analysis that we brought to our second-by-second data. Based on 2½ minutes of data per dyad, this approach predicted attachment outcomes at one year. We used our results to characterize the nature of the 4-month infant's procedural, presymbolic representations of "how interactions go," or emerging "internal working models" of communication relevant to attachment.

The specificity of our approach allowed us to identify new patterns of communication disturbances. We identified intermodal discrepancies, which may be intrapersonal or dyadic. For example, we identified infant "discrepant affect," smiling and whimpering in the same second.

Our approach allowed us to "unpack" interactions which might be coded as interactive errors (Tronick, 1989) or communication errors (Lyons-Ruth et al.,

1999), such as maternal smiling while infants are distressed. It led to the identification of different forms of maternal emotional withdrawal, such as lowered emotional coordination with the infant's positive and distressed moments; or over-stabilizing the face and becoming inscrutable. We also identified difficulties in the regulation of attention, such as instability in the maternal "attentional frame," resulting in patterns of looking and looking away that are hard to predict.

Thus this approach allows us to understand better what the nuances of the infant's experience might be. It provides a language for describing nonverbal communication in the mother–infant face-to-face exchange which can also be useful in describing aspects of nonverbal communication in adult treatment, which we discuss in the next chapter.

Brief Review of Our Findings on the 4-Month Origins of Disorganized Attachment

This section briefly reviews the fruits of our new approach in generating new ways of understanding mother–infant communication disturbances that predict disorganized attachment. We describe the "headlines" of the 4-month origins of disorganized attachment, discussed in detail in Chapter 7. We used our 4-month microanalyses of mother and infant communication patterns to predict secure (N = 47 dyads) compared to disorganized (N = 17 dyads) attachment at one year.

Figure 3.3 summarizes the 4-month communication patterns that predicted one-year disorganized attachment. Following each finding described below we offer an inference about the infants' experiences. See Chapter 7 for more extensive inferences about the mothers' experiences.

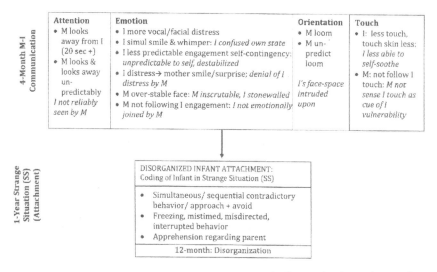

Figure 3.3 Summary of findings predicting 12-month disorganized attachment from mother–infant interaction at 4 months (see Beebe et al., 2010)

Attention Dysregulation in Future Disorganized Attachment Dyads

Compared to future secure dyads, in future disorganized dyads mothers gazed away from the infant's face excessively (30 seconds or more across the 2½ minutes coded), and they did so in a less predictable fashion. *These future disorganized infants may not feel reliably seen by their mothers.*

Affect Dysregulation in Future Disorganized Infants

Compared to future secure infants, future disorganized infants showed more vocal and facial distress. At times this distress became frantic. For example, one pair showed the pattern of "mutually escalating overarousal." Both mother and infant escalated the ante, as the infant built to a frantic distress. Even after extreme distress signals from the infant, such as 90-degree head aversion, arching away and screaming, the mother kept going. At the end the infant vomited. *These infants may experience frantic states of over-arousal, without repair. The mother may feel desperate to reach her infant.*

Future disorganized infants also showed more *discrepant affect*, such as smile and whimper within the same second. *Infant discrepant affect suggests affective conflict, confusion, and struggle. Discrepant affect may lead these future disorganized infants to feel confused about their own emotional state. Mothers may also feel confused.*

Future disorganized (vs. secure) infants showed lowered self-predictability of facial-visual engagement. *It may be harder for future disorganized (vs. secure) infants to sense their own next engagement "move;" they may feel "destabilized."*

Affect Dysregulation in Mothers of Future Disorganized Infants

Mothers of future disorganized (vs. secure) infants lowered their interactive coordination with infant facial-visual engagement, a form of maternal withdrawal. These mothers were less likely to follow infant direction of gaze, to become facially positive as their infants became facially or vocally positive, and to dampen their facial affect toward interest, neutral, or "woe face" as their infants sobered or became facially or vocally distressed. This pattern indicates a lowered maternal ability to emotionally "enter" and "go with" infant positive as well as distressed moments. *We infer that infants will not feel emotionally joined by mother.*

Mothers of future disorganized (vs. secure) infants showed heightened facial self-contingency, remaining overly facially stable, or inscrutable, similar to a momentary "still-face." *The infants may feel "stonewalled" and unable to read the mother.*

Mothers of future disorganized (vs. secure) infants were more likely to show smiles or surprise faces while infants were facially or vocally distressed: an emotional "denial" of infant distress. *Infants may feel "opposed" or "countered"* as mothers literally go in the opposite affective direction, as if attempting to "ride negative into positive." *We infer that it is difficult for infants to feel that their mothers sense and acknowledge their distress. We infer that it is difficult for mothers to empathically acknowledge infant distress.*

Comment on affect dysregulation findings: We suggest that future disorganized infants construct contradictory models of self-in-relation-to-other. For example, self as smiling at mother and whimpering to mother in the same moment, or self as protesting and grimacing as mother smiles or shows a surprise face, constitute contradictory expectancies. As Lyons-Ruth, Dutra, Schuder, and Bianchi (2006) note, these contradictions constitute a lack of integration in strategies for seeking comfort when distressed and may confer a vulnerability to dissociative processes (see Liotti, 1992).

Orientation Dysregulation in Future Disorganized Attachment Dyads

Mothers of future disorganized (vs. secure) infants showed excessive looming (30 seconds or more across the 2.5 minutes coded) into the infant's face. In addition, the *self-contingency process* of moving among the orientation positions of sitting upright, leaning forward, and looming in was less predictable in these mothers. Thus these mothers not only loomed more, but they did so relatively unpredictably. Looming into the infant's face often elicits a protective response: infants put their hands in front of their faces and turn their heads away (Bower, Broughton, & Moore, 1970). Loom behavior is postulated as frightening by Main and Hesse (1990). *These infants may be frightened by unpredictable maternal looming into their faces.*

Infant Touch Dysregulation in Future Disorganized Attachment Dyads

Infant touch was coded per second as not touching, any one type of touching [self, mother, or object], and two or more types of touch. Future disorganized (vs. secure) infants were less likely to touch. They spent less time specifically in touching their own skin, and they were more likely to be in the state of "no touch." In addition, in the *self-contingency process* of moving among touch states, future disorganized infants were more likely to get "stuck" in extended periods of not touching. These distressed infants thus have less access to self-comfort through touch, disturbing their agency, which may add to *a sense of helplessness in their distress.*

Maternal Touch Dysregulation in Future Disorganized Attachment Dyads

Mothers of future disorganized (vs. secure) infants lowered their contingent touch coordination with infant touch, a form of maternal withdrawal. As infants showed more touch efforts, mothers of future secure infants were likely to touch more affectionately and tenderly (and to use more active, rousing types of touch only when infants were not engaged in a lot of touch efforts). In contrast, mothers of future disorganized infants were less likely to show this pattern. *We infer that future disorganized infants come to expect that their mothers will be unavailable to help modulate states of affective distress through maternal touch coordination with their own touch efforts. Infants are left too alone, too separate, in the realm of touch.*

In Chapter 7 we suggest that the procedural representations of these interactions in future disorganized infants will be characterized by expectancies of emotional distress and emotional incoherence, difficulty predicting what will happen, both in the self and the partner, disturbance in experiences of recognition, and difficulty in obtaining comfort.

Mothers of disorganized infants are thought to be suffering from unresolved loss, abuse, or trauma, and to be in a continuing state of fear (Lyons-Ruth et al., 1999; Main & Hesse, 1990). Although we make more extensive inferences about the mothers' experiences in Chapter 7, here we note that mothers of future disorganized infants also have profoundly confusing, disturbing experiences of their infants. They do not obtain from their infants the "recognition" they need, that is, the happy, smiling "welcoming" infant. They frequently make comments to their distressed infants of "Don't be that way," "You don't want to be like that," "Smile for mommy," "No fussing, no fussing, you should be very happy." Thus these mothers notice their infant's distress, but this distress may trigger ongoing unresolved fears in the mothers that, in turn, gain expression in their complex and contradictory behavior. Their own difficulties with distress seem to make it extremely difficult for these mothers to relate empathically to their infants' distress.

Disturbances in Knowing and Being Known in the Origins of Disorganized Attachment

In these early interactions the organization of intimate relating is at stake (see Lyons-Ruth, 2008). Intimate relating entails the fundamental issue of how the infant comes to know, and be known by, another's mind. "Mind" is construed from the point of view of the infant, that is, expectancies of procedurally organized action sequences. Our findings allow us to describe *how* the future disorganized infant's ability to know, and be known by, another's mind, as well as to know his own mind, may be disturbed.

We propose that the future disorganized infant will have difficulty *feeling known* by his mother:

- in moments when he is distressed, and she shows smile or surprise expressions;
- in moments when the mother looks away repeatedly and unpredictably, so that he does not feel seen;
- as mother does not coordinate her facial-visual engagement with his "ups" and "downs" in facial-visual engagement;
- as mother does not coordinate her affectionate-to-intrusive touch patterns

with his frequency of touch, generating infant expectations that mother does not *change* with him.

We propose that the future disorganized infant will have difficulty *knowing* his mother's mind:

* as he has difficulty integrating mother's discrepant smile or surprise face to his distress into a coherent percept;
* as he has difficulty predicting whether mother will look or look away, and for how long; whether she will sit upright, lean forward, or loom in;
* as she "closes up" her face and becomes inscrutable;
* as mother's lowered engagement coordination makes it difficult for the infant to "influence" mother with his facial-visual engagement, leading to the infant's expectation that mother does not join his direction of attentional and affective change; and
* as mother's lowered contingent touch coordination makes it difficult for the infant to "influence" mother with the frequency of his touch behaviors, leading to the infant's expectation that mother does not "follow" his touch behaviors by touching him more affectionately as he touches more (and vice versa).

We propose that the future disorganized infant will have difficulty *knowing himself*:

* in his moments of discrepant affect, for example as he smiles and whimpers in the same second;
* as his own engagement self-contingency is lowered, making it more difficult to sense his own facial-visual action tendencies from moment-to-moment;
* as he has difficulty touching (self, object, mother), and specifically difficulty touching his own skin, and as he gets "stuck" in states of "no touch," all of which disturb his visceral feedback through touch, and disturb his own agency in regulating distress through touch.

In the next chapter we propose that these communication disturbances can be translated into new analogies and parallels in adult treatment.

4

INFANT DISORGANIZED ATTACHMENT, YOUNG ADULT OUTCOMES, AND ADULT TREATMENT

In this chapter we move to adulthood. In the past decade a new view of development has emerged which reaches from infancy to young adulthood. We discuss research which specifically predicts young adult dissociation from disorganized attachment at one year. We then link our findings on the 4-month origins of infant one-year disorganized attachment to research which links disorganized attachment at one year to young adult dissociation.

Disorganized attachment provides an important new way of thinking about psychopathology and its developmental course across the first two decades of life. Disorganized attachment cuts across many major diagnostic classifications (Lyons-Ruth, 1998a; Lyons-Ruth & Jacobvitz, 2008). In the general population, 15% of infants will be classified disorganized attachment; in high-risk populations, the percentage is higher. Thus it is likely that well over 15% of our adult patients may have had the relational dynamics in infancy leading to disorganized attachment that are documented in this book.

We then turn to the adult clinical situation. We review the nonconscious procedural dimension of face-to-face communication in adult treatment, also known as "implicit relational knowing" (Lyons-Ruth, 1998b, 1999). We consider what self- and interactive regulation might look like in face-to-face adult treatment.

The mother–infant patterns identified in the origins of disorganized attachment provide new ways of understanding and interpreting relational patterns as they emerge in adult treatment. Particularly contradictory patterns of communication in the context of distress, and difficulties in knowing and being known, which emerged from our findings on mother–infant communication, provide parallels and analogies for mismatches and communication difficulties that may appear in adult treatment.

Early interaction disturbances inevitably color adult treatment. How the therapist and the patient together co-create their patterns of relatedness, their ways of knowing and being known, both verbal and nonverbal, can ameliorate or exacerbate current-day "shadows" of early interaction disturbances. Knowledge of this research can alert the therapist to modes of nonverbal relatedness that can ameliorate the shadows of early interaction disturbances and facilitate engagement and therapeutic action.

In the final section we provide several case vignettes of adult treatment. We are particularly interested in how to facilitate engagement and therapeutic action in the shadow of early interaction disturbances. We focus on the repair of disturbances in knowing the partner, being known by the partner, and knowing oneself, in adult treatment.

Disorganized Attachment in Infancy Predicts Young Adult Dissociation

We have known for some time that secure attachment at one year is associated in childhood with better peer relations, school performance, and capacity to regulate emotions, as well as less psychopathology (Sroufe, 1983). We have also known that disorganized attachment at one year predicts childhood difficulties, particularly controlling behavior, either punitive or caregiving, and externalizing behavior and aggression (Dutra, Bureau, Holmes, Lyubchik, & Lyons-Ruth, 2009).

But only recently have we learned that disorganized attachment at 12 to 18 months predicts young adulthood outcomes. A remarkable series of longitudinal studies in the last decade show that infant attachment status sets a trajectory in development that predicts young adult outcomes (for example Dutra et al., 2009; Fraley, 2002; Grossmann, Grossmann, Winter, & Zimmermann, 2002; Shi, Bureau, Easterbrooks, Zhao, & Lyons-Ruth, 2012; Sroufe et al., 2005; Waters, Merrick, Treboux, Crowell, & Albersheim, 2000). We also note that there are some studies which failed to predict attachment in young adulthood from attachment in infancy (see for example Lewis, Feiring, & Rosenthal, 2000). We focus here on those studies which predict young adult dissociation from disorganized infant attachment.

These remarkable predictions do not mean, however, that development is "set in stone" in infancy. Instead, we view interactions in infancy as setting a transformational trajectory. In this transformational model, development proceeds through a process of regular restructurings of the relations within and between the person and the environment (Sameroff, 1983). Disorganized attachment represents an extreme end of attachment possibilities. Within a transformational and nonlinear model of development, this prediction from disorganized attachment in infancy to young adult outcomes thus operates at an extreme end of the range (see Kagan, 1997).

"Map" of Research Linking 4-Month Mother–Infant Communication, 12–18-Month Infant Secure vs. Disorganized Attachment, and Young Adult Outcomes

In Figure 4.1 we link our work on the 4-month origins of disorganized infant attachment to longitudinal studies predicting young adult dissociation from disorganized infant attachment. These studies show that disorganized attachment, and maternal "disrupted communication" (measured within the attachment assessment)

60

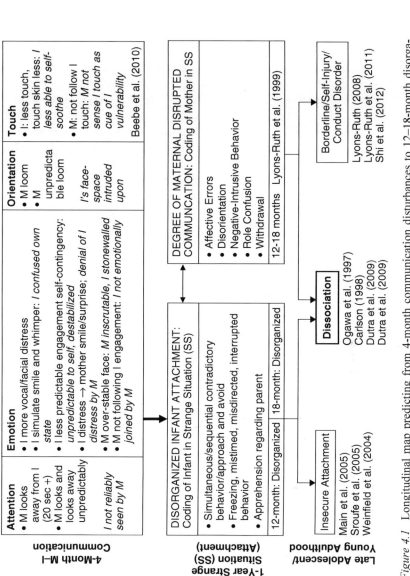

Figure 4.1 Longitudinal map predicting from 4-month communication disturbances to 12–18-month disorganized attachment to young adult outcomes

which is associated with disorganized attachment, predict young adult attachment insecurity and dissociation. In addition, maternal disrupted communication itself predicts a number of other problematic outcomes in young adulthood.

The top third of Figure 4.1 is the same as Figure 3.3 presented in the last chapter. It summarizes our findings on the 4-month origins of 12-month disorganized attachment. The middle third of Figure 4.1 depicts disorganized attachment on the left, and maternal disrupted communication on the right. Patterns of maternal disrupted communication identified within the attachment assessment were associated with disorganized attachment at 18 months (Lyons-Ruth et al., 1999).

The lowest third of Figure 4.1 shows studies which predicted young adult outcomes. We list several studies which predicted young adult insecure attachment and dissociation from infant disorganized attachment. Lyons-Ruth's measure of disrupted communication likewise predicted young adult dissociation, as well as borderline psychopathology, self-injury, and conduct disorder.

Because different studies using disorganized infant attachment and maternal disrupted communication converge in predicting young adult dissociation, we focus on dissociation. The definition of dissociation, following the research we describe, is based on the Dissociative Experiences Scale (Bernstein & Putnam 1986), a self-report measure. In this scale, the symptoms that reflect dissociation include amnesia, so that the person is unaware of what he is doing or how he got to where he is; absorption to the point that the person is unaware of the surroundings; and depersonalization, so that the person experiences events as though he is a third party or the person feels disconnected from his body.

In Figure 4.1, note that we have no direct link from our 4-month communication patterns to young adult outcomes; our own study followed these 4-month infants only to 12 months. Instead we infer this link. We propose that the contradictory patterns of communication we document at 4 months, which predict infant disorganized attachment at one year, set the stage for the developmental trajectory from disorganized attachment in infancy to dissociative forms of adaptation in young adulthood identified by other researchers.

As we proposed in the previous chapter, future disorganized infants at 4 months cannot develop an expectation of feeling "sensed" or "known," particularly when distressed. Disturbances of recognition were identified in all communication domains examined. In attention, the infant may feel not seen; in emotion the infant may feel not joined, and stonewalled when distressed; in orientation the infant experiences looming impingements; and in touch the infant is not touched more tenderly when he shows more aroused touch patterns. At times these infants may feel alarmed or threatened. We argued that the remarkable intrapersonal and dyadic contradictory communications and conflict disturb the coherence of the infant's experience. Thus we propose that the 4-month patterns documented in the origins of disorganized attachment are likely to set a trajectory in development which disturbs the fundamental integration of the person.

We hypothesize that dissociative experiences during times of distress later in life have their origins in experiences in infancy of not being sensed, met, known, and recognized, particularly in moments of distress. The difficulties in integrating contradictory communications and experiences identified in our data at 4 months are echoed in Spiegel and Cardeña's (1991) definition of dissociation as a separation of mental processes, such as thoughts, emotions, memory, that are ordinarily integrated.

The intense distress experience of future disorganized infants is often agitated and frantic, and at moments alarmed or threatened. When threatened we change from a state which is open to social engagement to states of fight-flight, freeze, or collapse (Porges, Doussard-Roosevelt, & Maiti, 1994). Clinically we observed such behaviors in future disorganized infants at 4 months. For example, after one mother greeted her intensely distressed infant with a big smile, we observed highly active, forceful infant movements of jerking the body while turning away from mother in the chair, which could be considered a precursor of "fight-flight." We observed moments of "freezing" when one mother poked and pushed her infant's face and head, but other than a blink, nothing in the infant's face or body moved. We also observed moments of infant "collapse." For example after multiple maternal intrusions with looming, chasing, and pulling the infant's arm to re-orient him after he turned away, the infant collapsed his head into his belly, with his body limp like a ragdoll. His mother raised and lowered his arms, but they fell back limp at his side. We also observed a pattern of mutually escalating over-arousal, in which mother and infant each upped the ante, the infant becoming more and more distressed, and the mother frantically trying to engage him by escalating her tempo and voice; eventually the infant vomited.

Main and Solomon (1990) describe disorganized infants as alarmed by the parent. The unresolvable dilemma of the disorganized infant is that the very parent that he needs for comfort is the parent who alarms him. Siegel suggests that the infant's direct response to such dyadic disruption is a neurologically "non-organized" or disrupted state (Siegel, 1999, 2012, personal communication, September 23, 2012). There is no adaptive strategy available. As these interactions repeat, the infant experiences a powerful loss of efficacy and helplessness. He learns that, at such moments of intense distress and dyadic disruption, he will not be able to get help and he will not be able to help himself. Later in development these moments may be experienced as helplessness, hopelessness, or shame. They may be associated with a fragmentation of attention and memory. Ultimately experiences of numbing, freezing, collapse, derealization, and depersonalization associated with dissociation succeed in altering the person's state of terror. Similarly Schore (2011) suggests that intense distress without repair is at the core of the disintegration that occurs in dissociative responses to overwhelming experiences. Thus the intense distress experiences of future disorganized infants in our data, characterized as often agitated and frantic, and at moments alarmed or threatened, are echoed in the descriptions of Main and Solomon, Siegel, and Schore.

We now turn to a brief description of a few of the studies which show that disorganized attachment at 12–18 months in the Ainsworth Strange Situation, and maternal disrupted behavior in this same context, predict young adult dissociation. We review two studies from the Minnesota longitudinal cohort: Ogawa, Sroufe,

63

Weinfeld, Carlson, & Egeland (1997) and Carlson (1998). We also review the work of Lyons-Ruth that specifically predicts young adult dissociation (Lyons-Ruth, 2003; Lyons-Ruth, 2008; Lyons-Ruth et al., 2006, 2011). For a review of this literature, see Lyons-Ruth and Jacobvitz (2008). For a collection of key papers, see Grossmann, Grossmann, and Waters (2005).

We begin with a caveat. The field of longitudinal studies from infancy to adulthood is relatively new, in the past decade or so. Although there have been striking predictions from infancy to adulthood, there have also been a few failures of prediction (Lewis et al., 2000). Moreover, although these studies show that early experience casts a long "shadow" on development, at least through early adulthood, later experiences also play an important role. If the environment changes, the quality of a child's adaptation is likely to change (Sroufe, 1983, 2005). These studies use a transformational rather than linear model of development (Sameroff, 1983). Most take into account the role of changing life circumstances, such as the occurrence of trauma, in predicting development. Thus transformations from secure to insecure are likely with trauma (Waters et al., 2000). Transformations from insecure to secure are also likely with special developmental advantages (Saunders, Jacobvitz, Zaccagnino, Beverung, & Hazen, 2011). Nevertheless, infant experience unquestionably has a special role. It frames the child's subsequent interactions with the environment, and it becomes the basis for various strategies for coping with stress, most prominently young adult dissociation (Carlson & Sroufe, 1995; Sroufe, Carlson, Levy, & Egeland, 1999).

Ogawa, Sroufe, Weinfeld, Carlson and Egeland (1997)

The Minnesota longitudinal cohort is a lifespan study from birth to young adulthood of a sample of children considered high risk for psychopathology due to poverty, single parenthood, younger age mothers, and low education status. Assessments were conducted at birth, every three months until 3 ½ years; grades 1, 2, 3, 6, and 7; ages 16, 17 ½, and 19 years. Sources of information included interviews with mothers and children, self-report scales, videotaped assessments of attachment at 12 and 18 months, and teacher reports.

Ogawa et al. (1997) predicted outcomes at five time-points from birth to age 19 in 126 children. We describe here only those findings which pertain to the prediction of dissociation at age 19 from measures in infancy. Dissociation was measured with a subset of items from the Dissociative Experiences Scale (Bernstein & Putnam, 1986) which captured more severe forms of dissociation, such as amnesia for dissociation, identity confusion, depersonalization, and derealization.

Ogawa et al. (1997) documented that trauma in infancy predicted higher levels of dissociation in young adulthood. Trauma in infancy was defined as experienced or witnessed abuse, a 1-month separation or longer, or the death of an immediate family member. Ogawa et al. suggest their findings indicate that early trauma is important for dissociation in young adulthood, but trauma at later points in development may have less impact.

In this study disorganized attachment in infancy predicted dissociation in high school and young adulthood. Moreover, disorganized attachment predicted the more extreme forms of young adult dissociation. Dissociation was predicted by maternal psychological unavailability (detached or uninvolved) in infancy, infant disorganized attachment, and lower infant attention span. Ogawa et al. were surprised that the predictors of young adult dissociation were all measures from infancy. These findings strongly support the importance of early experience for young adult development. As Lyons-Ruth noted about the Ogawa–Sroufe findings, "The consistency of the relation between early disorganization and later dissociative symptomatology at all ages was striking and unexpected" (2003, p. 893).

Carlson (1998)

The same cohort reported in Ogawa et al. (1997) was examined in a different way by Carlson (1998). She studied 157 mother–child pairs from birth to 19 years. She examined antecedents and consequences of disorganized attachment assessed at 12–18 months.

Regarding antecedents, the "biological" factors assessed did not predict 12–18-month infant disorganized attachment. "Biological" factors included mother's medical history, infant anomalies at birth, 7-day and 10-day Brazelton Neonatal Behavioral Assessment Scale measures, and maternal ratings of infant temperament (Carey, 1970) at 3 months.

A number of "environmental" factors did predict disorganized infant attachment, such as single-parenthood, maternal risk for parenting difficulties (assessed at birth), lower maternal caretaking skill during a 3-month feeding in the home (insensitive or intrusive caretaking), lower maternal cooperation and sensitivity (lower ability to adapt timing and quality of her stimulation to infant state, mood, and interest) during feeding and play assessed at 6 months in the home, and abuse (physical abuse, psychological unavailability, neglect) in the first year of life.

Regarding the consequences of 12–18-month disorganized infant attachment, Carlson documented that 12–18-month infant disorganized attachment predicted difficulties in mother–child relationship quality at 24 and 42 months; behavioral problems in preschool, elementary, and high school; and teacher reports of dissociation in elementary and high school.

Of central interest here, Carlson also found that 12–18-month disorganized infant attachment predicted severity of psychopathology at 17 years (Kiddie Schedule for Affective Disorders and Schizophrenia Rating, "K-SADS;" Puig-Antich & Chambers, 1978) and dissociative experiences (Carlson & Putnam, 1993) at 19 years. Moreover, a combined measure of early caregiving prior to one year (caretaking skill, cooperation/sensitivity and abuse) directly predicted dissociation (but not psychopathology) in young adulthood.

These two studies of one cohort of subjects show strong predictions from 12–18-month disorganized infant attachment to young adult dissociation (Carlson,

1998; Ogawa et al., 1997). Moreover the Carlson study found that early caregiving prior to one year also predicted both disorganized infant attachment, and young adult dissociation. Although the Carlson methods of assessing early caregiving are different from ours, and focus on the mother, they do provide an important parallel to the findings we report in this book, namely that factors in the mother–infant relationship early in the first year predict disorganized attachment.

Lyons-Ruth

Lyons-Ruth, Bronfman, and Parsons (1999) have taken an innovative approach to the assessment of infant attachment in the Ainsworth Strange Situation at 12–18 months. In addition to examining the infant's behaviors in the reunion episodes, which yields the attachment categories, they examined the mother's behavior in the reunion episodes. They developed scales of maternal *disrupted communication* (Lyons-Ruth, 2003; Lyons-Ruth et al., 1999) which follow:

- affective errors, such as smiling when the infant is distressed, or conflicting affective cues, such as inviting approach but then distancing;
- withdrawal, such as creating physical or verbal distance at the reunion, or failure to greet the infant at the reunion;
- role confusion: role reversal, such as attempts to elicit reassurance from the infant at the time of the reunion; or sexualization, such as hushed, intimate tones;
- negative-intrusive behavior, either physical, such as pulling the infant by the wrist; or verbal, such as mocking and teasing; and
- disorientation behaviors, in which the mother seems confused or frightened by the infant.

At 12–18 months, overall degree of maternal disrupted communication (based on all scales) is associated with concurrent disorganized attachment. In addition, several subscales of disrupted maternal communication are associated with disorganized attachment: affective errors, withdrawal, disorientation, and role confusion (Lyons-Ruth et al., 1999). Of central interest here, Lyons-Ruth (2003, 2008) predicated young adult dissociation from overall degree of maternal disrupted communication in infancy and two subscales: affective errors and role confusion. Degree of disrupted maternal communication at 18 months was a stronger predicator of young adult dissociation than disorganized attachment per se (Lyons-Ruth et al., 2006).

Similar to Ogawa et al. (1997) and Carlson (1998), Lyons-Ruth (2003) also found that broad social risk factors such as poverty or single parenthood did not predict young adult dissociative symptoms. Other variables that did not predict later dissociation in Lyons-Ruth's cohort were maltreatment from birth to age five, clinicians' judgments of risk for maltreatment during the first year, or psychiatric symptoms of the mother such as dissociation, depression, and post-traumatic stress disorder.

Lyons-Ruth et al. (2006) see the origins of young adult dissociation in the early mother–infant interactive process itself. They suggest that ongoing forms of par-ent–child disrupted and discrepant communication, which continue to organize contradictory mental processes, may be the key. Lyons-Ruth was among the first to argue that parental inconsistency, and maternal unavailability to respond to infant distress, were key components of the picture of disorganized attachment. Her data are strikingly consistent with our prediction of disorganized attachment from discrepant and conflictual mother–infant communication, and maternal emo-tional withdrawal from distressed infants, at 4 months.

Lyons-Ruth et al. (2006) suggest that mother–infant interactive dysregulations are "hidden traumas" in which the child becomes shut out of the process of dialogue itself. One cannot know one's experience until it is seen, recognized, and reflected on by the other (see Lyons-Ruth et al., 2006; Whitmer, 2001). Similarly, the 4-month interaction patterns that we document in the origins of disorganized attach-ment share this feature: infants are not seen, recognized, and empathized with.

Addressing the implications of this research for adult treatment, Lyons-Ruth et al. (2006) emphasize the need for an affectively alive, collaborative dialogue with the therapist, in which the patient can feel seen and recognized. The collaborative nonverbal action-dialogue proceeds hand-in-hand with the collaborative narrative dialogue. Later in this chapter we illustrate with case vignettes our own (BB and FL) attempts to create affectively alive, collaborative dialogues with our patients.

In summary, the field of developmental psychology is now able to predict from infancy to young adulthood, using mother–infant communication patterns, and attachment status, among other variables. The implications are startling. This lon-gitudinal predictability implies that the very idea of who we are, our identity, is embedded in early dyadic interactions. To understand ourselves dyadically is to see ourselves as more porous and vulnerable to the state and behavior of the other than we would often like to think.

Comment on Dissociation in Adult Treatment

The Ogawa et al. (1997) group considered dissociation to be a distortion of a core self-process. They defined self as the integration and organization of diverse aspects of one's experience, and dissociation as difficulties in the integration of one's experience.

In Lyons-Ruth's work (2003, 2008; Lyons-Ruth et al., 1999) early maternal with-drawal and affective errors at 12–18 months interfere with the infant's developing ability to organize experience, leading to young adult dissociation. Likewise in our own data at 4 months, there are many patterns of discordance and contradiction, both within the infant's own behaviors (smiling and whimpering in the same second) or between mother and infant (infant distressed, mother smiling), which interfere with the infant's ability to organize and integrate experience. Patterns of maternal with-drawal from infant distress are salient. These patterns disturb the infant's ability to feel sensed, known, and recognized, particularly in moments of distress.

Thus dissociation may have its origins in early difficulties in integrating experi-ence in the context of failures of maternal recognition, and intense distress that remains unrepaired. These difficulties are evident in our data during face-to-face interaction at 4 months. They are also evident at 12–18 months during the Ains-worth attachment assessment (see Porges et al., 1994; Schore, 2011; Siegel, 2012). The unresolvable dilemma of the disorganized infant is that the very parent that he needs for comfort is the parent who alarms him (Main & Solomon, 1990). The outcome is a process in which the very person on whom the infant depends for recognition of his states of attention, emotion, orientation, and touch, is the person who cannot recognize them.

We suggest that dissociation functions as an attempt to alter self-experience and the subjective world. It performs survival functions at the cost of loss of flexibility in the ability to deal with stress. If we put ourselves into the shoes of the young adult, we can imagine that dissociation can make the world more controllable, predictable, and thereby safer in the face of overwhelming threat. It constitutes a kind of "time out" experience, reported by some victims of rape, for example.

The research suggests the need to recognize the leading edge of dissociative symptoms, particularly in young adult patients. Leading-edge and trailing-edge interpretations were distinguished by Kohut (see Lachmann, 2008; Miller, 1985). Trailing edge interpretations address what the therapist believes the patient is attempting to ward off, or unconsciously cannot accept. The emphasis is on the negative effect of the patient's behavior on the self and the other.

In contrast, leading edge interpretations refer to what the therapist infers the patient is attempting to attain or maintain. For example, dissociating may help the patient tolerate an unpredictably responsive world, avoid distress or terror, and thus feel more secure. The leading edge recognizes that the patient is attempting to establish a world with some sense of safety, security, and predictability.

Ghent (1990) described Milner's (1952) treatment of an 11-year-old girl which illustrates leading-edge and trailing-edge interpretations. This child, in Ghent's words, "…fervently and defiantly scribbled on every surface she could find. Although it looked as if it were done in anger, interpretation in terms of aggression only led to increase in the defiance. In fact, the apparent defiance did not change until (Milner) began to guess that the trouble was less to do with faeces given in anger and meant to express anger, than with faeces given in love and meant to express love" (p. 106).

In treating adult patients who dissociate, it is inevitable that the treatment will re-evoke aspects of the very experiences that contributed to early developmen-tal difficulties. The key therapeutic question has to do with the balance between repetition and repair. If the therapist fails to recognize dissociative symptoms as containing some remnant of what the child originally needed, the treatment may tip toward the recreation of interactive patterns too similar to those in the patient's childhood.

Based on our research, as well as that of Lyons-Ruth, we propose that what the infant originally needed was to be protected from the threat of failures of recognition. This formulation is strikingly consistent with that of Bromberg (2011), working with adult patients. In our data, failures of maternal recognition included failures to join the infant's positive as well as negative feelings, to empathize with the infant's distress, to provide the infant a predictable feeling of being seen, to protect the infant from looming impingements, and to meet the infant's increasing use of touch with more tender and affectionate forms of touch. These failures of recognition set a trajectory in development that may lead to an inability to integrate experience.

Bucci (2011) suggests that purpose of dissociation is to turn the person's attention away from the source of the threat. There may be a disruption in the original encoding of the memory (primary dissociation) or an incomplete encoding of the memory (secondary dissociation). She suggests that the dilemma of dissociation is that the person is left with many unexplained potentially overwhelming bodily, motoric, or affective responses to stimuli that are unknown, unrecognized. The person has lost the connection to what she fears and how to respond (Bucci, 2011).

The therapeutic task is to acknowledge the impact of cumulative experiences of threat, which began in infancy. Silence, an unvarying vocal tone, asking for free associations, not answering questions, or turning questions back to the patient may all be experienced as a withdrawal by the therapist. The patient can experience these behaviors as too similar to a parent who had an inscrutable face, who looked away unpredictably, who did not join his or her positive or negative emotional states, or who stonewalled him in his distress. Whereas these reactions of the patient can be seen as lending themselves to analytic investigation and interpretation, they are not based on "distortions" or "fantasies." Instead they are shadows of early interaction patterns. The patient may thus be alarmed by the entire therapeutic context. In contrast, below we address patterns of interaction in adult treatment that may tip the balance toward repair.

There are many meanings of dissociation, and many interpretive strategies, a discussion of which goes beyond our scope. We note, however, that there is a striking fit between our findings at 4 months, and those of Lyons-Ruth at 12–18 months, both of which document maternal failures of recognition in disorganized attachment, and the theories of Bromberg (2011) and Benjamin (1995) in adult treatment, as well as theorists in neurobiology (Schore, 2009, 2011; Siegel, 1999, 2012; Porges et al., 1994). Bromberg (2011) proposes that the developmental trauma of non-recognition is so enormous that it is continually dreaded, like the shadow of a tsunami. Benjamin (1995) proposes that adult treatment requires a mutual recognition process in which both partners must find a way to recognize the different other. Many authors locate the origins of dissociation in unbearable, overwhelming experiences and unresolvable threat (Bromberg, 2011; Schore, 2011; Porges et al., 1994). The most common understanding of this threat in the picture of infant disorganized attachment is that the very parent that he needs for comfort is the parent who alarms him (Main & Solomon, 1990). But failures of recognition at 4 and 12 months provide an expanded view of the kinds of threat that may lead to dissociative processes.

69

The Adult Clinical Situation

Research on mother–infant communication might seem very far from the clinician's day-to-day concerns in the practice of adult treatment. But the moment-to-moment self- and interactive processes of relatedness documented in infancy are the bedrock of adult face-to-face communication as well. They provide a largely out-of-awareness background frame for the verbal narrative in the foreground. The subtleties of mother–infant communication disturbances have analogous forms in adults and thus have much to teach us as therapists of adults. Moreover, as the longitudinal research shows, modes of relatedness in adulthood are built on those of infancy.

Paralleling the linguistic, narrative dialogue in adult treatment, there is a simultaneous implicit, procedural action–dialogue. Although this action–dialogue is largely out of awareness, at times one can notice one's bodily experiences, so that some glimmers of it can become more conscious (Downing, 2011). If the therapist can understand the power of this nonverbal dialogue, and not inhibit its emergence, therapeutic action is facilitated. The therapist's use of the nonverbal action–dialogue emerges through spontaneous changes in bodily arousal, somatic sensations, and affective reactions (Bucci, 2011). These are the processes that allow the therapist to change with her patient's action sequences, to enter into her patient's experiences.

Because the shadows of early interaction disturbances are re-evoked in the treatment setting, the research can help us to be more aware of the kinds of interactive mismatches in the action dialogue that the patient may be sensitive to. It may help us be more aware of specific ways in which longings to know the partner, and be known by the partner, were derailed and may be re-activated. We may be more able to create "model scenes" (Lachmann, 2000) which capture current "shadows" of early interaction disturbances. And we may be able to become more aware of parallel or analogous processes in our own histories that help us empathize with the dilemmas of our patients (see Slavin, 2010, 2012). However, this "awareness" may not be a conscious awareness in the moment, a topic to which we now turn.

The Nonconscious Procedural Dimension of Face-to-Face Communication in Adult Treatment: Modes of Entering the State of the Other

Self- and interactive regulation in the treatment situation capture expectable patterns to which both partners actively contribute (Beebe & Lachmann, 2002). Each partner senses and anticipates her own as well as the partner's moment-to-moment process. This sensing occurs largely out of awareness, in a nonconscious, procedural format, although we can at times have glimmers of it. This procedural format provides a key dimension of therapeutic action (Beebe, 1998; Beebe & Lachmann, 1998, 2003; Beebe et al., 1992; Stern et al., 1998). We reserve the term unconscious for the dynamic unconscious, that which is kept out of awareness for dynamic reasons, such as conflict. In contrast, nonconscious processes can usually be brought into awareness by calling attention to them.

Lyons-Ruth (1998b, 1999) offers the concept of knowing how to proceed in intimate relationships, knowing the moment-by-moment sequences. She terms this "implicit relational knowing" (Lyons-Ruth, 1998b). In infancy, knowing how to proceed in intimate relationships is constructed through the procedural action–dialogue conducted through gaze, face, voice, orientation, and touch. In adult treatment, knowing how to proceed in intimate relationships is constructed through the procedural action–dialogue of facial expression, head orientation shifts, postural tonus, breathing rhythms, self-soothing, shifts in the chair, as well as the narrative dialogue.

Facial communication is used by a variety of researchers to explicate adult mechanisms of sensing and entering the state of the other in the procedural mode. Ekman, Levenson, and Friesen (1983; Levenson, Ekman, & Friesen, 1990) found that a particular facial expression is associated with a particular pattern of physiological arousal. Matching the expression of the partner therefore produces a similar physiological state in the onlooker. As partners match each other's affective patterns, each recreates a psychophysiological state in himself similar to the partner, thus participating in the subjective state of the other (Beebe & Lachmann, 1988, 2002). This process typically goes on outside of awareness.

Another example of nonconscious procedural knowledge is found in the work of Dimberg, Thunberg, and Elmehed (2000), "Unconscious facial reactions to emotional facial expression." They demonstrated that, out of awareness, adults cannot escape responding to the emotion of another person's face. In this experiment, the researchers used a taschistoscopic presentation of emotional faces by a "masked technique." Facial electrodes were attached to the subjects' faces (no pain is involved), and subjects were misled by being told that their sweat glands were being measured. Three slides of one face were sequentially presented for 30 milliseconds (30/1000 second) in a neutral pose, 30 milliseconds in an emotional pose (e.g., anger, or joy), and then 30 milliseconds in a neutral pose. The neutral poses "mask" the emotional pose. The total amount of time of the three sequential presentations is almost 1/10 second, approximately the amount of time required for the human brain consciously to perceive a stimulus. The brain registers a stimulus of 30 milliseconds, but 30 milliseconds is too fast to consciously perceive. Subjects report seeing the neutral face. The subjects' facial electrodes showed that the subjects mimicked the emotional face (e.g., anger), but they were unaware of having seen it. Thus, emotional reactions can be evoked out of awareness, so that important aspects of face-to-face communication occur on a nonconscious level. This may be one mechanism of projective identification.

The work of Heller and Haynal (1997; see Heller, 2012), "The doctor's face: A mirror of his patient's suicidal projects," provides a striking example of nonconscious procedural knowledge. Fifty-nine patients who had attempted suicide in the previous three days were given an initial interview by the same psychiatrist, while two videotape cameras recorded the faces of doctor and patient. One year later, 10 of these 59 patients had made another suicide attempt: the "re-attempter" group. The psychiatrist's own written predictions of which patients were likely to make another attempt were random. But fine-grained microanalyses of the videotapes of the psychiatrist's face identified 81% of the re-attempters. With her patients who would later try another suicide attempt, the psychiatrist frowned more, showed more vis-à-vis orientation and looking at the patient, and showed more overall facial activation and increased speech. The psychiatrist's greater activation and negative expressiveness can be seen as regulating her own inner state as well as communicating with her patient, both out of her awareness (Beebe & Lachmann, 2002; Beebe et al., 2005). Thus the psychiatrist "knew" something procedurally, through her non-verbal behavior, that she did not "know" at an explicit, linguistic level. This process characterizes adult treatment as well: much of what we "know" in the procedural mode is never translated into words (see Lyons-Ruth 1994).

Mirror neurons provide another mechanism for sensing the state of the other. Rizzolatti found that the same neurons activated as a monkey reaches for an ice cream cone are also active when the monkey simply observes the researcher reaching for an ice cream cone. Mirror neurons provide an "action-recognition" mechanism: the actor's actions are reproduced in the premotor cortex of the observer (Rizzolatti et al., 1996). Through mirror neurons, the observer has an enhanced capacity to recognize the intention of the actor (Wolf et al., 2001). Pally (2000) suggested that mirror neurons can be seen this way: I understand your intention by understanding (in a procedural format) what my own intention would be, if I were doing what you are doing. This process may be completely out of awareness.

A new area of research termed "embodied simulation" builds on Ekman's findings (Ekman et al., 1983) and mirror neuron research to address how emotions are communicated during social interactions. During social interactions, usually out of awareness, people tend to mimic the behavior of others, such as gestures, body postures, and facial expressions (Chartrand & Bargh, 1999; Dimberg et al., 2000; Kendon, 1970). Sometimes this mimicry is so rapid that it is not visible, such as facial mimicry which may occur within ½ second (Niedenthal, Mermillod, Maringer, & Hess, 2010). Thus observing an action can elicit the performance of that action, that is, mimicry.

Embodied simulation research shows the reciprocal effect: performing the action of the partner influences one's perception of the partner's action and facilitates recognition of the partner's action. This effect may operate consciously or nonconsciously. The effect is greatest in contexts of subtle nuances of emotion. Theories of embodied simulation suggest that mimicry reflects an internal simulation of the perceived expression (gesture, posture) of the partner, which then facilitates an understanding of its meaning. Action observation, action execution, and action recognition share the same neural substrates, including the brain's reward, motor, somatosensory and affective systems (Niedenthal et al., 2010; Oberman, Winkielman, & Ramachandran, 2007).

Compared to passive perception of a facial expression, mimicry is accompanied by greater activation in brain regions related to emotion processing. Reciprocally, blocking mimicry impairs recognition of expressions, perhaps especially those using facial musculature (Oberman et al., 2007).

Oberman et al. (2007) blocked the capacity for facial mimicry by asking the subjects to bite on a pen, which blocked the facial muscles associated with facial expression. Subjects were then asked to identify various emotional facial expressions. "Mimicry blocked" subjects were impaired in their verbal recognition of happy (but not sad) faces. Oberman et al. suggest that their findings are consistent with the proposal that people's ability to understand emotions in others involves simulating their states. This study documents that the blocking led to an impairment in conscious verbalized recognition of emotions.

Hennelenlotter et al. (2008) used a different method to block mimicry, a botox injection, producing a temporary paralysis of frown muscles, blocking facial mimicry. Subjects were then shown sad and angry expressions. With the reduced facial feedback from botox, during imitation of angry (but not sad) expressions, the activation of the limbic system was reduced, compared to control individuals without the botox injection. Hennelenlotter et al. (2008) conclude that peripheral feedback from facial muscles and skin during imitation modulates the neural activity known to be involved in the neural processing of emotional states. This is a potential physiological basis for the transfer of emotions during social interactions. This study documents that botox led to an impairment in the nonconscious bodily activation of emotion. Niedenthal et al. (2010) comment that by blocking the muscle pattern associated with anger, part of the embodied (nonconscious) meaning of the anger is lost, so that the emotion is experienced less intensely.

This research points to a largely unexplored territory, that is, what aspects of her bodily experience can the therapist become aware of? How might a therapist, out of awareness, block her own bodily-based emotional responses to her patient? How might a therapist's intensely positive or negative experiences with a patient bias the ways she may be able to activate and "live in," vs. withdraw and dampen, her body during the session? What kinds of experiences or training might facilitate a therapist's use of her own bodily-based emotional reactions in the service of therapeutic action?

Consistent with this research, Bucci (2011) suggests that a key aspect of therapeutic action is the way the therapist experiences the patient in her own body as well as through language-mediated responses. For example, as the patient speaks about a topic, the affective experience of the topic may be largely dissociated. "The language that the analyst speaks needs to be connected to the patient's affective core; this must be through the analyst experiencing the patient in him/her self" (Bucci, 2011, p. 255). In this process, the therapist is able to evoke within herself the affect that is missing in the patient's description (see also Bromberg, 2011). Again, this process may be out of the therapist's awareness.

Similarly Slavin and Kriegman (1998) argue that therapeutic action is found in a mutual influence process between patient and therapist. Not only does the patient need to be changed by the process of the interaction, but so does the therapist. Slavin (2012) suggests that the therapist has to be changed by deepening her awareness of her own struggles that are parallel in some way to those of the patient. For example, in discussing a patient who suffered from a painful preoccupation with being an outsider, Slavin suggested that the therapist find ways of evoking parallel experiences in her own life. In recalling her own experiences of being an outsider, a process in her own body is set in motion in which aspects of her own painful affect and arousal can be integrated into the patient–therapist dialogue. Slavin addresses this process from the perspective of conscious experience. But embodied simulation, largely out of awareness, is likely to be another way in which the therapist's own parallel emotions are evoked.

We can use these concepts to understand more of the experience of the mother of the future disorganized infant. When her infant is distressed, she may, out of awareness, inhibit or block this process of embodied simulation. Because of her own traumatic background, she cannot afford to allow the painful affects and arousal of distress to be evoked in her own body. She blocks her own mimicry of the infant's distressed emotions, through closed up faces, looking away, or competing expressions of smile and surprise. This reduces the intensity of her experience of the infant's distress.

When this mother consults us as an adult patient, we need to make it safe enough for her to experience her own largely dissociated distress. As the therapist listens to the mother's traumatic history, told in a dissociated, affectless way, the therapist does not inhibit her own bodily distress. In this way, the mother's distress can make its way into the dialogue.

Self- and Interactive Contingency in Face-to-Face Communication in Adult Treatment

For mother–infant as well as adult–adult face-to-face exchanges, each partner senses, in a nonconscious, procedural format, the other's feelings and purposes without words and language, by coordinating communicative expressions and gestures (Beebe et al., 2005; Trevarthen, 1998). Largely out of awareness, each person experiences being experienced, split-second by split-second (Beebe et al., 2005; Ruesch & Bateson, 1951). This layer of the communication continually influences, and is influenced by, the verbal narrative.

Let's imagine a therapist–patient interaction where the patient sits up. The therapist listens closely, visually attentive, as the patient talks. Occasionally the therapist interjects a sound, a word, a phrase or several sentences. Listening and speaking constitute a rhythm of sound and silence within each person's own behavioral stream. The individual's degree of self-predictability of that rhythm illustrates our measure of self-contingency. As therapists we can learn to be more aware, at moments, of the degree of predictability of our own rhythms.

The degree to which each person's rhythm of speaking and pausing affects that of the other illustrates our measure of interactive contingency (Holtz, 2004; Jaffe et al., 2001). For example, do the durations of one person's pauses affect the durations of those of the partner, so that each roughly matches the other's rate of speaking? And how do partners coordinate turns? Is each sensitive to the brief pause that occurs at the moment of the turn switch? This "switching" pause regulates turn-taking (Jaffe et al., 2001). In "polite" adult conversation (compared to arguments, for example), adults "match" the duration of the switching pause. That is, each waits for a similar duration at the moment of the turn switch.

Badalamenti and Langs (1992) showed that patterns of vocal rhythm coordination in adult treatment were linked to depth of narrative imagery, a measure developed by Bucci (1997). More narrative imagery was considered a "deeper" form of narrative. With patients who had less narrative imagery, therapists tended to interrupt more. With patients who showed the most narrative imagery, therapists tended to talk less, but to give a lot of "uh-huh" responses.

Those therapists who interrupted the least (without lowering their speech rate) were the most likely to have patients who "followed" or "joined" (contingently coordinated with) their therapists' speech rhythms. This research illustrates how variations in the coordination of vocal rhythms are an important aspect of adult treatment (see Holtz, 2004). Becoming more aware of interruptions, on the part of the therapist or the patient, is likely to facilitate the therapist's understanding of the communication.

Whereas sound–silence rhythms are familiar to analysts, other dimensions of the exchange are less familiar and may be more outside of awareness. Nevertheless all therapists use these procedural dimensions of the communication, and most therapists are very talented at it.

Usually out of awareness, both therapist and patient sense their own rhythms of looking and looking away, those of the partner, and how the two sets of rhythms affect one another. This constitutes the self- and interactive regulation of attention in the dyad. Patients who do not look upset the therapist's expectation of more familiar looking rhythms, as illustrated in the case vignettes at the end of this chapter.

Similarly both individuals sense their own rhythms of facial changes and facial "pauses," those of the partner, and how the two sets of facial rhythms affect one another. In this process each person senses (largely out of awareness) how the partner is responding to one's own facial changes. The same process can be seen in vocal affect, head orientation shifts, hand movements, foot movements, crossing and uncrossing the legs, torso shifts, and so on.

At various moments in the treatment, the interactive coordination of movements (of face, vocalization, etc.) may be organized by correspondences. Beebe and Lachmann (1988, 2002) called this pattern "matching the direction of affective change." Stern (1985) described tracking and coordinating with slight shifts in the partner's level of activation of face, voice or body as *changing with* the partner, a way of "feeling into" what the partner feels.

At other moments in the treatment, differences in the patterns of therapist and patient may be more prominent (Beebe et al., 2005). Differences may be optimal or nonoptimal. Mismatched facial expressions, where for example one partner is positive, and the other one is rather neutral or dampened, may signal some difficulty in the communication. On the other hand, escalating over-arousal toward panic in the patient is likely to be met by a difference in the therapist, an empathic but steadying pattern (see the case vignette of Daniel, Chapter 8).

Each person can also sense the degree of stability (self-contingency) of the rhythms of each, and how over-stabilization (such as the over-stabilized, inscrutable faces of the mother of the future disorganized infant) or lability may affect the interactive process. In most discussions of the role of interaction in adult treatment, the focus is on the interactive exchange itself. The concept that self-organizing processes within the individual (self-contingency as well as other forms of self-regulation) are an important component of the interactive process is often left out.

In this nonconscious procedural format, each partner constructs expectations of degrees of interactive efficacy and receptivity, as well as degrees of stability within one's own and the partner's behavioral stream. Most of these expectations are never verbalized, yet they exert a powerful impact on the verbal exchange and the therapeutic action of the treatment (Beebe & Lachmann, 2002; Lachmann & Beebe, 1996; Lyons-Ruth, 1999). Some of these processes can at times be brought into awareness when focused on.

Across the lifespan, both individuals in a face-to-face encounter are very affected by whatever the partner does, or does not do. The particular pattern of each individual's communication, for example in attention, affect, orientation and touch, powerfully affects the ongoing behaviors of the partner. This is the fundamental nature of face-to-face communication. It is not possible not to be affected on a moment-to-moment basis, even if the nature of the response is one of inhibition, or a temporary "frozen" state (Watzlawick et al., 1967).

In contrast to dyadic face-to-face interaction, a triadic interaction has a different organization. For example, toward the end of the first year, when toys are introduced into mother–infant face-to-face play, the attention structure becomes triadic, among the partners and the toy. This structure potentially generates "joint attention" to a third object, the toy.

Such a triadic structure is used in forms of psychotherapy using video feedback, such as mother–infant treatment, where a third focus is introduced, the videotape (Beebe, 2005). Below we describe a method of video feedback therapy applied to an adult treatment. When patient and therapist together watch a videotape, the two individuals are dramatically shifted out of the face-to-face encounter into a "joint attention" structure. They are no longer as organized by the mutual moment-to-moment responsivity. This may free them to reflect together on the videotape.

Thus like the early mother–infant face-to-face exchange, conducted without toys, in adult face-to-face treatment each individual is inherently vulnerable to the nature of the other's moment-by-moment behavior. In the mother–infant exchange, the entire language is that of shifts of gaze, face, vocal rhythm and intonation, orientation, and touch. In the adult-patient exchange, this nonverbal language has receded way into the background, and the verbal narrative is in the foreground. Thus it is easy to lose sight of the power of the moment-to-moment mutual regulation patterning as the context for the entire narrative exchange in adult treatment.

When applied to adult treatment, the concepts we present illuminate how easy or difficult it is for therapist and patient to come to understand each other; subtle differences in the manner in which the therapist comments, interprets, inquires, and expresses empathy; and subtle differences in the ways in which the patient initiates, responds, and elaborates; or withdraws, becomes anxious, or angry. The self- and interactive processes we describe are powerful aspects of therapeutic action of face-to-face treatment and can facilitate or disturb the co-created relatedness.

Not only can the therapist learn to observe more of the patient's bodily communication, but she can learn to observe her own, and learn not to inhibit her own. The therapist's own bodily arousal, attention, affective, orientation, and touch patterns are key. Her own bodily visceral feedback, usually out of awareness, allows her to change with her patient's action sequences, to enter into her patient's experiences. This nonverbal process feeds our ability to process our patient's emotions in the implicit mode. It also facilitates our ability in the linguistic, narrative mode to become aware of parallel or analogous experiences in our own lives that help us empathize with the dilemmas of our patients (see Slavin, 2012).

The Relational Patterns of the Origins of Disorganized Attachment Provide New Analogies for Adult Treatment

"Shadows" of early interaction disturbances associated with disorganized attachment may emerge in adult treatment conducted face-to-face. Modes of preverbal communication documented in infant research can, by metaphor or analogy, describe modes of nonverbal and implicit communication in adult treatment (Beebe & Lachmann, 2002).

In our previous work we described the mother–infant pattern of "chase and dodge" (Beebe & Lachmann, 2002; Beebe & Stern, 1977). As the mother looms into the infant's face, the infant moves his head back and away. The mother then "chases" by moving her head and body toward the infant. As she chases, the infant simultaneously moves his head still further away. This pattern was used as a metaphor for adult treatment by Sorter (1996), who treated a young woman for whom a chase and dodge pattern had become a central organizing feature of her life. This pattern emerged in the first session when Sorter rolled her chair forward to her usual position, facing the patient, and the patient reared back as her eyes became "big as saucers." As this pattern continued to unfold in the analytic dyad, Sorter was able to use the chase and dodge pattern as a metaphor to understand their mutual engagement and disengagement, and to facilitate therapeutic action.

Similarly, we use the mother–infant communication patterns identified in the origins of disorganized attachment as analogies for relational patterns in adult treatment. As a caveat, we are not interested in "classifying" a patient as showing patterns of disorganized attachment. We do not assume isomorphic correspondences between infancy and adult patterns. Nor do we assume that the adult patients we discuss necessarily show dissociative symptoms.

Instead we take each pattern from the research on the origins of disorganized attachment and use it to propose patterns of interactive dynamics and potential mismatches in adult treatment. We are interested in how the relational patterns revealed in the origins of disorganized attachment may provide additional analogies and metaphors for adult treatment. These analogies may help us understand and explain mismatches, communication difficulties, and aversive reactions on the patient's part as co-created in the moment-to-moment analytic process. They may also alert us to ways of interacting with our patients that facilitate "knowing, being known, and knowing oneself" in the shadows of early interaction disturbances. For each pattern we speculate about what it would be like if the therapist, or the patient, engaged in the pattern. These patterns are likely to be out of the awareness of both therapist and patient. Or either individual may have a vague intuition of sense of unease, but find it difficult to put it into words. It is likely to be helpful if the therapist can eventually become aware of such patterns.

Our new analogies follow.

In the realm of *attention regulation:*

- One individual may look and look away in an unpredictable way, generating an unpredictable "attention frame." This pattern leads to unpredictability in mutual gaze, generating an experience of *uncertainty about the partner's attention, and uncertainly about the emotional connection.*
- This unpredictable pattern of looking and looking away may be associated with long periods of looking away. If so, it may generate a feeling of *not being seen* by the partner.

Comment: The therapist is unlikely to be involved in such a looking pattern; therapists usually are steadily gazing partners, much like mothers with infants. However, if the patient is involved in this kind of looking pattern, it will likely disturb the therapist's sense of engagement with the patient.

In the realm of *affect regulation:*

- Our adult patients with early disturbances are often very distressed, sometimes with an agitated or frantic quality. This distress may or may not be overt.
- For either individual, the partner may not follow the individual's positive and negative facial and/or vocal affect, generating a feeling (out of awareness) in the individual of *not being emotionally joined* or empathized with, or a *feeling that the partner is remote.*
- One individual presents a closed up, inscrutable face, generating in the partner a feeling (out of awareness) of *not being sensed, not being acknowledged,* or being *"stonewalled."*

Comment: Either the patient or the therapist could participate in the last two patterns. The therapist could contribute particularly if expressive or affective neutrality is one of her goals. *However,* there are subtleties and variations in the neutral face that are not captured by this research. For example, a rather stable face which is nevertheless "kindly," that is, alert, interested, attentive, with a hint of positive expressiveness, "positive attention," may be a facilitating frame. Especially if this positive attention face is accompanied with head nods synchronized with the rhythm of the partner's speech, this kind of stabilization might have a therapeutic function (see case vignette of Daniel, Chapter 8).

So when does the overly neutral face actually become a problem? We suggest that when the face approaches a purely neutral expression which could be experienced as blank, facial stabilization may be a problem. Such a neutral face has no hint of empathy, no "holding environment." It is particularly a problem if no other modality carries the coordination of the dialogue, such as head nod rhythms which synchronize with the partner's speech rhythms. A frozen smile might also be a problem, because it does not shift and vary in nuance as the partner shifts. It thus has a "fake" quality, as if it is "held" rather than emergent. Like the blank over-stabilized face, the positive over-stabilized face may also become "unreadable," "inscrutable," leaving the partner too alone. An over-stabilized face is particularly problematic if the partner is distressed, generating a feeling in the partner of being "stonewalled."

• One individual may manifest discrepant positive and negative affect in the same second, or in rapid succession, generating a sense of *emotional confusion* in both partners.

Comment: Either patient or therapist could participate in this pattern. A common example is a patient who tells a painful story, but with a smile. Another example comes from my (Beebe) study of my behavior in videotaped sessions with Sandra, one of the treatment vignettes below. It was the fourth session of my consultation to "Dr. S's" ongoing treatment of Sandra. Sandra and I were just figuring out if, and how, we would continue to work together. In response to her question about this, I replied that I did plan to continue working with her, but our sessions would only be every couple of months. Examining the video, I discovered that as I said "yes," I shook my head "no." In retrospect, the "no" was probably a comment on the fact that the sessions would not be frequent. I was worried that it was less than what she might need.

• One individual is distressed, while the partner shows surprise, or smiles, generating in the individual *a feeling of being mocked, humiliated, or derogated.*

Comment: It is probably rare for therapist or patient to participate in this pattern. However, if the patient has a great deal of difficulty accepting empathy, the patient may show this pattern.

In the realm of *orientation regulation:*

- Either individual may generate an unpredictable spatial "frame," moving around a great deal with head or torso, and in an unpredictable way, which may generate a *feeling of destabilization* in both partners, as well as *wariness, an uncertainly about what will happen next.*
- Either individual may convey a "looming" quality, for example by coming in very close to the partner's face during greeting or parting moments, which may generate a feeling of *being intruded upon, possibly threatened.*

Comment: These patterns of spatial orientation are likely to be rare. However, it is possible that either therapist or patient may show anxiety, or possibly cultural differences, through these patterns. If the patient participates in either of these patterns, particularly the looming pattern, it will likely alarm the therapist.

In the realm of *touch*:

- Either individual may be unable to soothe himself or herself through touch, which may generate a *feeling of helplessness to calm one's own arousal.* Reciprocally, either individual may be very involved in soothing through touch, generating in the partner a sense of the individual's vulnerability.
- When the individual is touching herself, or an object such as the chair, or clothing, the partner may not sense the individual's touch patterns as a cue of arousal, agitation, or vulnerability. If so, the individual may feel that her *unease or agitation is not being sensed.* The partner is not available to notice and help transform the individual's agitated state.

Comment: Either therapist or patient may participate in these touch patterns.

In summary, in applying these patterns to adult treatment, we describe ways of communicating that can disturb either partner's experience of knowing and being known by the other, and of knowing herself. In the extreme, these patterns may generate moments of alarm or threat in either partner.

Case Vignettes from Adult Treatment

In the following vignettes we are particularly interested in how to facilitate engagement and therapeutic action in the shadow of early interaction disturbances. We focus on the repair of disturbances in knowing the partner, being known by the partner, and knowing oneself. We use some of the patterns derived from the research on the origins of disorganized attachment as analogies for adult treatment, but we do not assume that the patients we discuss would necessarily have had a disorganized attachment in infancy.

Case Vignette (Lachmann)

In a paper that I (FL) presented at a conference, I included a video of Tronick's (2007) still-face study. The video shows a mother holding a still face for 2 minutes, as instructed, and her infant's reaction of distress and "non-comprehension" to her mother's still face. A man approached me after the presentation and said, "I was really struck by that video. It made such a strong impact in my guts when I saw that ... although the verbal description of the study made no impact on me at all. I wondered, was that like my mother?" He is now in his 80s.

He began treatment with me. In retrospect he inferred that his mother may have suffered from a postpartum depression. He may have experienced her not looking at him much in her periods of listlessness or depression. He remembers his mother's lack of facial animation. He feels that she did not respond to him. Together he and I infer that she could not follow and join either his positive moments or his more distressed moments. He reports that he felt isolated and emotionally alone. He does recall a better relationship with his father, who held fast to his own beliefs and rebelled against his wife's religious orthodoxy. For example, on the mornings of the High Holy Days when he and his father dressed in holiday clothes, and should have been in Synagogue, they walked to the subway for a day of fun in Manhattan, and then they returned at sundown along with the throng of returning observant men.

He told me about his analysis many years earlier. Like the film I showed in my talk, he feels that his analyst also maintained a "still face" in demeanor, tone, and response throughout the treatment. It ended about 20 years ago. He has had a longstanding feeling that it was unsuccessful.

In the sessions now in their second year, he speaks continuously—with animation and humor—about his successes and disappointments, past and present. He speaks with an expressive face and hand gestures. He has often been thinking in advance about what he wants to talk about. When I comment, he politely waits until I am finished, and then continues. Gradually I have begun to talk less.

Well into the therapy I began to understand that the main thing he wants is to see my facial reactions. The words are much less relevant to him. The key is how I respond to him. As he said to me, "I realize I boss you around the way I boss everybody around. I'm here because what I need is your attention and your response to me." This comment was made somewhat facetiously. Had I taken it literally, and addressed his not treating me as a "separate subject," I would have interfered with an ongoing reparative process that was carried on interactively, on a nonverbal, affective level.

For much of his life this man has lived with the sense that his accomplishments (which are considerable) are not real to him. He feels that he is not engaged in his life. Perhaps not having felt that he made an affective impact on his mother, nor she on him, his experience has lacked a sense of reality. Without early validating experiences, he hoped for redress in his first marriage and analysis. But these efforts came to naught. He looks at my face to see my affective responses to him and to disconfirm his fear that he is again with a "remote" partner, like his first wife, and his first analyst. When he sees my animated facial reactions, he says that he feels that what he is speaking about is "real."

81

Initially, I had not been aware of my facial or postural reactions but, after I became aware of their importance to him, I tried to notice what I was doing. I find his "monologue" interesting, with humor and inventiveness. I am generally listening intently with concern, compassion, or a hint of a smile of approval. When he recounts painful memories with his mother, first wife, or first analyst, I, no doubt, show some momentary alarm and concern in my face. I notice I move my body toward and away from him as he speaks—toward him as he speaks about a particularly enjoyable evening with his second wife, and away as he provides a background narrative. But I generally say very little. Perhaps I make a comment or two toward the end of the session. A benefit of the research presented in this book is that I am able to feel comfortable in my facial and bodily responses without having to provide a verbal accompaniment, knowing that there is potentially direct therapeutic action in the nonverbal realm.

By the end of the session he is often in tears. He speaks about the loneliness that he has felt for years. None of his achievements have felt as though they are his own. Or he tells me about a letter he received from his son in which his son recalled some happy childhood experiences with him, such as making sandwiches together. Occasionally he remembers an aspect of his previous analysis. For example, he recounted a time when he experienced a profound sense of deflation in his analysis. He described an event that made him feel proud of his courage, and his analyst suggested that he was naïve, rather than courageous.

As the patient speaks I have become aware that I am being watched, not suspiciously, but for my facial responses and signs of encouraging support. In his prior analysis he had a feeling of being alone. In his treatment with me he tells me that he has the emotionally engaged responses, the audience, that he has always longed for. Moreover he has become more ready to expose himself and his ideas to his professional community, perhaps an indication of his increasing courage.

My consistent, intent visual attention, affective engagement and animated facial responsiveness seem to have increasingly enabled this man to feel seen, known, and appreciated. His experience seems more "real" to him. My function is analogous to maternal interest in, and enjoyment of, a child's experience. It is primarily my nonverbal, rather than verbal, modes of communication that helped the patient feel less alone, thereby offering a path toward greater self-integration.

We have no way of knowing whether or not this patient's attachment to his mother in his infancy would have met the criteria for "disorganized attachment." However, his strategy for repairing the effects of early maternal disruptions makes his actions in the treatment eminently understandable. His efforts at repair are particularly illustrated by his speaking for the full session, while watching my face intently for my affective responses to him. He does not need my verbal comments, but rather my affective reactions. These provide an incontrovertible validity that he is being seen and felt in a positive, affirming light. My understanding of this strategy enables me to listen and follow him without feeling that he is taking over the session or controlling it, based on an inability to recognize me an a subject. If I had interpreted his reparative strategy, and pathologized it, we would have repeated aspects of his core traumatic experiences. We would have repeated his feeling that he is not the author of his experience and his sense of not feeling that his experience is his own. These experiences characterized his childhood and were repeated in his previous analysis.

If this case description seems somewhat simplistic to you, you are not alone. I feel the same way. And I wonder, why? I think it seems simplistic because there is little verbalized interactive process, and almost no dialogue. All the therapeutic action is in the nonverbal, visual, and affective realm. If we had access to videotapes, I believe it would appear to be quite different.

Here is some process that may speak to this issue. The patient entered a session and said:

> "I was excited about coming here today. Last night my wife came back from a weekend at her college reunion. She told me she sat at a table with the woman who was her dorm counselor when she was in college and who is now Dean of Women."
>
> "This former counselor told of an incident while she and my wife were both at college. Another girl had been severely injured in a car accident and the dorm counselor drove the roommate of that girl to the hospital so she could visit her critically ill roommate. They had a very emotional visit. Soon afterward the injured girl died. The counselor continued to meet with the roommate to help her deal with her loss."
>
> "My wife was so moved as she told me that story that she cried. I cried as well. I asked, 'Why are we crying now?' My wife shrugged. I said, 'Because your mother would never have been that caring of *you*. And we both cried because that counselor was so emotionally engaged with the roommate.' My wife said, 'But I have known that about my mother. That's why I was so glad to get away to college.'"

My patient continued, "Yes, but to know it is one thing; to tell it to another person is different. That's what psychotherapy is about." Looking at me, he said "That's what I have with you. When you can tell someone how you feel and they can feel it too, that's what makes the difference."

Case Vignette: Dolores (Beebe)

Dolores was a brilliant and accomplished professional woman, and capable at times of highly articulate self-reflection (see Beebe, 2004). She was preoccupied with the faces of her childhood, and she wanted to be able to find her own face in mine. But she could not look at me, her own face was dampened, and she was often silent. Extremely fearful, withdrawn, and dissociated, she nevertheless longed for attachment. But she was deeply shut down and difficult to engage.

Much of the progress of creating the attachment occurred through the implicit "action–dialogue" of face, voice, and orientation. Although most of the treatment was conducted as an ordinary psychoanalytic dialogue, I made an unusual intervention, derived from my background with videotape microanalysis of mother–infant interactions. During a period in which she was quite withdrawn, I took a series of videotapes of my face only, while interacting with her. She welcomed my taking the videos, but she did not want to be in it. We watched the tapes together.

Because she did not look at me at this time, seeing my face seeing her, and hearing my sounds responding to her, heightened her experience of my response and her own visceral experience. She came to recognize herself in my face recognizing her. I tracked the shifts in rhythm and activation of her body and voice, "going with" each shift. I strained to catch her barely audible words, drastically lowered my level of activation, and frequently held my body (but not my face) perfectly still. My speech rhythm matched her slowed pace; I tolerated very long pauses. Most of these adjustments were made out of my awareness. Only after reviewing the videotaped interactions did I become aware of my nonverbal behavior with Dolores. Much later, Dolores commented, "You were honoring the potential over-arousal of my longing." In the 10th year she described, "You insinuated yourself into an interaction with me, into my closed system, where I had shut everything out."

In early infancy Dolores lost her biological mother. At approximately age 2 years Dolores lost her loving foster mother. This loss was further compounded by the substitution of an abusive mother at this time. One aspect of the trauma that Dolores suffered was a profound violation of her expectancies of "how the faces go." She expected a warm and loving face, the face of the first (foster) mother that she could make happy—and instead she was "faced" with the angry, hostile mother who told her she was bad. But she eventually went mute, at approximately age 4 years. She described this experience as "going away, going dead, defeated, lost, in the quiet place." This profound disruption in the dyadic organization of her experience threatened the dialogic organization of her mind, which continued to threaten her as an adult.

About a year and a half into the treatment, when Dolores was having a great deal of trouble adjusting to seeing me less in person, after her unwanted but necessary move to another state, she herself had first brought up the idea of videotaping some sessions. We were both interested in the idea. Because Dolores could not look at me, I thought the videotape might help her sense more of my feeling for her. I believed that her ability to engage with my face would be essential in reclaiming her relatedness and aliveness.

Only after I examined the videotape did I realize how completely quiet I had become in the session, to adjust to Dolores's level of fearfulness. In the videotape my body was still, but not frozen or collapsed. My face showed slow, soft, subtle shifts of expression. In my research life I am aware that I also slow down and reduce my level of activity when I interact with infants. But for Dolores I did this in an even more dramatic fashion. This adjustment illustrates my stabilizing the orientational frame, which is destabilized in the mothers of future disorganized infants. Dolores was like a frightened deer, ready to run. Intuitively, I sensed the importance of remaining highly predictable to her.

Analyzing the videotape, my visually intent, soft face conveyed the intensity of my listening. With each sentence, I slightly changed the pattern of the way my hand was self-soothing my face, registering my own efforts to regulate my intense feelings with Dolores. At one point I said, "But you're planting a flower before you leave?" My chin moved upward, in a greater focus of attention, and my body was still. This may have conveyed to Dolores how intent I was on what she was saying and feeling. Then she said, "Yes, before I turn to concrete." My eyebrows went up in a very concerned expression. Leaving was excruciating.

In the next session that we videotaped a few months later, we were more playful. She said, "Your face jumped into my eyes, for one little second." I said, "Really? [pause] Well, that's good." My eyebrows went up, and I had a big smile. The phrase "Well, that's good" had a "sinusoidal" contour, known as a "greeting" contour. I greeted her playful effort at engagement.

But then there was a big shift; I saw something in her face. My face dampened. I said, "You feel sad." Dolores said something, and I repeated what I thought I heard, "Leaving is the worst thing that could happen?" As her positive feelings rapidly moved to sadness, I matched the rhythm of her words, including her emphasis on "worst." I added a slight questioning intonation at the end. My body became very quiet. I briefly closed my eyes, and I let out a soft sigh. This interaction illustrates a form of distress regulation, close to a matching of her state. I elaborated in two subtle ways: the questioning intonation, which left open the possibility of other feelings, and the sigh, which elaborated on the sense of loss.

A year later, while she was alone, Dolores had been looking at the videotapes we had taken. These are notes that I took during a session on the telephone. Dolores said, "I was looking at your face looking at me. I saw the way it's different when I'm with you." I asked, "What did you see?" She replied, "I saw that you were seeing me. I wasn't seeing you, when I was with you in person, but later, when I was watching the video, and I saw you, I felt much more real." I said, "Wow." She replied, "Yes. In a way that, when I am with my feelings alone, sometimes I don't. But when I saw my feelings on your face, I felt more, feeling my feelings. I felt kind of familiar. But I don't feel them, necessarily, when I'm alone. When I'm alone with them I feel more confused. When I see them on your face, I can read them better. When I'm having them all by myself, there isn't any sense to them—that's part of what feels so bad, nobody to make any meaning." She goes on, "I need to see, or I need to feel. I have the picture of you, looking at me, and I like it; you never take your eyes away from my face. But now, on the phone, your voice floats on the ear, floats away."

Dolores probably had visceral as well as facial responses as she watched my face. In parent–infant communication, one function of facial mirroring may be an amplification of the infant's own inner state (Gergely & Watson, 1996). Seeing her own facial expression reproduced or elaborated on my face may have helped her register her own face and associated proprioceptive feedback. Dolores was learning more about her own feelings by watching me experience her. Her inner registration and identification of her feelings had been difficult for her. When she was able to "see" herself in my face, she was able to sense her own inner state more clearly (George Downing, personal communication, July 18, 2001). She was also better able to register her own response to me in a verbal mode: she liked the feeling of my face watching her so closely. Using the work on mirror neurons, simply by watching my actions, for example a moment of tender response on my face, her own brain may have been activated in the premotor cortex, as if she were herself performing these actions of tender empathy.

Continuing this conversation a week later over the telephone, Dolores told me, "When I was *watching* you, on the video while I was alone, I was interacting with your face. When I wanted to have certain feelings, I called up the feeling of your face. I was making your faces on my face."

I said, "Like imitating?" She replied, "Yes, but not imitating exactly. More remembering the feeling of your face talking to my face—not the words. I said your 'face-talk' on my face. I was getting the feeling for what was happening in the faces, and that's how I remembered certain feelings, certain good feelings— how I remembered feeling comforted—during watching the video, and after."

Research on mirror neurons indicates that when subjects actively mimic an observed face, the activation of mirror neurons is greater than simply viewing the face (Carr, Iacoboni, Dubeau, Mazziotta, & Lenzi, 2003; see Rustin, 2013). Thus Dolores allowed herself an intensified way of knowing my experience of her through her own active facial correspondences.

She continued, "You have such good faces. I have those good face-feelings. That is what is inside me. I sometimes have bad face-feelings too. Your good faces, the 'still-lake-face,' the 'resting-face,'—I like best your 'just-watching-all-the-time-face,' it makes me safe."

I said, "I'm so happy that you can see what my face feels for you. And how did you remember us after you watched the video?" She replied, "I wanted the feeling again. One strange thing: afterwards I made your face. I said, "Oh! Which one?" She replied, "A certain face. A picture of my feelings. Deep. Like when you see I'm worried or sad." I said, "Then you made my 'worry-sad-face'?" She replied, "Yes. I moved my face. I could just feel you." I said, "You could feel me responding to you?"

She replied, "If I don't have a responder, I can't even have that feeling. It's you, feeling me, and it's me, seeing myself on your face. Then I can feel more real, then I know that it is me. On the video, when I let myself be with your face, then I knew that your face was for me. I could see that your face was not bad or scared or mean. The face is the beginning of a person. This faces loves me; I'm ok." I said, "I think you felt this once before, with the face of the first good mother, and now you feel it again with me."

In this exchange Dolores was able to describe some of the subtleties of my facial responsiveness with her, and how she used them in a process of internalization.

About eight years later, Dolores told me she was thinking about the "good" between our faces, and how she holds on to that feeling: "When I have to leave you, I feel on my face the feeling on your face, saying 'good, but sad'… I feel you on my face. I see your eyebrow furrowed, trying to see something, you're listening to me so intently. And I can feel it on my face, in my body-face. I use it on my own face, the good mother face, your face. [pause] When you have the good-face-in-relation-to-the-good-face, you get to be the good face, you get to have the good face." And I said, "You remember this, and it became the foundation for your beautiful capacity to love."

The central dilemma in the early stages of the treatment was finding a way into Dolores's "closed system," as she later described it. A great deal of the work of "finding" Dolores was based on variations in nonverbal correspondences which provided the most basic ways in which I sensed and entered her experience, promoting a feeling of "being with," and "shared mind" (Beebe, 2004; Beebe et al., 2005).

Each partner is able to be aware of the other's feelings and purposes without words and language, by matching communicative expressions through time, form and intensity (Trevarthen, 1998). Stern's (1985) concept of tracking slight shifts in the partner's level of activation of face, voice or body, and changing with the partner, as a way of "feeling into" what the partner feels, was critical to the therapeutic action of the treatment. I felt my way into Dolores's experience through the way her lower lip might tremble, through her rapid foot jiggle when she was anxious, through the muted quality of her face and movements, through her drastically lowered level of bodily activity—the "deadness." I matched her very reduced activity level, her pausing rhythms and long switching pauses, the rhythm and contour of her words.

Since Dolores initially did not make much use of the facial-visual channel of communication, the early phases of the treatment were carried through my rhythms of voice and body rather than my face. My contingent coordination with her rhythms constituted the process of how I reached for her, how I tried to sense her state, and she could come to sense mine. Both Stern (1985) and Trevarthen (1998) argue that matching of communicative expressions simultaneously regulates both interpersonal contact and inner state. Dolores gradually came to sense a "comforted" inner state as she became more aware of how I matched her and coordinated with her. Thus correspondences of expressions through time, form, and intensity provided a powerful nonverbal mode of therapeutic action. My coordination simultaneously gave me a greater feeling of "being with" her.

Dolores discovered that I was seeing what she herself "carried" in her face and body, or "sensed" about herself, without being able to describe it verbally. Seeing my face seeing her, and hearing my sounds responding to hers, alerted her to her own inner affective reality. After reading the paper that I wrote about us, she declared, "I recognized myself in your face recognizing me, for example, when you said, 'good but sad,' and I came to feel myself more, and to feel more alive. I saw myself, and I saw you, recognizing me, and I felt the promise of an 'us' as a new possibility. And I came to feel an inner sense of feeling comforted."

87

Case Vignette: Sandra (Beebe)

For the past half decade, I (BB) have been a consultant with an ongoing therapeutic role to a two-decade long psychoanalytic treatment of a traumatized adult
patient, Sandra. Dr. Larry Sandberg is the central therapist. When I agreed to
become involved in the treatment, I also suggested that she see a dance movement
therapist, Dr. Suzi Tortora, who has continued to see Sandra weekly. Thus it is
a collaborative treatment among three therapists, each of whom sees the patient
individually. When I began seeing Sandra, she had not looked at her therapist,
"Dr. S" thus far in the treatment (Beebe, Orfanos, & Sandberg, 2012). I describe
portions of my first two years of involvement in the treatment. Sandra began her
treatment with Dr. S after a psychotic depression which culminated in a serious
suicide attempt and several rounds of shock treatment.

I call my consultation with Sandra a "video feedback consultation." Every couple of months we meet for 2 hours. In the first hour, I conduct a psychoanalytically
oriented session sitting up, and I videotape my face only. Sandra does not want
to be in the videotape. In the second hour Sandra and I both look at the videotape
together and try to understand more about our interaction, by watching me, and
listening to what we both say.

Sandra does not want to look at me. She tells me in our first session prior to
videotaping, "If I look at you, you might see parts of me you won't like, scary parts
of me." She tells me that her mother told her she had "lethal" eyes. Her mother
warned everyone not to look into her eyes. "My mother said, be careful of her
because when she's angry, you will see her eyes… [she cries]. I did not feel I was
so dangerous. I don't want to hurt people." When I ask Sandra if she believes her
mother, she responds, "This is what I am working on with Dr. S. He thinks I still
have the idea, if I look at you, you might be scared of me."

Already in the first session Sandra told me that she is worried she will disappoint me. I later learned that everything she did seemed to have disappointed her
mother. She worries in this first session, "I'm not worth your time. I don't have
much to say."

Although Sandra does not look at me in person, she is happy to look at the videotape of my face. This strategy seems to provide her with a feeling of more safety
than looking at me in the actual session *in vivo*. By watching my face afterward,
after the session has already happened, she knows that nothing dangerous has
occurred, and she is less worried about disappointing me.

During the first session that we videotaped, Sandra sat very still, shoulders
hunched forward. Her head was down, chin tucked in. Her thumbs twisted against
each other with considerable energy and at times agitation. As the very first video
session began, I listened intently, speaking very little. My face had a deep frown
and intense concern for long periods. My shoulders were slightly hunched, echoing hers. My thumbs gently rubbed one another in an echo of her gesture.

Only by examining the videotape did I become aware of these behaviors in
myself. I was entering her very distressed state with my intense frown and hunched

shoulders. I was soothing myself with my thumbs, out of awareness, in a remarkable entry into her thumb movements. My psychoanalytic colleagues and friends who know me well are surprised by the level of distress on my face. In retrospect I am not surprised, but I simply did not know that my face carries this level of distress. The videotapes have been essential in my attempt to learn more about my own nonverbal communication during sessions. I have been studying myself as I interact with infants, in my interest in "stranger–infant" interactions. But I have had relatively little opportunity to study my nonverbal communication in adult treatment, with the exception of a brief period of videotaping in the case of Dolores described above. My intensely distressed face reminds me of the Heller and Haynal (1997) finding that the intensity of the facial distress in the therapist identified the more seriously at-risk patients.

Later as Sandra and I discussed this section of the video, Sandra said, "You put yourself in my shoes. You allow me to be sad, a new experience. You made me live with my sadness. It was important to allow me to watch you. I saw you have concern, empathy." The intense distressed concern in my face was important in helping her sense her own state of sadness.

Sandra was very affected by seeing my face in that first video feedback session. A year later she told me she had not really looked at someone's face since she was about 12 years old. A few days after our first videotaped session I learned from her therapist that Sandra had had a "shock" of recognition in this session. She felt that her mother's face was so different from mine; that something really was wrong with her mother's face. The fact that I was not like her mother was liberating, as well as terrifying. She had a further recognition of her mother's face as cruel and full of hatred. She had been holding onto the idea that her mother was hitting her to put her on the right track.

This vignette illustrates the role of the distressed face of the therapist which reflects the profound distress of the patient. The therapist's distress communicates to the patient that her pain is recognized, experienced, shared. Unlike the Lachmann case vignette above, where the patient craved an affectively alive and responsive face, here the patient began the consultation not knowing that my face existed, much less that my face could help her. But immediately she was able to see something in my face that helped her identify more of her mother's cruelty. In this process Sandra brought a remarkable openness and responsiveness.

This session also illustrates the role of self-touch. Sandra saw me regulating myself though rubbing my thumbs together gently. Together we noted the similarity to the way she rubs her thumbs, but her way is agitated, whereas mine is slow and soft. The therapist's forms of self-touch and self-soothing are another route through which the patient can sense the therapist's own level of distress, as well as the therapist's response to the patient. Moreover, we both needed self-soothing. Her story is so painful.

In watching the videotapes of my face in sessions with Sandra, I have been struck by my freedom to express my ideas and emotions with my hands. I talk with my hands. But she cannot. She is stuck in one type of self-touch, analogous to the future-disorganized infants who are stuck in states of "no touch." My use of my hands is consistent with Norbert Freedman's discussion of the use of hand gestures to support the symbolic function (Freedman, Barroso, Bucci, & Grand, 1978).

In the second video session (our fourth session) we discussed our plan to continue working. Dr. S and I had begun this series of consultations not knowing if Sandra would like it. But by this point Sandra has indicated to Dr. S that she wants to continue. I told Sandra that I enjoyed working with her and I was very happy to continue. After a long pause she told me that it was hard to take a compliment, because she was afraid of bothering people or taking their time. I said, "That's sad." She told me, "It's not easy to identify with the person that you feel sorry for." Then after a long pause I saw something in her face which I was not sure of. Her head was down, and her face was hard to see. I asked if she if feeling sad right now. After a very long pause she said, in a slow, uneven, unpredictable rhythm, "Not quite, ... because ... you gave me the idea ... to grow my hair." Although we were in the middle of a serious discussion, Sandra's non-sequitur here illustrates her sense of humor, as well as a deflection from the painful discussion. She was also letting me know how much I have already affected her. She identified with me and wanted to have hair like mine. Many sessions later I learned that her mother had abruptly cut off her long, beautiful hair when she was a teenager, and she had worn it short ever since. But she has continued to let it grow longer since this session.

As we watched this video of our second session, Sandra said, "I felt like a person in front of you, a regular person, not nothing. I had to identify with that person. As the session goes on I am more able to identify with this person that you feel sad about. As I am talking about all this I realize it is past. I could not go through that again. I am not telling you everything about how terrible it was." As she said this, she became teary. She continued, "I am going back to some feelings I had in the past. But here I am sitting in front of you, I feel safe. Now I am not in the same world as before. The experience of watching your face, you felt sad, I know my past is not happy."

I asked, "Was there some feeling of shock of seeing my face, feeling sad for you?" Sandra said, "I know it was a shock. Destabilizing. An opening. Like, your past is sad, ok, you have to own this sadness, and now, you are in another world or else you would not be sitting here." I said, "Watching my face feel sad for you helps you own the sadness, and helps you know that this is new, now, another world." Sandra said, "It is easier to see your face sad in the video than in reality. Because at that moment you are not looking at me. If it is in the moment, I could disappoint you." I said, "You feel protected from that issue while you watch the video."

Between the first and second sessions there was a considerable shift. Dr. S told me that before she met me, she had a dream of me with a harsh face with dark cropped hair. In the first video session she saw that my face was not like her mother's face. By the second session she wanted to grow her hair longer like mine.

Moreover the theme of being bad or dangerous shifted to being sad. When she said, "You made me live with the sadness," she seemed to recognize that I had entered her experience: "You put yourself in my shoes." In this moment she was feeling known by me. She then entered her own experience more deeply and became more aware of her sadness. She felt she could identify with the sad person that she experienced me experiencing. In this moment she knew herself in a more visceral way, a self-expansion.

In a session 2 years later, Sandra was talking about a moment in which she was very happy and excited about something. But immediately she felt a suicidal urge: "There was not a second in between." At that point in the film, I repeat, "There was not a second in between, not a second in between," and one of my hands slapped the other one fiercely, in an uncharacteristic gesture. When Sandra and I were watching the film afterward, I asked her about it. She said, "Your hands—you are trying to understand what I am feeling, the *violence* that is involved." She described my hands as "working hard." My hands were working to represent the terrible moment of the shift. She identified the "violence," represented by my hands, in the moment of her shift from positive to negative (her potentially suicidal moment).

Out of awareness, I was enacting her feelings with my hands, dramatizing the emotion. In this process I entered her state and made it more available, helping us both sense it more vividly. Sandra felt more known by me in this moment, because my hands understood the violence. The "hand dialogue" is a highly evocative aspect of the nonverbal communication in adult treatment. The loss of access to this dimension, on the part of either partner, will constrict the ability of the pair to communicate.

The feedback portion of the session has a "joint attention" structure: Sandra and I shift our chairs to sit side-by-side, and jointly pay attention to the video. We are both freer. We are not in the direct micro-momentary contingency system of face-to-face interaction in which each is partially organized by the other. The interchange can go more slowly. Each partner has more time to observe, and to think. Sandra has more control, more capacity to titrate the "dose" of the relatedness. It is safer, the session has already happened, and we can stop time. We can go back and forth in the videotaped session. As we both try to find words to describe what we see, we translate back and forth between the verbal narrative and the implicit action dialogue. The task is collaborative observing and thinking together about the video. It provides a rich forum for reflective functioning for both partners. It is associative and playful. There is no right answer. Both partners are on more of an equal footing.

Because Sandra did not want to be in the video, we were of necessity using only one camera, on my face. It turned out to have a great advantage. With only one camera, the patient must enter the analyst's experience first, in order to then enter her own. Thus only by entering the bi-directional field, and observing my response to her, can Sandra use the video feedback session. If there were two cameras in the usual split-screen set-up, the patient would not have to work as hard. The patient could enter her own experience directly through watching her own image. In the one-camera set-up, Sandra was able to see the deeply distressed sadness on my face, and to use it to sense her own. Together we observed my emotions through my face, hands, head, and body postures. Sandra increasingly allowed herself to use my emotions to imagine her own corresponding states. She has come to have much more access to her own states, and potentially, to her mother's states.

The therapist's own nonverbal communication is a pivotal aspect of the therapeutic action of adult treatment. While we are in a session we cannot easily observe it, because it is largely out of our awareness. Examination of the therapist's nonverbal communication is an important, largely uncharted territory. Video feedback can heighten the patient's ability to use the analyst's nonverbal communication. This process is particularly helpful with certain kinds of patients.

Lyons-Ruth (1999) argues that the non-interpretive, procedural modes of therapeutic action are identified through moment-by-moment action sequences. In infancy, knowing how to proceed in intimate relationships is constructed through the action dialogue of gaze, face, voice, orientation, and touch. In adult treatment, knowing how to proceed in the intimate therapist–patient relationship is constructed in the procedural action-sequence mode, as well as the symbolic, narrative mode. In watching the video, Sandra and I together try to figure out how I proceed in this intimate relationship. Sandra has shown a remarkable ability to enter my moment-by-moment action–dialogue with her, as we discuss the video. This process facilitates her ability to sense me, to sense how I know her, to feel known by me, and ultimately to sense and know herself more deeply.

Conclusion

The case vignettes we offered emphasize modes of therapeutic engagement in the shadow of early interactive disturbances. We used the research to try to fine-hone our own awareness of these shadows, and how the patient may be attempting to repair these early difficulties. In recognizing the patient's efforts to do so, we attempt to facilitate, or not interfere, with the kinds of engagement that they may need to repair early difficulties.

In considering the relevance of our research on the 4-month origins of disorganized attachment to adult treatment, our goal is to view the patient through an adaptive lens rather than a pathological one. The patient attempts to cope with the stress of a developmental trajectory that began with contradictory and conflicted patterns of communication and engagement, patterns which at times generated alarm and threat. These patterns disturbed the patient's most fundamental processes of knowing the partner, being known and recognized by the partner, and of knowing herself.

In considering parallels and analogies between mother–infant communication and therapist–patient nonverbal communication, we offer a caveat. It is not to our advantage to become self-conscious about our nonverbal behavior. When doing video feedback in a mother–infant treatment, I (BB) tell the mother at the end of the session to trust herself and to have confidence that she has learned something. She does not have to consciously "try" to make herself behave differently. That is, she can put it in the background rather than the foreground. Similarly for us as therapists, our nonverbal behavior is necessarily in the background, and mostly out of awareness. Nevertheless, an understanding of nonverbal behavior can inform our treatments.

In creating bridges from the data of infant research to the language of adult treatment, in this chapter we made an effort to make inferences that remain as close to the data of our findings as possible. The metaphors of knowing the partner, being known by the partner, and knowing oneself are powerful ones which emerge from the research findings. They are relevant both to the infant's emerging procedural expectancies, as well as to adult forms of experience.

Next we turn to Part II where we present our findings on the origins of future secure, resistant, and disorganized dyads. At the end of Part II we return to the relevance of our research to adult treatment.

Part II

MOTHER–INFANT COMMUNICATION, THE ORIGINS OF ATTACHMENT, AND IMPLICATIONS FOR ADULT TREATMENT

Despite considerable research, we still lack a full understanding of how attachment is formed and transmitted prior to 12 months (De Wolff & van Ijzendoorn, 1997; Lyons-Ruth, 1998a; Lyons-Ruth et al., 1999; Madigan et al., 2006; Pederson & Moran, 1996). Through a detailed microanalysis of mother–infant face-to-face communication at 4 months we take up the challenge of investigating in a more fine-grained and precise way the process of attachment formation between mother and infant.

Chapters 5 to 7 describe patterns of mother–infant interaction at 4 months which predicted patterns of attachment at 12 months. Chapter 5 addresses the findings of future secure dyads. Chapter 6 addresses the findings of future resistant dyads. Chapter 7 addresses the findings of future disorganized dyads. These analyses were conducted on groups of mothers and infants. For example, we compare future resistant dyads to future secure dyads. Thus any particular infant may not exemplify all of the findings of the group.

A total of 84 mother–infant dyads visited our laboratory at 4 and 12 months. At 4 months, mother–infant face-to-face interaction was videotaped. Mothers were instructed to play with their infants as they would at home, but without toys. At 12 months the separation-reunion paradigm, the Strange Situation (Ainsworth et al., 1978) was videotaped to assess attachment classification (see Chapter 3). The participants were a low-risk, ethnically diverse community group of primiparous women delivering full-term, singleton, first-born infants without major complications. The mothers turned out to be highly educated (for details see Beebe et al., 2010).

Of the 84 infants who participated in the attachment assessment, 56% ($N = 47$) were secure, 5% ($N = 4$) were avoidant, 19% ($N = 16$) were resistant, and 20% ($N = 17$) were disorganized. Of the 84 infants, 37 were insecure (including avoidant, resistant, and disorganized). Of 47 male infants, 24 were insecure; of 37 female infants, 13 were insecure. Because the percentage of avoidant infants was so low, we did not analyze them as a separate category.

This is an unusual distribution of attachment classifications for a community sample. The proportion of secure infants (56%) is similar to other samples (see van Ijzendoorn, Goldberg, Kroonenberg, & Frenkel, 1992). However, the proportion of avoidant infants is unusually low (5%), compared to the rate of 15% reported by van Ijzendoorn, Schuengel and Bakerman-Kranenburg (1999); and that of resistant (19%) is high compared to the rate of 9% reported by van Ijzendoorn et al. (1999), or 7–15% by Cassidy and Berlin (1994). The proportion of disorganized (20%) is somewhat high compared to the rate of 15% reported by van Ijzendoorn et al. (1999). The participants are also unusual in the high level of education: 87.4% of mothers completed some college or more. The participants thus represent a high-risk attachment group, highly educated, in a selected low-risk community sample in the neighborhood of a large urban teaching hospital.

The first 2½ minutes of the 4-month mother–infant interaction were coded second-by-second for each of the modalities listed below, separately for mothers and infants (for details see Chapter 3; for coding see Appendices):

- Mother and infant gaze (at and away from partner's face)
- Mother and infant facial affect
- Infant vocal affect
- Mother spatial orientation
- Infant head orientation
- Maternal touch
- Infant touch

For each communication modality we created a behavioral scale ordered in gradations, as required by time-series methods (except gaze at or away from partner's face). For example, the infant facial affect scale is ordered from high positive affect, to medium or low positive facial affect, to interest or neutral face, to mild negative facial affect (grimace, frown), to the lowest point of the scale, negative (pre-cry face, cry face). We also created composite facial-visual "engagement" scales for mother and infant, which capture a holistic gestalt of facial and visual behaviors. In addition we examined two dyadic codes, "mother chase–infant dodge," and "mother positive face or surprised face while infant is distressed."

We used the behavioral scales to analyze self- and interactive contingency, and behavioral qualities, in relation to attachment outcomes (see Chapter 3). Addressing behavioral qualities, we tested associations between the means of 4-month behavior scales (e.g., mothers' mean level of touch) and future infant attachment status (such as secure vs. resistant). Because the means of behaviors yielded little, we also examined the *extremes* of the distributions of the behavioral scales, termed "behavioral extremes." For example, the behavioral extreme of maternal touch was rough touch and/or intrusive touch.

In each chapter we first describe the results, followed by an interpretive discussion of the origins of internal working models of attachment at infant age 4 months. Documentation of the results presented in Chapters 5, 6, and 7 can be found in Beebe et al. (2010). In Chapter 8 we turn to the relevance of this research for adult treatment.

5

FUTURE SECURE DYADS

This chapter presents our findings on the patterns of mother–infant communication at 4 months which predict secure infants at 12 months. We then infer the procedural expectations developed in future secure dyads at 4 months, if the action patterns could be translated into words. Thus we attempt to describe the procedural representations, or "internal working models" of future secure infants at 4 months. We use the term coordination interchangeably with interactive contingency where it increases clarity. For the findings of the all-insecure group (avoidant, resistant, and disorganized) see Beebe et al. (2010).

Although a review of this literature is beyond our scope, mothers of secure infants are described as more responsive and "sensitive," more consistent and prompt in response to infant distress, more likely to hold their infants, less intrusive, and less tense and irritable, than mothers of insecure infants. Secure (vs. insecure) infants are described as more responsive in face-to-face play, better able to elicit responsive caretaking, more positive, and more able to express distress (Ainsworth et al., 1978; De Wolff & van Ijzendoorn, 1997).

Future Secure Dyads at 4 Months

First we address all self-contingency findings together. Then we address interactive contingency findings organized by communication modality.

Self-Contingency

Within the subset of future *secure* dyads, all 4-month mother and infant *self-*contingency values are significant, indicating that both mothers and infant do have predictable individual rhythms of behavior. Thus all mother behaviors (gaze, facial affect, facial-visual engagement, touch, and spatial orientation) and all infant behaviors (gaze, facial affect, vocal affect, facial-visual engagement, touch, and head orientation) have predictable individual rhythms. These predictable rhythms facilitate predictability within each individual's experience, and "readability" of each individual for the partner.

Interactive Contingency of Visual Attention

In future secure dyads, mothers and infants each follow the partner's direction of attention as each looks and looks away from the partner's face. This is a bi-directional pattern. If the procedural expectation developed in secure dyads could be translated into words, it might be: "We follow each other's direction of attention as we look and look away from each other's faces." The infant's procedural representation or internal working model might be, "I know your rhythms of looking at me; I feel seen by you."

Interactive Contingency of Facial and Vocal Affect

We examined mother and infant facial affect, ordered from high positive to negative, and infant vocal affect, ordered from high positive to negative. In future secure dyads, mothers facially follow the direction of infant facial and vocal affect as it becomes more and less positive, and more and less negative. Infants reciprocally follow the direction of maternal facial affect with their own facial and vocal affect. This is a bi-directional contingent facial and/or vocal mirroring process: each can predict the other's affective behavior, and each can anticipate that the partner will follow his or her own direction of affective change.

The expectation developed in secure dyads might be: "We follow each other's faces up into big smiles, and down into interest expressions and sober faces, as we become more and less positive. We go all the way up to the top positive peak together, and then we come back down bit by bit together." The infant's procedural representation might be, "I can count on you to share my state, to go up with me as I get excited and happy, and to come down with me as I become sober or distressed. I can influence you to follow me and join me. I can count on you to 'get' what I feel. I feel known by you. I know how your face goes, I know you."

Interactive Contingency of Facial-Visual Engagement

Facial-visual engagement is a composite measure of visual attention and facial affect. For infants it includes vocal affect and head orientation. In future secure dyads, mothers follow infant direction of engagement as infants become more and less engaged, but infants do not follow mothers' facial-visual patterns, a unidirectional contingency pattern. This finding indicates that mothers of future secure infants are sensitive to how their infants "package" together their gaze and facial and/or vocal affect. Infants do not show this same sensitivity to maternal facial-visual engagement.

Future secure infants may develop the expectation, "As I look at you, and as I feel more positive, I can expect that you will follow me, reciprocally looking at me and feeling more positive (and vice versa)."

Interactive Contingency of Mother Touch–Infant Behaviors

We asked whether mothers of future secure infants coordinate their touch (ordered from affectionate to intrusive) with three infant behaviors: facial-visual engagement, vocal affect, and touch. Mothers of future secure infants coordinate their touch behaviors with infant vocal affect and touch, but not with infant engagement. As infant vocal affect is more positive, maternal touch patterns are more affectionate (and vice versa). As infants touch more (from none, to one, to more than one touch behavior per second), maternal touch patterns are more affectionate (and vice versa).

Thus future secure infants can anticipate that mothers will follow their vocal and touch behaviors with corresponding maternal touch patterns. They can anticipate that when they are doing a lot of touching, their mothers will "read" this behavior as a more "vulnerable" state, requiring more tender, affectionate maternal touching. Future secure mothers, however, do not contingently coordinate their touch patterns with infant facial-visual engagement.

Future secure infants coordinated their facial-visual engagement with maternal touch. As maternal touch patterns are more affectionate, infant engagement is more positive (and vice versa). But infants do not contingently coordinate their vocal affect or touch behaviors with mother touch. Thus mothers can sense that their touch behaviors "influence" infant engagement. Mothers can anticipate that infants will follow their touch patterns with corresponding engagement changes.

This system is uni-directional rather than bi-directional. Where mothers coordinate their touch with infants (vocal affect, touch), infants do not coordinate; where infants coordinate with maternal touch (through infant engagement), mothers do not coordinate through touch. Thus mothers and infants "carry" different aspects of the predictability in the maternal touch domain. Perhaps future secure infants do not coordinate with mother touch with their own vocal affect or touch because maternal touch is "good enough," and thus in the background. Only in the gestalt variable of infant facial-visual engagement do we see infant coordination with mother touch.

If the developing expectations could be translated into words, infants may come to expect that, as their vocal affect is more positive, and as they touch more, their mothers will touch in more affectionate and tender ways (and vice versa): "I can influence you to touch me in more tender ways when I need it." However, infants come to expect that, as their facial-visual engagement becomes more positive, mothers are *not* more likely to show more affectionate touch patterns (and vice versa).

For their part, mothers may come to expect that, as their touch patterns are more affectionate, they can influence infant facial-visual engagement to become more positive, and vice versa. However, mothers come to expect that they cannot influence infant vocal affect and touch by the degree to which their touch is more vs. less affectionate. Thus more to less affectionate maternal touch influences some aspects of infant behavior but not others.

BEATRICE BEEBE AND FRANK M. LACHMANN

Interactive Contingency of Mother Spatial Orientation–
Infant Head Orientation

In future secure dyads, maternal spatial orientation influences infant head orientation, but infant head orientation does not influence maternal spatial orientation, a
uni-directional process. As mothers move from sitting upright to leaning forward
to looming in, infants contingently coordinate head orientation away, from vis-à-
vis to orienting away to arch; as mothers move back toward upright, infants move
toward vis-à-vis. Thus mothers come to expect that, as they approach toward loom,
their infants withdraw, orienting away toward arch; as mothers sit back upright,
infants reorient into vis-à-vis.

However, as infants orient toward and away, from vis-à-vis to arch, mothers
of future secure infants do not coordinate their spatial behavior with infant head
orientation. Thus infants come to expect that their head orientation behavior does
not affect mothers' spatial orientation.

Infant Intrapersonal Contingency of Vocal Affect and Touch

Rather than examining the association of mother and infant, this pattern examines
the association of two infant behaviors, vocal affect and touch. Thus it is a different way of thinking about infant "self-regulation." It follows Tronick's (1989)
suggestion that infants may use touch to manage vocal distress. The association
between infant vocal affect and infant-initiated touch carried a positive sign. In
future secure infants, as infant vocal affect is more positive, infant touch is more
likely; as infant vocal affect is more distressed, infant touch is less likely. Thus
infant touch is facilitated by a climate of positive infant vocal affect. Reciprocally, as infant touch is more likely, infant vocal affect is more positive (and vice
versa).

Thus future secure infants learn to expect that their own touching maintains
positive vocal affect, and positive vocal affect facilitates more touch. This pattern
constitutes an infant coping mechanism.

These findings do not confirm the usual assumption that infants use touch when
they are vocally distressed. The findings indicate the opposite: infants are less
likely to use touch when vocally distressed, and more likely to use touch when
vocally positive. However, the findings do confirm that more infant touch facilitates more positive infant vocal affect.

Origins of Internal Working Models of Future Secure Dyads

Overall, future secure infants and their mothers may develop a procedural representation, or internal working model, of face-to-face interactions that includes the
expectations that, "I can anticipate when you will look and look away; I know your
rhythms of looking at me; I feel seen by you. I follow your feelings up and down
as I feel more happy or more distressed; we go up to the top positive peak together.

102

What I feel and what I do resonates in you" (Estelle Shane, personal communication, November 12, 2006). In addition, future secure infants may come to expect, "I can count on you to share my feelings, to 'get' what I feel. I feel known by you. I know how your face goes, I know you. I know I can influence you to touch me more tenderly when I need it." Mothers of future secure infants may come to expect, "I know that when I touch you more affectionately, you will look at me and smile more. I know that moving forward and looming in is hard for you, and you orient away. I know that when I move back, you come back to me."

Lest the above descriptions seem too idealized, we note that extensive clinical observation of the secure subset showed a great deal of variability among these dyads, with many seeming far from ideal, yet "good enough." We compared these findings within the future secure 4-month subset ($N = 47$) with our prior findings in this data set across the full 4-month group ($N = 132$), which can be conceptualized as the "average" infant in the data set (Beebe et al., 2013). The future secure subset is less than half the full group, yet infant self-contingency findings are identical, and interactive contingency findings are very similar, compared to the average dyad. Thus at 4 months, the future secure infant and the "average" infant are very similar. The future secure subset are "average" dyads rather than ideal.

6

FUTURE RESISTANT DYADS

How are 4-month mother–infant face-to-face interactions organized in dyads that will turn out to be resistant, as compared to secure, at 12 months?

In the Ainsworth separation–reunion paradigm at 12 months (Ainsworth et al., 1978), the insecure-*resistant* infant is very distressed at separation but cannot be comforted by the mother's return and does not easily return to play. In prior research, mothers have been shown to be inconsistent in their response, sometimes non-nurturant, but at times sensitive and caring (Cassidy & Berlin, 1994). These infants show limited exploration of the environment. They seek proximity to the mother and maintain contact. But at the same time they are angry, petulant and often cry. They seem inconsolable in spite of efforts by their mothers to comfort them.

Mothers of future resistant infants bring their own difficult attachment histories. Cassidy and Berlin (1994) suggest that, because of a history of not being able to trust attachments, mothers of future resistant infants emphasize attachment and minimize autonomy. These mothers are overly attentive to their infant's emotional responses, and they feel more comfortable when the attachment system is activated, to be sure that their infants need them. But they provide inconsistent maternal availability. Such inconsistency activates greater infant bids for attention, which might assure the mother of her importance to the infant. But resistant infants have difficulty using the comfort they clamor for, and they show an ambivalent pattern.

Based on Cassidy and Berlin's (1994) description, we hypothesized that future resistant dyads show "ambivalence" patterns at 4 months. This ambivalence might manifest as a dyadic "approach–withdrawal," in which one partner heightens, and the other partner lowers, coordination within the same communication modality-pairing. Or the ambivalence might manifest as an individual approach–withdrawal pattern, as the individual shows both heightened and lowered coordinations. We also hypothesized that mothers of future resistant (vs. secure) infants use forms of touch that interrupt the infant's ongoing activity (see Cassidy & Berlin, 1994).

Future Resistant Dyads at 4 Months

We first give an overview of findings of self-contingency, interactive contingency, and behavioral qualities, comparing future resistant dyads with future secure. We then discuss differences in future resistant (vs. secure) dyads by communication modality, integrating differences in behavioural qualities and in degrees of self- and interactive contingency. The second part of the chapter offers an interpretive formulation of the origins of working models of attachment in future resistant infants at 4 months. Formal presentation of the results of the data analyses can be found in Beebe et al. (2010).

Self-Contingency

Self-contingency generated few findings. Future resistant (vs. secure) infants differ only in facial-visual engagement self-contingency; mothers of future resistant (vs. secure) infants differ only in spatial orientation self-contingency. Thus the degree of predictability of the individual rhythms of behavior are very similar in future resistant and future secure dyads.

Interactive Contingency

Regarding interactive contingencies, future resistant (vs. secure) infants differ in engagement coordination with mother engagement, engagement coordination with mother touch, and vocal affect coordination with maternal touch. In contrast, mothers of future resistant (vs. secure) infants do not differ in any interactive contingencies. Maternal interactive contingency is thus entirely intact in these dyads, and mother and infant self-contingency are largely intact. We discuss these findings in detail below.

Behavioral Qualities

Mothers of future resistant (vs. secure) infants tend to show progressively less affectionate, more active touch, as well as chase and dodge, discussed below; otherwise they do not differ. Future resistant (vs. secure) infants do not show *any* differences in behavioral qualities.

Differences in Resistant Compared to Secure Infants, by Communication Modality

Attention Dysregulation in Future Resistant Dyads

There were no differences.

Touch Dysregulation in Future Resistant Dyads

Mothers of future resistant (vs. secure) infants tended to show progressively less positive touch. This finding indicates an increasing likelihood of less affectionate and more active touch patterns as the play session progressed. We construe this less positive maternal touch to be a central disturbing factor in the picture of future resistant dyads.

Spatial Dysregulation in Future Resistant Dyads

"Mother chase–infant dodge" was more prevalent in future resistant (vs. secure) dyads. This intrusive spatial pattern was accompanied by lowered maternal self-contingency of spatial orientation, a disturbance of the "spatial frame." As mothers move from sitting upright to leaning forward to looming in, to chase, they are less predictable: a form of "unpredictable chase."

Thus mothers of future resistant (vs. secure) infants tended to show a coherent constellation of progressively less positive touch, less self-predictable spatial orientation, and disturbance of the infant's freedom to look away by "chasing" with their head and body in the direction of infant "dodges" (movements away from vis-à-vis). These findings differ from the usual description of mothers of resistant infants as remote and under-involved (Belsky, 1997; Cassidy & Berlin, 1994). However, our findings of maternal spatial and tactile intrusion are consistent with the literature reviewed by Cassidy and Berlin (1994) which documents maternal interference with infant autonomy, exploration or ongoing activity.

Engagement Dysregulation in Future Resistant Infants

Consistent with our hypothesis, future resistant infants demonstrated approach–withdrawal discordance (conflict) in facial-visual engagement. These infants lowered their engagement coordination with maternal touch. That is, they were less likely to show facial and/or vocal distress as maternal touch became more intrusive, and they were less likely to become positive as maternal touch became more affectionate. But at the same time, these infants heightened their engagement coordination with maternal engagement, an infant vigilance for maternal facial-visual shifts. This is a remarkable discordance, in which the same behavioral constellation, infant engagement, is both *inhibited* in relation to maternal touch and *activated* in relation to maternal engagement.

Future resistant infants also showed lowered vocal affect coordination with maternal touch. Thus future resistant infants withdrew from maternal touch through both facial-visual engagement and vocal affect.

The engagement findings indicate an imbalance in self- and interactive contingency in future resistant infants. Not only did they heighten their engagement coordination with maternal engagement, but they also lowered their engagement self-contingency. This imbalance tilts toward interpersonal involvement at the

106

expense of self-stability. The lowered engagement self-contingency makes it harder for infants to anticipate their own next move, as well as harder for mothers to anticipate infant engagement shifts. It is striking that infants showed "destabilized" self-contingency in precisely the channel in which they heightened their contingent coordination with mother. Infant intrapersonal and interpersonal engagement dysregulation are linked here.

Infant intrapersonal vocal affect and touch

There were no differences in future resistant infants in the ways that they coordinated their vocal affect and their touch.

In summary, the findings identified a number of new patterns in the 4-month origins of resistant attachment. Compared to future secure dyads, future resistant dyads showed:

* progressively less affectionate and more active forms of maternal touch as the session goes on;
* dyadic maternal "chase" and infant "dodge";
* less predictable maternal spatial orientation patterns, a disturbance of the maternal spatial "frame," which also indicates a relatively unpredictable maternal "chase" pattern;
* infant inhibition of emotional coordination with maternal touch such that infants are less likely to protest as maternal touch becomes more intrusive, and they are less likely to become positive as maternal touch becomes more affectionate;
* infant vigilant engagement coordination with maternal engagement, at the expense of infant engagement self-stability;
* the last two findings together indicate an infant discordance: infant engagement coordination is inhibited with maternal touch but activated with maternal engagement.

Origins of Internal Working Models in Future Resistant Infants

Based on the work of Bretherton (1980) and Main et al. (1985), we began this study with the proposal that 4-month infant procedural expectancies of contingent patterns of self- and partner contingency, as well as of specific behavioral qualities, provide ways of defining processes by which patterns of intimate relating and attachment security are constructed: the origins of working models of attachment. We suggest that the patterns identified for future resistant (vs. secure) dyads form the basis for emerging infant "working models" of attachment, procedurally organized expectancies of action sequences, as early as 4 months. In this section we infer what the experience of future resistant infants may be like. We also

107

discuss ways in which the findings may suggest disturbances in the infant's ability to "know" and be "known" by his mother's mind, as well as to know his own mind.

As noted above, because of histories of not being able to trust attachments, mothers of resistant infants may feel more comfortable when the attachment system is activated. This may allow mothers to feel that their infants need them (Cassidy & Berlin, 1994). In the Strange Situation at 12 months, these mothers often linger as they leave, activating the child's request that the mother stay, perhaps in an effort to be sure that they are needed. At 4 months, mothers of future resistant infants may become upset and may "chase" when their infants "go away," for example, when their infants inevitably at times look away and orient away. Perhaps these mothers then feel abandoned or unimportant. Clinically, we observed these mothers saying things like, "What are you looking at?" "Hey, look at me," or "Where are you going?"

Following Cassidy and Berlin, the maternal "chase" behavior and tactile intrusion in mothers of future resistant infants are interpreted as ways of saying to the infant "Come here, don't go away, I need you" (Jude Cassidy, personal communication, October 18, 2006). We interpret these mothers as being overly concerned with the infant's attention and emotional presence; we interpret their intrusion behaviors as their wish for infants to stay with them. However, mothers of future resistant (vs. secure) infants showed intact interactive contingency across all communication modalities, safeguarding the infant's interactive agency. Like that of the future secure infant, the internal working model of the future resistant infant will preserve the expectancy that he can influence maternal behaviors to coordinate with his own, so as to match his direction of behavioral change.

Maternal Touch Dysregulation

Mothers of future resistant (vs. secure) infants showed a disturbance in their touch patterns. These mothers used progressively less affectionate and more active forms of touch as the session progressed, which may indicate the mother's increasing need for the infant to stay with her. Less affectionate maternal touch occurred in the context of lowered maternal spatial self-predictability. The constellation of less predictable orientation as mother reaches in to touch, and progressively less affectionate maternal touch, is likely to disturb the infant's development of a confident expectation that maternal touch will be affectionate and comforting. The infant's procedural representation of "state transforming," the expectation of being able to transform an arousal state through the contribution of the partner (see Stern, 1985), is likely disrupted with respect to maternal touch. Difficulty with state transforming is construed as an "ongoing dysregulation," a recurrent pattern across the session.

Infant Inhibition of Emotional Coordination with Maternal Touch

Future resistant (vs. secure) infants inhibited their vocal affect and engagement coordination with maternal touch. They were not as likely to signal vocal and engagement distress as maternal touch patterns became less affectionate. Nor were they as likely to become more positive (in vocal and engagement patterns) as maternal touch patterns became more affectionate. Thus these infants resisted being emotionally organized by maternal touch: a remarkable demonstration of agency. This infant inhibition also indicates that infant ability to use maternal touch for "state transforming" will likely be disrupted. Thus both infant and mother contribute to a disruption in the infant's expectation of being able to transform arousal states through mother's touch.

Infant inhibition of coordination with maternal touch is linked to the disturbance in maternal touch patterns. Thus future resistant infants down-regulate by using engagement and vocal affect to inhibit response to maternal touch, in an effort to manage intrusive maternal stimulation. However, infant inhibition of a distressed response to maternal touch may lead to a disturbance in the infants' ability to communicate what they "like" or do not "like," ultimately a confusion in sensing their own state in relation to maternal touch. Future resistant infants learn to mask their distress, which may lead to a dissociative loss of awareness of distress in relation to maternal touch, and to later somaticization of distress (Mary Sue Moore, personal communication, July 2, 2007).

This finding has a parallel in the Strange Situation at one year, in which resistant infants may be upset but passive, not doing anything to ameliorate their distress, or ineffective in getting comfort from mother (Cassidy & Berlin, 1994; Jude Cassidy, personal communication, October 18, 2006). Although by 4 months future resistant infants have learned to "tune out" maternal touch, this "tuning out" may disturb the 12-month infant's ability to use maternal touch to be soothed in the reunion following the separations of the Strange Situation (George Downing, personal communication, October 25, 2006). Future research could analyze the moment of reunion in the Strange Situation for infant response to maternal touch. Infant "tuning out" of maternal touch can be seen as a premature separation from mother's touch, which may have later implications for infant autonomy (John Kerr, personal communication, July 11, 2007).

Dyadic Approach–Avoid: "Chase and Dodge"

Future resistant dyads tended to show a spatial "approach–avoid" pattern termed "chase and dodge": as mothers pursued ("chased"), infants oriented away ("dodged"), and vice versa (Beebe & Stern, 1977; Stern, 1971). In this pattern, which clinically conveys painful moments, the infant has "veto" power, through myriad dodging maneuvers, over maternal efforts to establish mutual gaze. This pattern generates an infant expectation of misregulation of spatial orientation patterns, such that, "As you move in, I move away; as I move away, you move in." This pattern disturbs infant freedom to look away. As infants look and orient away, mothers pursue by following in the infant's direction of movement. Because infant looking away is a key method of down-regulating arousal (Field, 1981), maternal chase also disturbs "state-transforming," the expectation that one's arousal regula-

109

tion will be facilitated by the partner. Chase and dodge occurred in the context of maternal lowered self-predictability of spatial movements across upright, forward, and loom. This pattern generates infant difficulty in being able to anticipate when this intrusion might occur, which might be frightening for infants. This lowered maternal spatial self-predictability is a disturbance in the stability of the maternal "spatial frame" of the face-to-face encounter, a background sense of spatial structure that mothers usually provide (George Downing, personal communication, October 25, 2006).

The maternal behaviors of progressively less affectionate touch, lowered predictability of spatial position, and maternal chase–infant dodge, define a coherent constellation of maternal spatial and tactile intrusion. But the future resistant mother does not seem to sense that her spatial and tactile intrusion may be forcing her infant to withdraw emotionally from her touch. This maternal intrusion will likely disturb the infant's feeling of being sensed or acknowledged by her. Perhaps the mother of the future resistant infant cannot grasp these consequences because she herself is so preoccupied with her needs to be important and needed by her infant (John Kerr, personal communication, July 11, 2007). In the Adult Attachment Interview, the "preoccupied" mother (the adult classification parallel to the resistant infant) tends to be so self-preoccupied that she may lose track of the interviewer (Main, Hesse, & Goldwyn, 2008).

What might the infant's procedural experience be, if we could translate it into words? Beebe and Lachmann (2002; see also Beebe & Lachmann, 1988) previously suggested that the *infant's* experience in the chase and dodge pattern might be, "As you move in, I move away; as I move away, you move in … I feel overaroused and inundated … No matter where I move in relation to you, I cannot get comfortable" (Beebe & Lachmann, 2002, p. 114). The *mother's* experience might be, "When I want to connect with you, I become aware of how much I need to be responded to. I feel you move away from me as I show my wish to engage. I cannot find a comfortable place in relation to you. I feel anxious and rejected" (Beebe & Lachmann, 2002, p. 114). Although this interpretation of the chase and dodge pattern was originally written in 1988, without reference to attachment patterns, it is strikingly consistent with Cassidy and Berlin's (1994) description of the mother of the resistant infant as vulnerable to feeling abandoned and unimportant when the infant goes away. We now add that the future resistant infant's experience of chase and dodge is further colored by the relative unpredictability of the mother's spatial movements as she moves in to chase.

Infant Simultaneous Inhibition and Activation of Engagement Coordination

In addition to the dyadic approach–avoid pattern of "chase and dodge," future resistant infants themselves made complex "approach–avoid" adaptations. These infants *simultaneously inhibited, and activated, the same behavioral configuration*, engagement, in the different contexts of maternal touch, and maternal engagement, respectively. The infant thus generates opposite expectancies of the ways he responds to the mother through his own engagement coordination. This pattern is construed as an "ongoing dysregulation" across the session. On the one hand future resistant infants *dampened* their emotional (engagement and vocal affect) coordination with less positive maternal touch, seeming not to be "reacting," or "tuning it out." They also dampened their coordination with more positive maternal touch. On the other hand, these infants *heightened* their engagement coordination with maternal engagement, a vigilance to mother's facial-visual state.

This infant intermodal discordance is a complex and confusing organization. In the touch domain, the infant seems to be forced into premature separation or autonomy; in the facial-visual domain, the infant seems to be forced into premature vigilance. The expectancy of the infant may be, "My mother really responds to me. But when will she move in toward me to touch me in that uncomfortable way? Uh-oh, I have to watch out when she touches me like that. I better not react. I better watch her carefully to see what she is feeling. What's going to happen next?"

Although the discordant use of engagement coordination in future resistant infants could be characterized as ambivalence, it is better characterized as an ethologically coherent, adaptive pattern. However, these difficulties may set the stage for infant confusion regarding his response to his mother, and for infant difficulties in sensing his own state. They may also set the stage for the resistant infant's later difficulties with autonomy (John Kerr, personal communication, July 11, 2007).

Emotional vigilance in future resistant infants has a parallel in the Strange Situation at 12 months. Unlike secure infants in the Strange Situation, resistant infants cannot count on mother's emotional availability, so that they do not have the luxury of *not* attending to mother (Cassidy & Berlin, 1994; Jude Cassidy, personal communication, October 18, 2006). At the point at which mother and stranger begin to talk, resistant infants are more likely than secure infants to look to mother, suggesting that resistant infants need to watch their mothers to be sure that they can get her attention (Dickstein, Thomson, Estes, Malkin, & Lamb, 1984).

If the 4-month infant's procedural experience could be translated into words, perhaps the experience of the future resistant infant's *inhibition* of emotional coordination with maternal touch might be, "I can't afford to 'go with' your touch; as your touch becomes less affectionate, I can't afford to be affected by you or to protest; as your touch becomes more affectionate, I can't trust it to be comforted or to feel good. I can't rely on your touch." If the mother's procedural experience could be translated into words, the mother might feel: "I can't affect you with my touch. I can't reach you. You don't need me. I have to try harder." This interaction pattern presumably also disturbs the mother's own sense of agency through her touch.

If the future resistant infant's procedural experience could be translated into words, perhaps the experience of *heightened infant engagement* coordination with maternal *engagement* might be, "I need to pay very careful attention to you. I struggle to stay with you emotionally. As you are looking at me and becoming facially positive, reciprocally I look at you and become more positive with you; as you dampen your face, I stay with you and dampen my own. I feel too affected by you. But I better make sure that I know what you feel" (Estelle Shane, personal communication, November 12, 2006). This heightened infant engagement coordination might be interpreted as infant efforts to see what mother wants (needs), and to stay with her, to "cooperate" to keep them both happy (Cassidy & Berlin, 1994; Jude Cassidy, personal communication, October 18, 2006). The mother might feel, "Wow, I have so much effect on you; I have so much power." This power may be comforting to these mothers, who need reassurance that their infants need them. However, the combination of lowered maternal ability to affect infants in the tactile realm, but heightened ability to affect infants in the facial-visual realm, is likely to be confusing to both partners. This confusing intermodal discordance in the infant's coordination with mothers may exacerbate the mother's sense of insecurity as to whether her infant really needs her, and whether she can really influence her infant.

Thus future resistant infants at 4 months are vigilant to mother's emotional state, and coordinate very carefully with her facial-visual engagement, which enables them to anticipate what both the self and the mother will feel next. We suggest that this vigilance is an attempt to cope with maternal tactile and spatial intrusion. We imagine a spiraling sequence in which, as mother's touch becomes progressively less affectionate, and as the infant inhibits his response to maternal touch, mother may become insecure about feeling needed by her infant, and may "chase" as the infant looks and turns away. In this process, the infant dampens his distress response to maternal less affectionate touch (not telling her that she upsets him), and instead he stays vigilant to mother's attention and affect (Mary Sue Moore, personal communication, July 2, 2007).

Lowered Infant Engagement Self-Predictability: Infant "Destabilization"

In the context of this vigilant infant engagement coordination with mother engagement, future resistant infants experience lowered self-predictability in their ongoing rhythm of facial-visual engagement. We infer a decreased sense of self-familiarity and coherence over time, metaphorically an emotional "destabilization" (Doris Silverman, personal communication, November 6, 2006). One cost of this complex adaptation is that from moment-to-moment it is more difficult for future resistant infants (and their mothers) to anticipate the next infant state of engagement, an "ongoing dysregulation" which is potentially confusing to both infants and mothers.

Knowing and Being Known in the Origins of Resistant Attachment

We now return to the topic of the organization of intimate relating which is at stake in these early infant working models or representations. Intimate relating entails the fundamental issue of how the infant comes to know, and be known by, another's mind, as well as how the infant comes to know his own mind. We construe "mind" here from the point of view of the infant, that is, expectancies of procedurally organized action sequences, our definition of presymbolic representation.

Regarding *feeling known* by mother, intact maternal interactive contingency safeguards the future resistant infant's interactive agency and expectation that mother will contingently "go with" his direction of affective change, thus sharing his states. However, we propose that the future resistant infant will nevertheless have difficulty *feeling sensed and known* by his mother in the arena of her spatial and tactile intrusion. Perhaps because of her own needs to feel needed, the mother of the future resistant infant does not seem to sense that her spatial and tactile intrusion may force her infant to withdraw emotionally from her touch.

We propose that the future resistant infant will have difficulty *knowing* his mother's mind as he has difficulty predicting what mother will do next spatially: sit upright, lean forward, loom in, or chase.

We propose that the future resistant infant will have difficulty *knowing himself* as his own lowered engagement self-contingency makes it more difficult to sense and come to expect the rhythms of his facial-visual action tendencies from moment-to-moment. He will have difficulty knowing himself as he simultaneously inhibits his engagement coordination with mother touch, but activates his engagement coordination with mother engagement.

The future resistant infant thus generates opposite expectancies of the ways he responds to mother with his engagement, a complex, confusing, but nevertheless adaptive organization. We note that these difficulties of the future resistant infant are identified not through disturbances in maternal affective correspondence and state-sharing (see Meltzoff, 2007; Stern, 1985; Trevarthen, 1998). Instead, these difficulties of the future resistant infant are identified through dysregulated tactile and spatial exchanges.

Internal Working Models of Future Resistant Infants at 4 Months

We propose that the intact maternal facial mirroring of infant facial and vocal affect in mothers of future resistant infants generates infant expectancies of feeling affectively "on the same wavelength." Overall the future resistant infant comes to expect a shared corresponding affective process, and to expect that he can influence maternal behaviors so as to match his own direction of behavioral change. These are important residual capacities in future resistant dyads.

Nevertheless, these infants also come to expect a maternal tactile and spatial impingement, which is compounded by its relative unpredictability. They come to expect that they will "dodge" as their mothers tend to "chase," an experience of "moving away" as their mothers "move in." They come to expect that they must manage mother's touch by tuning it out. This adaptation is costly, sacrificing infants' ability to communicate their distress response to increasingly less affectionate maternal touch, an important aspect of the infant's ability to regulate affect and arousal.

Thus future resistant infants come to expect that they cannot use mother's touch to help them regulate their arousal. They cannot rely on mother's help when they need to calm down, because looking away to down-regulate arousal is interfered with by maternal chase. They come to expect difficulty in state transforming.

At the same time future resistant infants come to expect their own vigilant pattern of engagement coordination with mother's engagement. This vigilance comes at the cost of engagement self-destabilization. High emotional coordination may be what their mothers need. Meanwhile, the future resistant infants come to expect a complex and confusing pattern. They are simultaneously facially-visually too "hooked-in" to maternal engagement, and yet facially-visually too "separate" or tuned-out to maternal touch. Thus they come to expect their own opposite patterns toward their mothers, as they struggle to make complex adaptations.

These dyadic patterns at 4 months shed light on how the mother's own self-preoccupation with being needed and loved is communicated to the future resistant infant as early as 4 months. They show how mother and infant both develop complex adaptations in this emotional context. The patterns we have described come to constitute internal working models of future resistant infants in the form of procedural self- and interactive expectancies. These expectancies bias the trajectory of how experience is organized, activating certain pathways and inhibiting others, ultimately limiting the range and flexibility of social experience.

7

FUTURE DISORGANIZED DYADS

Based on our detailed microanalyses, how are 4-month mother–infant face-to-face interactions organized in dyads that will turn out to be disorganized, as compared to secure, at 12 months?

In the reunion episodes of the Ainsworth separation–reunion paradigm at 12 months (Ainsworth et al., 1978), *disorganized* infants may simultaneously approach and avoid their mothers. They may also show incomplete movements and expressions, confusion and apprehension, and momentary behavioral stilling. These behaviors are considered to constitute a breakdown in behavioral organization under the stress of the heightened activation of the attachment system following separation (Main & Solomon, 1990; Solomon & George, 1999). For example, the infant may freeze as the mother enters, then start to move to greet her, but then fall down and curl into a ball. Or the infant may cling to the mother, but cry with face averted. These infants do not have a coherent strategy for dealing with the stress of the separation. The distress and threat activated by the brief separation do not subside once the mother returns. Unlike the secure infant, the disorganized infant does not return to exploring the environment and the toys.

Despite important recent progress in understanding disorganized attachment, we still lack a full understanding of how disorganized attachment is formed and transmitted prior to 12 months (De Wolff & van Ijzendoorn, 1997; Lyons-Ruth et al., 1999; Madigan et al., 2006). Traditional measures of maternal sensitivity do not predict disorganized infant attachment. However, important progress has been made in the last decade. Maternal behavior within the Ainsworth Strange Situation has been found to be frightened and/or frightening (Jacobvitz, Hazen, & Riggs, 1997; Lyons-Ruth et al., 1999; Schuengel, Bakermans-Kranenburg, & van Ijzendoorn, 1999; Tomlinson, Cooper, & Murray, 2005).

Lyons-Ruth et al. (1999) also found that maternal frightened and/or frightening behavior occurs in a broader context of atypical, disrupted maternal behaviors within the Ainsworth Strange Situation. At 18 months, degree of infant disorganization was associated with disrupted maternal behaviors: affective communication errors (such as mother positive while infant is distressed), disorientation (frightened expression or sudden loss of affect), and negative-intrusive behaviors (such as mocking or pulling infant's wrist).

Lyons-Ruth et al. (1999) suggested that the degree of derailment of communication seen in disorganized dyads "should be fear-arousing in itself because the infant will have little sense of influence over the caregiver at times of heightened fear or stress" (p. 69; see also Koos & Gergely, 2001). This concept is pursued in our current analyses, where little infant sense of influence can be translated into lowered maternal contingent coordination with infant behavior.

We hypothesized that mothers of future disorganized (vs. secure) infants lower their emotional coordination with infant emotional changes, not following or joining the infant's positive and negative shifts. This hypothesis integrates Lyons-Ruth et al.'s (1999) proposal that mothers of disorganized infants are unpredictable, so that the infants have little sense of influence. It also integrates their finding that these mothers are more likely to remain positive when infants are distressed. We hypothesized that mothers of disorganized (vs. secure) infants show greater prevalence of negative facial expressiveness, a parallel to the finding of greater frightened and/or frightening faces in mothers of disorganized infants (Main & Hesse, 1990). We hypothesized that future disorganized (vs. secure) infants use more discrepant affect (simultaneous positive and negative facial and/or vocal affect). This hypothesis is based on the simultaneous approach and avoidance behavior frequently shown by infants classified as disorganized in Strange Situation, and on clinical observation by the first author of videotapes of the Jaffe et al. (2001) data set.

Future Disorganized vs. Secure Dyads at 4 Months

In this section we discuss differences in future disorganized (vs. secure) dyads at 4 months, integrating differences in behavioral qualities and degree of contingency. We use the term "coordination" interchangeably with interactive contingency where it increases clarity. We then discuss our finding that male infants are overrepresented in the future disorganized infants in our sample. The second part of the chapter offers an interpretive formulation of the origins of working models of attachment in future disorganized infants at 4 months. The formal presentation of the results can be found in Beebe et al. (2010). In the third part of the chapter we compare the working models of future resistant vs. future disorganized infants.

Mothers of future disorganized infants bring their own difficult attachment history to their interactions with their infants. They are likely to suffer from unresolved loss, abuse, or trauma (Lyons-Ruth, 1999; Main & Hesse, 1990). In the Adult Attachment Interview these mothers may become emotionally incoherent or dissociated. Their difficulties with their own distress are likely to disturb their responses to distress in their infants.

Attention Dysregulation in Future Disorganized Dyads

Mothers who gazed away from the infant's face extensively (30 seconds or more across the 2½ minutes coded) were more likely to have infants with greater degree of disorganization at 12 months. Whereas 41.2% of mothers of future disorganized infants showed this pattern of extensive gazing away, 21.3% of mothers of future secure infants showed it. Moreover, mothers of future disorganized infants not only looked away extensively, but they did so in a less predictable fashion (lowered gaze self-contingency).

Spatial Dysregulation in Future Disorganized Dyads

Mothers of future disorganized (vs. secure) infants showed extensive looming (20% of the time or more) into the infant's face. Maternal loom was also relatively unpredictable (lowered self-contingency of spatial orientation). Looming into the infant's face elicits a protective response from the early weeks of life: infants put their hands in front of their faces and turn their heads away (Bower et al., 1970). Loom behavior is considered frightening by Main and Hesse (1990).

Dyadic Touch Dysregulation in Future Disorganized Dyads

Future disorganized infants (vs. secure) spent more time in "no touch," and less time in touching their own skin. They were more likely to continue in the behavior of "no touch" (heightened touch self-contingency). These findings indicate lowered infant access to self-soothing through touch, likely to interfere with infant arousal regulation of vocal distress, a hallmark of future disorganized infants.

In this context of difficulty in using touch in future disorganized infants, their mothers lowered their contingent touch coordination with infant touch: a reciprocal dysregulation. In the secure subset (Chapter 5), mothers are procedurally "aware" of and sensitive to infant touch behavior: the more likely infant touch, the more likely maternal touch was affectionate (and vice versa). This association was lowered in mothers of future disorganized infants. Perhaps they lowered their touch coordination because infant touch was a "weaker signal," in the sense that infants used it less. However, when future disorganized infants did touch more frequently, their mothers nevertheless showed lower touch coordination, a maternal withdrawal.

Affect Dysregulation in Future Disorganized Infants

Future disorganized (vs. secure) infants showed complex facial and/or vocal patterns of distress, largely consistent with our hypotheses. They showed more vocal distress, more combined facial and/or vocal distress, and more discrepant affect (simultaneous positive and negative facial and vocal affect within the same second). These multiple dimensions of infant distress are consistent with the finding that disorganized infants show the highest cortisol following the Strange Situation (Spangler & Grossman, 1993).

Future disorganized (vs. secure) infants also showed lowered self-predictability of facial-visual engagement. We infer that it is harder for these infants to sense

117

their own next engagement "move," as well as harder for their mothers to anticipate infant engagement shifts. Because future disorganized infants lowered their
engagement self-contingency in the context of lowered maternal engagement coordination (discussed next), we conjecture that these two findings are compensatory.
That is, infant engagement "self-destabilization" occurs in relation to maternal
failure to adequately coordinate with infant engagement (or vice versa).

Affect Dysregulation in Mothers of Future Disorganized Infants

Mothers of future disorganized (vs. secure) infants *lowered* their *engagement
interactive contingency* with infant engagement, a form of maternal withdrawal.
These mothers were not as correlated with the immediately prior infant engagement behavior. They were less likely to follow infant direction of gaze, to become
facially positive as their infants became facially or vocally positive, or to dampen
their facial affect toward interest, neutral, or "woe face" as their infants became
distressed. Because future disorganized infants were very distressed, lowered
maternal engagement coordination indicates a lowered maternal ability to emotionally "enter" and "go with" infant distress, via contingent changes.

Mothers of future disorganized (vs. secure) infants also heightened their facial
self-contingency, remaining overly facially stable, or inscrutable, like a momentary "still-face." The combination of lowered maternal engagement coordination
with infant engagement, but heightened maternal facial self-contingency, suggests
these mothers were procedurally (out of awareness) "preoccupied" with facial
self-management, at the expense of coordinating with the infant. Together, these
findings produced a coherent constellation of lowered maternal facial and visual
availability for the infant.

Following Lyons-Ruth et al. (1999), we showed that mothers who were more
likely to show positive expressiveness or surprise while infants were facially and/
or vocally distressed were more likely to have infants with greater degree of disorganization at 12 months. We suggest that infant simultaneous positive and negative emotion parallels maternal positive emotion during infant negative emotion.
Maternal interpersonal emotional discordance is thus echoed in infant intrapersonal emotional discordance (Jude Cassidy, personal communication, October 25,
2006).

Our finding has a parallel in the work of Madigan et al. (2006; Goldberg, Benoit,
Blokland, & Madigan, 2003), who found affective communication errors during
free-play in disorganized dyads at 12 months. Lyons-Ruth et al.'s finding was
evident within the Strange Situation at 12 months. In contrast, our finding is at 4
months, with a different method, indicating robustness of the phenomenon.

We failed to find differences in the frequency of negative facial affect (frown,
grimace, compressed lips) in mothers of future disorganized (vs. secure) infants.
We did not code anger or disgust, which would have been a closer parallel to
frightened and/or frightening faces, although clinically we observed instances of
anger and disgust in these mothers, particularly at moments of infant distress.

Infant Intrapersonal Vocal Affect–Touch

There were no differences in the ways that infants coordinated vocal affect and touch in future disorganized (vs. secure) infants.

Gender Differences in Future Disorganized Infants

Male infants were over-represented in future disorganized infants. Male infants are more emotionally reactive than female (Weinberg, 1992; Weinberg, Tronick, Cohn, & Olson, 1999). Lyons-Ruth et al. (1999) found that male (vs. female) infants showed more disorganized conflict behavior and avoidance when mothers showed high levels of frightening or withdrawing behavior in the Strange Situation.

Summary of Future Disorganized (vs. Secure) Dyads at 4 Months

In summary, 4-month infants who will be classified disorganized (vs. secure) at 12 months were more likely to be male and to show complex forms of emotional dysregulation:

- more vocal distress, and more combined facial and/or vocal distress;
- more *discrepant* facial and vocal affect;
- lowered engagement self-contingency, an emotional destabilization;
- more failure to touch, less touching one's own skin, and greater likelihood of continuing in a "no touch" state, all of which compromise infant access to arousal regulation through touch, in the context of increased distress.

Mothers of 4-month infants who will be classified disorganized (vs. secure) at 12 months were more likely to show the following patterns:

- extensive (20% of the time or more) gazing away from infant's face, and less predictable self-contingency patterns of looking at and away from the infant, compromising infant ability to expect and rely on predictable maternal visual attention;
- extensive (20% of the time or more) "looming" head movements, which were relatively unpredictable, interpreted as potentially threatening;
- greater likelihood of positive and/or surprise expressions while infants were distressed, interpreted as maternal emotional "denial" of infant distress;
- lowered emotional (facial-visual engagement) coordination with infant emotional ups and downs, interpreted as maternal emotional withdrawal from distressed infants;
- heightened maternal facial self-contingency, an overly stable face leading to a "closed-up" inscrutable face;
- lowered maternal contingent touch coordination with infant touch, a form of withdrawal.

119

The two findings of lowered maternal engagement coordination and lowered maternal touch coordination compromise infant interactive efficacy in these domains.

Origins of Internal Working Models in Future Disorganized Infants

The recurrent nature of the infant's experiences leads to the development of procedural representations or "working models" of self and others that influence the infant's emotional experiences and expectations (Bowlby, 1973; Bretherton, 1980; Bretherton & Munholland, 1999; Main et al., 1985). We proposed that 4-month infant procedural expectancies of patterns of self- and partner contingency, as well as of specific behavioral qualities, provide ways of defining processes by which patterns of intimate relating and attachment security are constructed: the origins of emerging working models of attachment. In this section we infer the experience of future disorganized infants at 4 months, who are more likely to be male. As noted above, mothers of future disorganized infants bring to the interaction their own difficult attachment histories, fears regarding intimate attachments, and difficulties managing their own distress.

Our findings show many forms of intrapersonal and interpersonal conflict, intermodal discordance, or contradiction, leading to confusion and incoherent working models in future disorganized infants. We propose that infant internal working models are characterized by expectancies of emotional distress and emotional incoherence, difficulty predicting what will happen, both in the self and the partner, profound disturbances in experiences of recognition, and difficulty in obtaining comfort. We infer that infants at moments experience alarm and threat. Our results provide one response to Madigan et al.'s (2006) call for better identification of the details of the elusive behaviors of anomalous parenting directly implicated in the development of disorganized attachment.

To set the stage, there many ways in which maternal contingent coordination with infants is intact in mothers of future disorganized infants. These mothers differed from mothers of future secure infants in interactive contingency of facial-visual engagement and touch, but not gaze, facial affect, or orientation. Thus there is no *overall* maternal failure to register infant states. However, lowered maternal contingent coordination of engagement and touch are important findings, discussed below.

Many of the difficulties of mothers of future disorganized infants occur at specific heightened moments in which they display contradictory behavior patterns, which are triggered at moments of infant distress (Lyons-Ruth, personal communication, October 17, 2008). Presumably out of their own unresolved fears about intimate relating, and fears of being re-traumatized by infant distress, at specific moments mothers of future disorganized infants mobilize complex contradictory behavioral tendencies, or "defensive" behaviors, that derail the infant. We use an ethological definition of conflict, in which behavior is organized simultaneously in opposing directions, rather than a psychoanalytic definition of conflict as impulse and defense. The infant's distress may be so over-arousing and terrifying to the mother of the future disorganized infant that she repeats aspects of her own childhood feelings through the procedural action-sequence mode, or defends herself against re-experiencing them (Mary Sue Moore, personal communication, July 2, 2007). Finally, we propose that many of the dysregulated patterns provide specific ways of defining *how* the infant's ability to "know" and be "known by" the mother's mind, as well as the infant's ability to "know" his own mind, become derailed.

Infant Distress and Discrepant Affect

Compared to future secure infants, future disorganized infants at 4 months show more vocal distress, and combined facial and/or vocal distress. They also show discrepant affect in the same second, especially positive facial affect such as smile, with distressed vocal affect such as whimper. These are painful moments to watch.

To our knowledge, this is the first such documentation of *simultaneous* discrepant infant affect, disturbing the usual inter-modal redundancy in communication channels (Bahrick & Lickliter, 2002). Infant discrepant affect suggests affective conflict, confusion, and struggle, a striking intrapersonal affective dysregulation. We conjecture that the infant's stress response is heightened at such moments, consistent with known heightened cortisol levels in disorganized infants following the Strange Situation (Spangler & Grossman, 1993). Moments of infant discrepant affect can be understood using the principle of *heightened affective moments*, which specifies that dramatic moments may become formative out of proportion to mere temporal duration or frequency.

This infant pattern of discrepant affect fits an ethological definition of conflict. For example, one future disorganized infant joined sweet maternal smiles with smiles of his own, but meanwhile he whimpered as mother pushed his head back and roughly smacked his hands together. This mother thus also showed an inter-modal discrepancy between her positive facial affect and her rough touch. We infer that the infant's discrepant affect reflects his need for affective contact with his mother, despite being distressed by her rough handling. Because of discrepant affect, it may be difficult for future disorganized infants eventually to know what they feel, or how to make sense of their contradictory feelings (Jean Knox, personal communication, March 3, 2009).

Infant contradictory positive and negative affect at 4 months is strikingly similar to infant contradictory approach and withdrawal behavior at 12 months, a key feature of disorganized attachment. Disorganized attachment, in turn, predicts contradictory and unintegrated mental processes, particularly dissociative processes, in young adulthood (Lyons-Ruth, 2008; Dutra et al., 2009). Infant emotional distress and discrepant affect is one central feature differentiating future disorganized infants from future resistant infants.

Dyadic Affective Conflict: Maternal Smile or Surprise to Infant Distress

Not only the infant but also the dyad was in affective conflict. Mothers of future disorganized (vs. secure) infants were likely to show smile and/or surprise faces specifically during infant facial and/or vocal distress: a maternal emotional "denial" of infant distress. Thus these mothers "opposed" or "countered" infant distress, literally going in the opposite affective direction, as if attempting to "ride negative into positive." This finding, too, can be understood using the principle of *heightened affective moments.* It can also be construed as a disruption, without repair. Moreover, the infant's expectation of matching and being matched in the direction of affective change, which lays the groundwork for feeling "attuned to" or "on the same wavelength," is disturbed. We propose that unresolved fears about intimate relating in these mothers trigger complex "defensive" maneuvers and contradictory behavioral tendencies that derail their infants (Karlen Lyons-Ruth, personal communication, October 17, 2008).

We infer that this maternal "countering" of infant distress confuses future disorganized infants and makes it difficult for infants to feel that their mothers sense and acknowledge their distress. By clinical observation, these are moments in which infants seem alarmed. We infer that these infants come to *expect* that mothers do not empathically share their distress. This finding evokes Winnicott's (1965) description of an impingement in which, instead of mirroring the infant's gesture (distress), the mother substitutes her own gesture (smile or surprise) (Lin Reicher, personal communication, December 2, 2008).

We propose that the intrapersonal discrepant affect of future disorganized infants is in part fueled by seeing their mothers' positive facial affect while they themselves are distressed. Maternal interpersonal affective discrepancy, such as maternal smile to infant distress, is echoed in infant intrapersonal affective discrepancy, simultaneous smile and distress (Jude Cassidy, personal communication, October 23, 2006). An alternative possibility is that the infant's discrepant signals regarding facial vs. vocal affect contribute to the mother's propensity to smile when infants are distressed.

Dyadic Conflict: Attention Dysregulation

A second form of dyadic conflict can be seen in the finding that, despite greater distress in future disorganized infants, their mothers showed extensive looking away from the infant's face (20% of the time or more), a striking finding. Moreover, these mothers showed less self-predictability in patterns of gazing at and away from the infant's face. These findings may lead to infant feelings of being too visually "separate" from their mothers, of not being "seen," and of being confused about mother's visual presence and availability. Extensive and relatively unpredictable looking away disturbs the "visual frame" of the face-to-face encounter, a background sense of structure that mothers usually provide (George Downing, personal communication, April 18, 2007). Thus infant ability to rely on a predictable maternal pattern of visual attention is compromised.

Extensive maternal looking away may reflect maternal discomfort with intimate engagement through mutual gaze (Karlen Lyons-Ruth, personal communication, January 12, 2007); or it may reflect moments of maternal dissociation (George Downing, personal communication, April 18, 2007). If the mother of the future disorganized infant looks at her distressed infant, there may be a greater likelihood that similar levels of distress will be activated in her. Looking away may reflect a maternal attempt to down-regulate arousal (Jude Cassidy, personal communication, October 23, 2006). Hodges and Wegner (1997) propose that individuals who become overwhelmed with the emotion of another can protect themselves from "automatic" forms of empathy with forms of "exposure control," such as looking away (see also Peck, 2003).

Clinically we observed moments of maternal dissociation. For example, as one infant became increasingly frantic, the mother looked down, with a blank, closed up face; she seemed very far away inside herself. In another example, one mother smiled more and more as her infant began to open his eyes, as if she were happy that her infant was looking at her. But simultaneously the infant had an intensely distressed pre-cry face. It seems as if this mother "split" her infant: she joyfully greeted his eyes as they opened to see her, but she ignored his intense distress. Finally the infant arched back forcefully, with a cry of protest, and a look of surprised disbelief. Maternal dissociation fits the literature on the adult attachment interview in which forms of dissociation such as lapses in attention, dysfluencies, or simultaneously entertaining contradictory facts about a person (both dead and alive) are characteristic of mothers classified as "unresolved," who are likely to have disorganized infants (Main et al., 2008).

Maternal Intermodal Discordance

Mothers of future disorganized infants themselves exhibited an intermodal discordance between extensive gazing away, thus "too far away;" and extensive looming, thus "too close in" (Karlen Lyons-Ruth, personal communication, January 17, 2007). We described two maternal loom sequences in future disorganized dyads in Chapter 1, illustrated in Figure 1.3b. Maternal loom is upsetting for infants. In the first loom sequence, the infant puts his hands up in front of his face (a defensive gesture available from the beginning of life) as mother looms in. In the next moment, the infant raises his hands still more as mother looms in further.

In the second loom sequence, the infant looks at mother with his bottom lip pulled in (a gesture of "uh-oh") as mother looms in, smiling. In the next moment, as mother looms further, the infant closes his eyes and pulls his lips into a full "compressed lips" expression. In the next moment, as mother looms in still further with a bigger smile, the infant dips his head down, with a slightly negative expression. In the final moment of this sequence, the infant shows an unhappy grimace; only now does mother's partial surprise face show that she senses something is wrong. At each point the infant signals discomfort, but mother overrides that signal until the final frame.

Mothers of future disorganized infants may reveal their desire for contact by looming. However, looming seems to be in conflict with their need to be visually "away" (Karlen Lyons-Ruth, personal communication, January 12, 2007). Looming may reflect the mother's need for control over the contact (Mary Sue Moore, personal communication, July 2, 2007). Both looking away and looming in disturb the potential for mutual gaze. Because eye contact is arousing, we conjecture that both these maternal behaviors reflect concerns about visual intimacy, which may be over-arousing.

It is striking that both maternal gaze away and maternal loom occurred in the context of lowered maternal visual and spatial self-predictability. Not only is there a maternal intermodal discordance (looming in and looking away), but these discordant behaviors unfold in relatively unpredictable ways. Thus mothers of future disorganized infants disturb both the "spatial frame" and the "visual frame," a background sense of structure in the ways mothers set the stage for the interaction (George Downing, personal communication, April 18, 2007). This loss of predictability further exacerbates infant difficulty in decoding and predicting maternal behavior, decreases infant sense of agency, and increases the possibility that the infant may feel unsafe (Mary Sue Moore, personal communication, July 2, 2007). It will be difficult for the infant to generate a coherent percept from the contradictory intermodal maternal discordance, coupled with lowered maternal self-predictability. Both infants and mothers will have difficulty sensing what mother feels and what she will do next. Is she or isn't she coming in to loom? Is she or isn't she "going away" visually, or "coming back"?

Dyadic Conflict: Lowered Maternal Engagement Coordination

A third form of dyadic conflict was seen in the finding that, despite infant distress, mothers of future disorganized infants lowered their facial-visual engagement coordination with infant engagement: an emotional and attentional withdrawal from contingently coordinating with infant positive as well as distress moments. They did not join the infant's attentional and emotional direction, disturbing the likelihood of shared affective processes (Beebe & Lachmann, 1988, 1994; Lyons-Ruth, 2008), consistent with our hypothesis. Although the prevalence of *behavioral qualities* of positive or negative facial affect did not differ in mothers of future disorganized vs. secure infants, the ways that mothers *contingently coordinated* their facial-visual behavior with that of the infants differed. Thus the difficulty is found in the *process* of relating over time, rather than the mere frequency of behaviors. This pattern was an "ongoing dysregulation."

This maternal withdrawal makes it difficult for future disorganized infants to come to expect that their emotional and attentional states can influence mothers to coordinate with them. They do not come to expect that their mothers will join their distressed or their positive states. In short, infants are relatively helpless to affect mothers with their facial-visual engagement processes, which disturbs the infant's sense of interactive efficacy. This finding is consistent with Koos and Gergely's

(2001) proposal that mothers of disorganized infants subject the infant to loss of contingent "control" over maternal behavior. Lowered maternal coordination in the context of infant facial and vocal distress may be fear-arousing. Such fear is another possible route to a frightening mother, which is one current description of a central dynamic of the disorganized category (Lyons-Ruth et al., 1999; Main & Hesse, 1990). A perceived lack of behavioral control in the future disorganized infant may be related to the finding that these infants may have over-controlling styles later in development (Lyons-Ruth & Block, 1996).

We noted that lowered maternal facial coordination with infant facial or vocal affect, or lowered maternal gaze coordination with infant gaze, was not found in mothers of future disorganized infants when these communication modalities were analyzed separately. Thus mothers of future disorganized infants *perceive* the infant's affect and gaze, and in many ways are adequately responsive. Instead, it is only when the overall gestalt of infant facial-visual *engagement* (which includes infant head orientation and vocal affect as well) is considered that we find lowered maternal coordination. Thus, although facial-mirroring seems intact, maternal mirroring of the entire infant engagement gestalt is not. These mothers do not seem to be able to relate to the overall gestalt of their infants.

Our findings of maternal facial-visual withdrawal here parallel those of Lyons-Ruth (2008), who found that maternal withdrawal from the infant's attachment-related cues at 12 months was the best predictor of adult borderline or conduct symptoms. Such maternal withdrawal, through failure to join the infant's affective direction, may disturb the developing child's ability to share attentional, affective, and mental states with others (Lyons-Ruth, 2008).

We theorize that mothers of future disorganized infants cannot coordinate with infant emotional ups and downs, and cannot acknowledge moments of infant distress, because they cannot bear to pay attention to their own emotional distress. The infant's distress may evoke their own distress, with ensuing efforts to manage their distress. Eisenberg (Eisenberg & Fabes, 1992; Peck, 2003) proposes that individuals who are skilled at regulating their emotions are free to focus on the distress of the other because they do not become overly emotionally aroused as they vicariously experience the other's distress. This picture might describe mothers of future secure infants. In contrast, less skilled individuals may experience their own personal distress in response to another's distress, and then need to manage their own distress. This picture seems consistent with mothers of future disorganized infants. However, the issue may not be maternal "skill" but a history of trauma.

We interpret the mother's lowered contingent engagement coordination with infant engagement, as well as maternal smile or surprise to infant distress, as maternal emotional "denial" of infant distress. Although minimization of distress has been associated with avoidant attachment styles (Belsky, 1997; Cassidy, 1994), the forms of maternal denial of distress documented here are different from minimization. Lowered emotional coordination communicates to the infant, "You can't affect me." Showing the opposite (positive) emotion to the infant's negative emotion constitutes an "opposing" of the infant's emotion, communicating, "I'm not going there." We propose that the infant represents these maternal responses to his distress through procedurally organized expectancies of action sequences. Moreover, one aspect of this representation is the infant's own distress and potential alarm.

Heightened Maternal Facial Self-Contingency: "Closing up One's Face"

Maternal lowered engagement coordination was accompanied by remaining overly facially stable or too "steady-state," like a momentary "still-face" (Tronick, 2007). We interpret this finding as mothers "closing up their faces," another way of not being available to the "play of faces," another way of saying "you can't affect me." We illustrated a mother "closing up" her face, across a 4 second sequence, in Figure 1.3a. As the distressed infant opens his eyes, mother's closed-up face remains stabilized, although her head angle shifts; likewise as infant distress increases, mother's facial affect remains stabilized.

Mothers of future disorganized infants may sense the risk of greater facial variability, which would facilitate greater facial coordination with the infant's facial affect. Clinically we observed that mothers' "closing up" their faces often occurred at moments of infant distress, as if mother is "going blank." To remain empathic to infant distress might re-evoke aspects of the mother's own original traumatized state.

The constellation of momentarily closing her face, lowering her ongoing coordination with the infant's emotional shifts, and extensive looking away from her infant's face, may be ways of shutting herself down in a self-protective effort, possibly dissociative (Mary Sue Moore, personal communication, July 2, 2007). Mothers of future disorganized infants may, out of awareness, be afraid of the facial and visual intimacy that would come from more gazing at the infant's face, more coordination with the infant's facial-visual shifts, and more "joining" the infant's distressed moments. These findings confirm and extend Lyons-Ruth's (2008; Lyons-Ruth et al., 1999) proposals that mothers of disorganized infants engage in disrupted and contradictory forms of affective communication, especially around the infant's need for comfort when distressed.

If her procedural experience could be put into words, we imagine that the mother of the future disorganized infant might feel, "I can't let myself be too affected by you. I'm not going to let myself be controlled by you and dragged down by your bad moods" (Karlen Lyons-Ruth, personal communication, October 17, 2008). "I refuse to be helpless. I'm going to be upbeat and laugh off your silly fussing." She might feel, "I can't bear to know about your distress. Don't be like that. Come on, no fussing. I just need you to love me. I won't hear of anything else. You should be very happy." And she might feel, "Your distress frightens me. I feel that I am a bad mother when you cry" (Estelle Shane, personal communication, November 12, 2006). Or she might feel, "Your distress threatens me. I resent it. I just have to shut down" (Mary Sue Moore, personal communication, July 2, 2007).

We conjecture that infants may experience the combination of maternal withdrawal of engagement coordination and "too-steady" faces as a kind of affective "wall." Maternal positive facial affect specifically at moments of infant distress further connote a "stone-walling" of infant distress: an active maternal emotional refusal to "go with" the infant, a refusal to join infant distress. This pattern disturbs the infant's ability to feel sensed and may generate alarm. We infer that future disorganized infants come to expect that their mothers do not "join" their distress with acknowledgments such as maternal "woe face," an empathic form of maternal facial mirroring. Instead they come to expect that their mothers are happy, surprised, or "closed" when they are distressed.

Lowered Infant Engagement Self-Predictability: Infant "Destabilization"

In the context of lowered maternal engagement coordination, future disorganized (vs. secure) infants lowered their engagement self-predictability. This finding indicates a more variable process in which the infant's ability to anticipate his own moment-to-moment action tendencies is lowered. Infants are metaphorically "destabilized." We infer a decreased sense of self-familiarity and coherence over time (Doris Silverman, personal communication, November 6, 2002). We note that lowered infant engagement self-contingency, an *intrapersonal* dysregulation, is linked to maternal failure to adequately coordinate with infant engagement, a maternal *interpersonal* dysregulation.

Dyadic Touch Dysregulation

Mothers of future disorganized (vs. secure) infants not only lowered their contingent engagement coordination with infant engagement, disturbing infant interactive efficacy in the facial-visual realm, but they also lowered contingent touch coordination with infant touch, disturbing infant interactive efficacy in the touch realm. Both patterns constitute examples of "ongoing dysregulations." These mothers were less able to acknowledge increasing frequency of infant touch as a cue for more affectionate, tender touch. In contrast, for mothers of future secure infants, infant-initiated touch behavior enters the interpersonal exchange as a communicative signal, a new finding (George Downing, personal communication, October 26, 2006). Perhaps the lowered touch coordination of mothers of future disorganized infants reflects maternal difficulty tolerating an infant behavior that involves self-soothing, because of their own difficulties with distress. Or perhaps these mothers lacked affectionate touch in their own childhoods, and have difficulty identifying infant need for more affectionate touch.

We infer that future disorganized infants come to expect that their mothers will be unavailable to help modulate states of affective distress through maternal touch coordination with their own touch behavior: an interpersonal touch dysregulation. Infants are left too alone, too separate, in the realm of touch (Anni Bergman, personal communication, November 16, 2006).

Simultaneously future disorganized infants showed an intrapersonal touch dys-regulation: less touch overall, specifically less touching of their own skin, and greater likelihood of continuing in states of "no touch," metaphorically "getting stuck" in states of "no touch." This configuration again depicts an infant intrap-ersonal dysregulation linked to a maternal interpersonal dysregulation. Lowered infant access to touch further disturbs infant arousal regulation of distress.

Given the heightened facial and vocal distress in these infants, we infer that these interpersonal and intrapersonal forms of touch dysregulation compromise infant interactive efficacy, and infant self-agency, in the capacity to self-soothe through touch. Getting metaphorically "stuck" in states of "no touch" may disturb the infant's visceral bodily feedback, laying one groundwork for the dissociative symptoms known to characterize these disorganized infants once they are young adults (Dutra et al., 2009; Lyons-Ruth, 2003). Future disorganized infants cannot rely on mothers to help in the touch domain, nor can they rely on themselves to provide self-comfort and modulation of vocal distress through touch.

Together, future disorganized infants and their mothers showed a dyadic touch dysregulation. This constellation of findings illustrates a disturbance in the interaction pattern of "dyadic state transforming," the expectation of being able to transform an arousal state through the contribution of the partner (Beebe & Lachmann, 2002; Stern, 1985). As a corollary, the infant findings (less touch, less touching one's own skin, getting "stuck" in states of no-touch, in the context of greater vocal distress) illustrate a disturbance in an infant "intrapersonal state transforming," the expectation of being able to help oneself transform arousal states.

Future disorganized infants thus come to expect that they are relatively helpless to affect mothers, in the realms of facial-visual engagement and touch. They are left too alone to manage potentially frantic distress on their own. Moreover they also come to expect that they are relatively helpless to help themselves by provid-ing touch self-comfort and touch modulation of vocal distress.

If their procedural experience could be put into words, we imagine future dis-organized infants might experience, "I'm so upset and you're not helping me. I'm smiling at you and whimpering; don't you see I want you to love me? When I'm upset, you smile or close up or look away. You make me feel worse. I feel con-fused about what I feel and about what you feel. I can't predict you. I don't know what is going on. What am I supposed to do? I feel helpless to affect you. I feel helpless to help myself. I feel frantic. I feel unsafe."

Infant self-contingency represented half of all mother and infant contingency findings in future disorganized (vs. secure) dyads. Infant touch self-contingency dysregulation (greater likelihood of continuing in "no touch" states) and infant engagement self-contingency dysregulation (facial-visual destabilization) gener-ated difficulties in sensing, predicting, and modulating one's own state. These infant intra-personal forms of dysregulation accompany the overt emotional dis-tress of these infants, and the maternal failures to acknowledge and respond to this distress.

Procedural Mechanisms of Sensing the State of the Other

In an effort to understand further mothers of future disorganized infants, we take up the topic of procedural mechanisms of sensing the state of the other. A facial expression produced by one person tends to evoke a similar expression in the partner, out of awareness (Dimberg et al., 2000), a powerful way of participating in the state of the other. This is such a robust phenomenon that some researchers dub it an "automatic" facial mimicry (Hatfield, Cacioppo, & Rapson, 1993; Hodges & Wegner, 1997; Peck, 2003). Perhaps mirror neurons, an "action-recognition" mechanism in which the actor's actions are reproduced in the premotor cortex of the observer, help explain why this is such a robust phenomenon. But as we have seen, mothers of future disorganized infants do not match or empathically join the facial distress of their infants.

Furthermore, we know from adult research that, as partners match each other's affective patterns, each recreates a psychophysiological state in the self which is similar to that of the partner, an additional way of participating in the subjective state of the other (Beebe & Lachmann, 2002; Ekman et al., 1983; Levenson et al., 1990). Recent work on embodied simulation (see Chapter 4) suggests that such matching facilitates sensing the other's emotions. By showing discrepant rather than similar expressions, mothers of future disorganized infants may prevent this embodied simulation.

We propose that these means of sensing the state of the other, highly biologically primed, are inhibited in these mothers for defensive reasons (Virginia Demos, personal communication, March 3, 2007). We conjecture that mothers of future disorganized infants cannot process and respond to emotional information in the moment because they are flooded by their experience of the infant's distress, which may re-evoke earlier traumatic states of their own. They may shut down their own emotional processing, and be unable to use the infant's distress behaviors as communications, in a momentary dissociative process (Mary Sue Moore, personal communication, July 2, 2007). For example, as one of the future disorganized infants showed a sharp increase in vocal distress and turned away with a pre-cry face, the mother's head jerked back, as if "hit" by the infant's distress; she then looked down with a "closed up" face. It is also possible that the mirror neuron system of these mothers is disrupted during moments of infant distress. Moments of maternal inability to participate in the infant's state arguably become "heightened affective moments." Such moments intensify infant negative arousal and may organize infant experience out of proportion to mere frequency or duration. In such heightened moments, infants may feel unsafe.

Knowing and Being Known in the Origins of Disorganized Attachment

The organization of intimate relating is at stake in these procedural representations, which form the early working models of attachment. Intimate relating entails the fundamental issue of how the infant comes to know, and be known by, another's mind. We construe "mind" here from the point of view of the infant, that is, generalized expectancies of procedurally organized action sequences. Our findings allow us to describe *how* the future disorganized infant's ability to know, and be known by, another's mind, as well as to know his own mind, may be disturbed.

We propose that the future disorganized infant will have difficulty feeling known by his mother:

- In moments when he is distressed, and she smiles or shows surprise expressions. These are akin to Stern's (1985) moments in which the infant learns that his distress states are not shareable. Such moments may accrue to later experiences of "not-me."
- In moments when the mother looks away repeatedly and unpredictably, so that the infant does not feel seen.
- As mother does not coordinate her facial-visual engagement with his facial-visual engagement. She is thus unable to coordinate with the shifting overall gestalt of her infant, his emotional and attentional "ups and downs."
- As mother does not coordinate her affectionate-to-intrusive touch patterns with his frequency of touch. This pattern generates infant expectations that his mother does not *change with* him, and that she does not match his direction of change, in the arenas of both facial-visual engagement and touch.
- As she looms into his face, relatively unpredictably, generating a feeling of alarm, or threat.

Clinically we observed that mothers did not seem curious about, and made no efforts to repair, powerful disruptions. This observation suggests maternal difficulty thinking about the infant's mind and motivation (Fonagy, Gergely, Jurist, & Target, 2002).

We propose that the future disorganized infant will have difficulty knowing his mother's mind in the following ways:

- As he has difficulty integrating mother's discrepant smile or surprise face to his distress into a coherent percept.
- As he has difficulty predicting whether mother will look or look away, and for how long.
- As he has difficulty predicting whether mother will sit upright, lean forward, or loom in.
- As she "closes up" her face and becomes inscrutable.
- As mother's lowered contingent engagement coordination makes it difficult for the infant to "influence" his mother with shifts in his own facial-visual engagement. He cannot use his own state to anticipate where she is going next. The infant comes to expect that his mother does not join his direction of attentional and affective change.

- As mother's lowered contingent touch coordination makes it difficult for the infant to "influence" mother with the frequency of his touch behaviors. He cannot use his own touch behavior to anticipate the nature of her next touch. This pattern leads to the infant's expectation that mother does not "follow" his touch behaviors by touching him more tenderly and affectionately as he touches more (and by touching him with more rousing patterns as he touches less).

We propose that the future disorganized infant will have difficulty knowing himself in the following ways:

- In his moments of discrepant affect, for example as he smiles and whimpers in the same second.
- As his own engagement self-contingency is lowered. This makes it more difficult to sense his own facial-visual action tendencies from moment-to-moment. This may also make it more difficult to develop a coherent expectation of his own body.
- As he has difficulty touching (himself, an object, or his mother), and specifically as he has difficulty touching his own skin, and as he gets "stuck" in states of "no touch." All of these difficulties disturb his visceral feedback through touch and disturb his own agency in regulating distress through touch.

As Sander (1977, 1995) notes, infant inner experience is organized in the interactive context. Sander argues that the infant–caretaker system may both facilitate, and constrain, the infant's access to and awareness of his own states, and his ability to use his states in organizing his behavior. We propose that the future disorganized infant experiences a disturbance in the experience of agency with regard to his own states.

One important aspect of these difficulties of the future disorganized infant's ability to know, and be known by, another's mind, as well as to know his own mind, is identified through disturbances in maternal affective correspondence and state-sharing (Meltzoff, 2007; Sander, 1977; Stern, 1985; Trevarthen, 1998). However, many other aspects of these difficulties are identified through dysregulated tactile, spatial, and attentional behaviors. These are important additions to disturbances in affective correspondence.

Lyons-Ruth (1999, 2008) proposes that the outcome of the process of coming to know and be known by another's mind is dependent on whether the partner is capable of a *collaborative dialogue*. Overall the mother of the future disorganized infant does not generate collaborative dialogues. Her infant will be unlikely to be able to generate internal working models in which both partners are represented as open to the full range of experiences of the other. Lyons-Ruth (1999, 2008) also suggests that failures of collaborative dialogue generate contradictory internal models. An example in our data are moments when infants whimper and smile in the same second, possibly generating an infant internal working model such as, "I smile to find your smile, while I whimper to protest your uncomfortable touch."

131

Another example of contradictory procedures are moments where infants are distressed but mothers smile or look surprised, possibly generating internal working models of, "While I am upset, you are happy; or "You are surprised at my distress." Contradictory procedures, intrapersonal or dyadic, disturb the ability to know and be known by the partner, and to know the self. They disturb higher-order coordinations essential to social and cognitive development. And they set the stage for dissociative defenses in which contradictory arenas of knowledge are entertained (Lyons-Ruth, 1999).

Internal Working Models of Future Disorganized Infants at 4 Months

We propose that future disorganized infants represent these individual and dyadic patterns as emerging internal working models in the form of procedural representations, based on expectancies of self- and interactive patterns. These expectancies bias the trajectory of how experience is organized, activating certain pathways and inhibiting others, ultimately limiting the range, flexibility, and *coherence* of experience.

One central feature of these expectancies is intense infant emotional distress and the inability to obtain comfort. In many ways future disorganized infants are alone with their facial and vocal distress, helpless to affect their mothers with their frantic distress. At critical moments they are opposed by their mothers. A second feature is an expectancy of difficulty predicting what will happen, both within the self and within the partner. A third feature is difficulty in knowing what the self feels and what the partner feels: a form of emotional incoherence. A fourth feature is the expectation of not feeling "sensed" or "known," particularly when distressed. These are profound experiences of non-recognition which may disturb the infant's sense of safety.

These future disorganized infants do not experience Sander's (1995) "moment of meeting," a match between two partners such that the way one is known by oneself is matched by the way one is known by the other (Lin Reicher, personal communication, November 8, 2007). They come to expect that their distress states are not shareable (Stern, 1985).

A further critical feature of these expectancies of future disorganized infants is the experience of intrapersonal and dyadic contradictory communications, conflict, and remarkable intermodal discrepancies. These contradictions disturb the coherence of the infant's internal working model. Our dyadic model of procedural representations holds that both roles are known to both people. We propose that the future disorganized infant will come to know both roles of mother and infant. This may account for why, later in development, the disorganized child plays out the mother's role of denial of distress, overriding the state of the mother with a controlling style.

In sum, we have described many fundamental disturbances in the processes through which infants may come to feel known and can recognize being recognized, through which infants may come to know their mothers, and through which infants come to sense their own states. This picture provides detailed behavioral mechanisms that could result in the lack of a consistent strategy of dealing with negative emotions, characteristic of disorganized infants in the Strange Situation by 12 months (van Ijzendoorn et al., 1999). The disturbance in individual and dyadic emotional coherence in future disorganized infants and their mothers offers a striking parallel to the contradictory and unintegrated affects of the disorganized infant in the Ainsworth paradigm, and to the contradictory evaluations of attachment relationships in the findings of their mothers in the Adult Attachment Interview.

Comparison of Internal Working Models of Future Resistant vs. Disorganized Infants

Pattern of Findings: Behavioral Qualities and Contingencies

Future resistant and disorganized dyads were remarkably differentiated in the pattern of findings. Regarding *behavioral qualities*, there was no finding in common, for mothers or infants. For *mothers*, behavioral qualities were altered in future resistant and disorganized dyads, but in entirely different ways. Mothers of future resistant infants showed progressively less affectionate and more active touch, and chase and dodge; whereas mothers of future disorganized infants showed extensive loom, extensive looking away from distressed infants, and mother smile or surprise face while infants were distressed. For *infants*, whereas the future resistant infant showed no difficulties in behavioral qualities, the future disorganized infant showed intense emotional distress, and difficulties in access to his own touch.

Regarding *contingencies*, again the findings were strikingly differentiated. Future resistant and disorganized infants shared only one finding: lowered engagement self-contingency, an emotional destabilization. Mothers of future resistant and disorganized infants shared only one finding: lowered spatial orientation self-contingency, generating infant difficulty in predicting mother's next spatial move.

Regarding *infants*, future resistant (vs. secure) infants differed not in behavioral qualities, but rather in the *contingent process* of relating, particularly in *interactive* contingency. In contrast, future disorganized (vs. secure) infants differed in *behavioral qualities* and in *self-contingency*, but not in *interactive* contingency. Future resistant infants still seem to have the capacity to try to manage maternal stimulation by altering their contingent coordination with their mothers. In a remarkable demonstration of agency, they resist being organized by progressively less affectionate maternal touch. But future disorganized infants do not alter their own contingent coordination with their mothers. Instead they show their difficulties in other ways, such as intense distress, destabilized engagement self-contingency, and difficulties with touch.

133

Regarding *mothers*, interactive contingencies of mothers of future resistant (vs. secure) infants were intact. Infant expectations that they can influence mothers to match the direction of their behavioral change were safeguarded. In contrast, mothers of future disorganized (vs. secure) infants disturbed the *interactive process*. They lowered their contingent coordination of engagement and touch, disturbing infant interactive efficacy in these arenas.

Different Central Difficulties in Working Models of Future Resistant vs. Disorganized Infants

Central Interaction Patterns

A comparison of the central interaction patterns in the findings of future resistant and future disorganized dyads shows that only mothers of future disorganized infants had difficulty in facial mirroring and the more general arena of affective correspondence. Thus only these mothers had difficulty in sharing the affect state of the infant, particularly distress. But only future resistant infants showed difficulty in affective correspondence, through heightened coordination of facial-visual engagement with maternal engagement, a vigilant form of mirroring. Both future resistant and disorganized dyads showed difficulties with infant and dyadic state transforming, although they manifested in different ways. Both future resistant and disorganized dyads showed patterns of spatial intrusion, but the specific patterns were different. Future resistant dyads showed spatial approach-avoid, in the pattern of maternal "chase" and infant "dodge." Future disorganized dyads showed maternal loom. In patterns of interactive contingency, future resistant dyads showed dysregulated *infant* interactive contingency, whereas future disorganized dyads showed dysregulated *maternal* interactive contingency.

A number of new patterns of disturbance were also documented. A disturbance in the predictability of the maternal "spatial frame" was common to mothers of both future resistant and disorganized infants, but the mothers of future disorganized infants disturbed the predictability of the "attentional frame" as well. "Destabilized infant engagement self-contingency" was common to both future resistant and disorganized infants. Infant "tuning out mother touch" (lowered infant coordination with maternal touch) was identified only in future resistant infants. The following patterns were identified only in future disorganized dyads: infant lowered access to touch, and specifically to touching his own skin; infant "simultaneous discrepant affect;" maternal "closing up the face;" and maternal "extensive looking away."

The central difficulty of future resistant mothers was a spatial-tactile intrusion, coupled with an unstable spatial frame. We interpreted this pattern as the maternal wish for infants to stay with them, in the context of their own preoccupation with the infant's attention and emotional presence. But the future resistant mother cannot see that her very attempts to keep her infant involved with her will compromise her infant's involvement. The maternal spatial-tactile intrusion leads to difficulties in infant state transforming, and complex "approach–avoid" patterns, both dyadic and intrapersonal, in future resistant dyads. In the dyadic approach–avoid pattern, infants "dodge" as mothers "chase," and mothers chase as infants dodge. In the infant intrapersonal approach–avoid pattern, infants activate their engagement coordination with maternal engagement, but inhibit their engagement coordination with their mothers' less positive touch. This inhibition masks their distress and sacrifices their ability to communicate about maternal touch.

We proposed that in their working models of attachment, future resistant infants will represent the experience of moving away from mother as she moves in with spatial and tactile intrusion. They will represent responding to mother by "going in opposite directions," their simultaneous activation and inhibition of their own engagement in relation to maternal facial-visual engagement and touch, respectively. Thus, they vigilantly coordinate with maternal engagement while they "tune out" maternal touch. And they will have difficulty communicating what they "like" or do not "like," a confusion in sensing their own affective and attentional state, and ultimately a difficulty in coming to know what they feel, in relation to maternal touch. However, two key arenas are intact. Because mothers showed no altered interactive contingency, infant interactive agency in this realm is not disturbed. And there are no difficulties in maternal facial mirroring or the more general arena of maternal affective correspondences. Thus considerable competence remains visible in these dyads.

The difficulties of future disorganized dyads at 4 months are at a fundamentally deeper level than those of future resistant dyads. All central interaction patterns showed disturbance: maternal affective correspondence, infant and dyadic state transforming, maternal spatial intrusion, and maternal lowered interactive contingent coordination which disturbs infant interactive efficacy. The new interaction patterns identify disturbances in the spatial and attentional frame, which disrupt the very foundation of the face-to-face exchange. The new interaction patterns also identify infant discrepant affect, and maternal methods of managing her own state, such as extensive looking away and closing up her face, which create further distance from the infant.

The central feature of future disorganized dyads is intrapersonal and interpersonal discordance or conflict, in the context of infants who are intensely emotionally distressed. We argued that *maternal withdrawal from distressed infants* compromises infant interactive agency and emotional coherence in future disorganized infants. We characterized these infants as "frantic," not sensed or "known" in their distress, and relatively helpless to influence mothers with their distress. We suggested that they are at moments alarmed or threatened. Moreover, we propose that infant attempts to manage distress become hierarchically organizing (Werner, 1948). That is, because mothers of future disorganized infants are unable to help infants with their distress, the infants' own efforts to manage distress become a priority, coloring all other domains. We interpreted maternal withdrawal from distressed infants as the mother's difficulty with her own unresolved loss, mourning, or abuse. We infer that these mothers have difficulty bearing their own distress, as well as that of their infants. We understood these mothers to be preoccupied with regulating their own state (by looking away or closing up their faces).

Knowing and Being Known

We propose that although both future resistant and disorganized infants will have difficulties in representing knowing and being known in these ways, these difficulties will be more modest in the future resistant infant, but extensive and serious in the future disorganized infant.

BEING KNOWN BY THE MOTHER'S MIND

The intact maternal interactive contingency safeguards the future resistant infant's interactive agency in this realm. However, the future resistant infant may have difficulty feeling sensed and known by his mother at moments of spatial and tactile intrusion.

In contrast the future disorganized infant, who is very distressed, will have serious difficulties representing being known by his mother's mind, as he encounters her difficulty in sharing his distress through her "countering" of his distress, and her inscrutable closed up faces. He will have difficulty representing being known by his mother's mind as he encounters her extensive and unpredictable looking away, generating a feeling of not being *seen.* Her unpredictable looming will generate a feeling of threat. Her difficulty following the direction of his own facial-visual engagement and touch behaviors will generate a feeling of not being joined, difficulty in anticipating what she will do next, and potential alarm.

Compared to the future resistant infant, the future disorganized infant will have great difficulty coming to represent an internal working model of, "you share my happiness when I am happy and you understand me when I am distressed; you know me; we are on the same wavelength; you are like me; we share the same states." Instead, future disorganized infants come to expect that mothers do not sense and join their states, a working model of *not being known and recognized by the mother*, accompanied by potential alarm, especially when distressed.

KNOWING THE MOTHER'S MIND

We propose that the future resistant infant will have difficulty knowing his mother's mind as he has difficulty predicting when mother will intrude (spatial and/ or tactile intrusion). But he is also working too hard to know mother's mind, as he vigilantly coordinates his facial-visual engagement with her facial-visual engagement.

In contrast, the future disorganized infant will have difficulty knowing his mother's mind across a broad range of arenas, especially her affective state. The future disorganized infant will represent a working model of attachment in which he may feel, "I don't know what you feel. You show me incomprehensible, indigestible smiling and surprised faces when I am upset; your face is inscrutable. I can't count on your attention. I don't know when you are going to loom into my face, I can't read your intent, and I feel threatened. I can't influence you to follow my facial-visual changes or my touch. I can't read you or predict you; you are not on my wavelength." Compared to the future resistant infant, these difficulties disturb the future disorganized infant's internal working model of "I know you; you are mine."

KNOWING ONESELF

Both the future resistant and future disorganized infant will have difficulty *knowing himself* as his own engagement self-contingency is lowered. This lowered self-contingency makes it more difficult to sense his own facial-visual action tendencies from moment-to-moment, and more difficult to develop a coherent expectation of his own body. Both future resistant and disorganized infants showed an affective discrepancy, generating difficulty in sensing and representing a coherent state. The future resistant infant represents opposing expectations of how he responds to mother with his facial-visual engagement: he is vigilant to her engagement but inhibited to her touch. The future disorganized infant represents opposing expectations of his own state in moments of discrepant simultaneous positive and negative affect, a more primal split in the organization of self-experience. Moreover, the future disorganized infant has difficulty touching in general, difficulty touching his own skin, and tends to get "stuck" in states of no touch. These patterns disturb his visceral feedback through touch. He will thus come to expect that he will have difficulty in being able to regulate his distress through touch. He will come to anticipate frantic and alarmed states.

Although the future resistant infant has difficulty *using mother's touch*, the future disorganized infant's difficulty *using his own touch* will accrue to difficulty sensing his own control over his own body. More generally, both future resistant and future disorganized infants have difficulty in knowing the self, and generate representations that "my body is not my own, I can't sense myself." However, because of the numerous difficulties with his own touch, and his more primal affective split, we propose that the future disorganized, as compared to resistant, infant experiences a more serious disturbance in the experience of agency with regard to his own states, and is more prone to represent himself as helpless to use his states in organizing his own behavior, and in regulating his distress.

We propose that the level of dysregulation in future disorganized dyads is thus of an entirely different order than that of future resistant dyads. The future disorganized infant represents *not being sensed and known* by his mother, particularly in states of distress: "You are not on my wavelength"; he represents *not knowing the mother*: "I can't read you, influence you, or count on you, especially when I am upset"; and he represents *confusion in sensing and knowing himself*, especially at moments of distress; "I can't tell what I feel, I can't sense myself, I can't help myself." Thus the emerging working model of the future disorganized infant

137

represents confusion about his own basic emotional organization, his mother's emotional organization, and his mother's response to his distress, setting a trajectory in development which may disturb the fundamental integration of the person.

In the next chapter we turn to a discussion of our findings and the implications for adult treatment.

8

DISCUSSION

Mother–Infant Communication, the Origins of Attachment, and Adult Treatment

It is remarkable that we can predict the trajectory of infant attachment patterns at 1 year from 2½ minutes of mother–infant face-to-face interaction at 4 months. By 4 months infants are already "dialogic," entering into exquisitely sensitive reciprocal bi-directional exchanges with their social partners. Despite the spurt in motor capacity and the onset of symbolic functioning and language that occur between 4 and 12 months, the trajectory begun at 4 months remained evident. Thus aspects of attachment are already in place at 4 months, in subtle processes of face-to-face communication.

How was the prediction of attachment from 2½ minutes of mother–infant face-to-face interaction at 4 months possible? Our conceptual framework captured the fine-grained second-by-second implicit procedural communication between mothers and infants as they interacted face-to-face. The level of detail with which the interactions were coded from split-screen videotape was the base of the study. We coded the domains of attention, emotion, orientation, and touch. Thus everything we studied had a tangible visual referent, precise to a second.

But our theory of face-to-face interaction led the way. It led our questions, data analyses and interpretations. In our dyadic systems view of face-to-face interaction, each person's action is constituted in coordination with that of the partner; each person's behavior is affected both by his own immediately prior behavior (self-contingency), and by that of the partner (interactive contingency). Both partners are active participants in the co-creation of patterns of relatedness. However, the contributions of the two partners are not necessarily symmetrical. The mother obviously has a greater range, control, and flexibility of behavior than the infant.

The basic unit of the mother–infant communication system is *action knowledge*, based on predictable patterns of behavior across time. These predictable patterns of interaction generate expectancies of actions and action sequences. Continuous moment-to-moment variation provides each partner an essential means of sensing the self and the other. Predictable patterns across these variations facilitate the anticipation of oneself, one's partner, and the ways that each coordinates with the other. These are processes of self- and interactive contingency.

In this book we argue that what is at stake in the infant's procedural expectancies of self- and interactive contingency is the organization of intimate relating (see also Lyons-Ruth, 1999, 2008). Intimate relating entails the fundamental issue of how the infant comes to know, and be known by, another's mind. We construed "mind" from the point of view of the infant, that is, generalized expectancies of procedurally organized action sequences.

Self-contingency taps one dimension of self-regulation, that is, the procedural anticipation of where one's own behavior is tending in the next second. It generates expectancies of the degree to which one can anticipate the rhythm of one's own behavior: how predictable, how stable, how variable one's behaviors are, from moment-to-moment. It spans the range from midrange degree of predictability; to overly stabilized, tending toward steady state; to insufficiently predictable or labile, tending toward loss of predictability. The process of self-contingency is so basic that it is rarely noticed, like breathing. It accrues to one's experience of temporal coherence over time.

Self-contingency turned out to be extremely important in the origins of insecure attachment. In our findings self-contingency could be too high, as in the overly stable infant state of "no touch" of the future disorganized infant, which we characterized as getting stuck in states of "no touch." And self-contingency could also be too low, as in the "destabilized," lowered self-predictability of facial-visual engagement in the future disorganized infant. In these findings, the infant's ability to use his states in organizing his behavior is constrained, tending toward either too steady-state, or insufficiently stable. Heightened and lowered patterns of self-contingency in the origins of insecure attachment helped us to conceptualize infant disturbances in *knowing oneself.*

It is easy to mistake self-contingency for an organismic variable, a process contained entirely with the individual. Actually it is a complex amalgam of the individual and the dyad. A person's self-contingency process is specific to a particular partner. For example, in another study we examined how these same infants interacted with strangers (graduate students) compared to how they interacted with their mothers. We found that changing the partner altered both infant self- and interactive contingency (Beebe et al., 2009).

Interactive contingency generates expectancies of whether, and how closely, each partner coordinates with the other. These are expectancies of "how I anticipate that I will affect you, and how I anticipate that you will affect me." We use the term *coordination* interchangeably with *interactive contingency* where it increases clarity. As the mother coordinates with the infant, how closely does she follow and join the infant's own process and direction of change? This coordination will affect the infant's sense of interpersonal agency. Reciprocally, how closely does the infant sense the mother's state, and follow and join the mother's process and direction of change? This coordination will affect the mother's sense of interpersonal agency. Heightened and lowered patterns of interactive contingency in the origins of insecure attachment helped us to conceptualize infant disturbances in *knowing the partner* and *being known by the partner.*

Self-contingency added an important new dimension to our understanding of how attachment disturbances proceed early in development. Sander (1977, 1995) argues that inner experience is organized in the interactive context. The dyadic system may both facilitate, and constrain the individual's ability to use his states in organizing his behavior. Self-contingency taps Sander's concept of the individual's ability to use his states in organizing his behavior. Sander's position is poignantly illustrated in our findings on the origins of disorganized attachment. Infant *self*-contingency dysregulations were linked to maternal *interactive* contingency dysregulations. Disturbances of infant self-contingency in engagement and touch occurred in the context of maternal interactive contingency disturbances in the *same modalities,* that is, engagement and touch.

For example, mothers of future disorganized infants lowered their facial-visual engagement coordination with infant facial-visual engagement. In this pattern infants came to expect that their mothers did not follow and join their own engagement; that they could not influence their mothers in facial-visual engagement. The infant dysregulation that emerged here was not in the way the infant responded to his mother (interactive contingency); instead infant self-contingency showed lower self-predictability. The infant's facial-visual engagement rhythms were "destabilized."

Self- and Interactive Contingency in Adult Treatment

These concepts of self- and interactive contingency are directly relevant to adult treatment. The concept of expectancies shifts the focus to the process in which patterns of interaction became organized in the patient's history, and to the process by which patterns of interaction are becoming organized and re-organized in the treatment relationship. Patterns of self- and interactive contingency in adults operate largely out of awareness, but glimmers of them can at times be brought into awareness when focused on.

Interactive contingency is a concept from infant research that has already been integrated into adult treatment, under the term "mutual regulation" or "interactive regulation" (Beebe & Lachmann, 2002; Beebe et al., 2005; Stern et al., 1998; Tronick, 1998). We reiterate that higher coordination is not necessarily "better." Nor does mutual regulation necessarily entail a positive form of "mutuality." Mutual regulation means reciprocal or bi-directional regulation: each partner affects the other. All patterns of interaction are co-created. For example, in the "chase and dodge" interaction, the mother's chase movements increase the likelihood that the infant will "dodge"; and the infant's "dodge" movements increase the likelihood that the mother will "chase." But the outcome of the interaction is far from optimal or positive.

Our previous research discovered that midrange mother–infant coordination predicted secure attachment; non-optimally high coordination, that is "vigilant," predicted some types of insecure attachment; and non-optimally low coordination, that is withdrawn, predicted other types of insecurity (Jaffe et al., 2001). We dubbed this the "optimum midrange model" of interactive coordination. Similarly in our current findings, interactive coordination could be too high, as in the future resistant infant's vigilant coordination with maternal facial-visual engagement; or too low, as in the future resistant infant's withdrawn, "tuned-out" coordination with maternal touch.

In adult treatment, similarly, greater coordination with the partner may not always be optimal, and may vary with the level of distress of the patient, the nature of the disturbance, and the phase of the treatment. For example, in the beginning stage of treatment with Dolores (Beebe, 2004) when she was very hard to reach, based on observation of the videotapes I experienced myself as a "hyper-tracker," vigilant to every slight shift in Dolores's body. Ten years into the treatment, I experienced myself as more "midrange" in my degree of coordination, more relaxed, less careful. That is to say, my degree of interactive contingency—detectable on videotape—had shifted from high toward midrange. These degrees of coordination with Dolores were out of my awareness until I studied the videotapes.

Self-contingency provides a new concept for the implicit, procedural dimension of adult treatment. It provides a new way of sensing and thinking about one's own body from moment-to-moment, as well as that of the patient. Although this process is largely out of awareness, glimmers of it can be brought into awareness when focused on. It can alert us as therapists to moments of high self-stability, moments of "steady-state," likely carefulness, wariness, or fear. It can also alert us to moments of destabilization, moments of unusually high variability or loss of predictability. The meaning of these moments can be interpreted only within the dyadic context of each particular instance.

Using the Jaffe et al. (2001) measures of vocal rhythm, Holtz (2004) found that self-contingency of vocal rhythms was more predictive of adult treatment outcomes than interactive contingency. The majority of her findings involved self-contingency of therapist or patient. For example, therapists who were midrange in their degree of self-predictability of the durations of pauses between words (which determines speech rate), and midrange in their degree of self-predictability of turn-taking pauses ("switching pauses"), tended to have patients who made more progress (based on judgments of patient's speech before and after interpretations regarding such constructs as insight, patient involvement, lack of resistance, and productive free-association). Patterns of self-contingency may be just as important in therapeutic action as patterns of interactive contingency (see also Badalamenti & Langs, 1992; Warner, 1992).

The idea that inner experience is organized in the interactive context (Sander, 1977) is very relevant to adult treatment. Self-contingency taps one aspect of the organization of inner experience in the interactive context. Depending on the nature of the interactive regulation in the treatment, the patient may re-organize her self-contingency processes. Such a shift accrues to the way she senses herself, in the procedural mode, out of awareness. For example, in the case of Dolores (Beebe, 2004), she entered the treatment fearful of looking at me. Her earliest mother, the "good face," had been lost at about age 2, when Dolores was abruptly transferred to a cruel mother, with whom she developed the expectation of danger and fear. Over the course of our 10-year treatment, and specifically through watching my face on the video as I interacted with her, her expectation of danger and fear of looking was transformed. She came to expect in me the "still-lake face," the "just watching me all the time face." She came to feel found, sensed, and known by me. She came to feel that she knew me, my different faces, my ways of regulating myself, and responding to her.

Dolores's self-contingency processes were simultaneously transformed. When she first came, in a state of fear, she was shut-down, inaccessible, unable to look or talk. Her "steady-state" indicated fear. Slowly she began to move and talk, and finally, to look. Much later in the treatment she described a transformation in which she came to expect an inner state of feeling comforted. It had initially occurred out of her awareness. This was a transformation in her experience of knowing herself, as well as in knowing me. She came to be able to anticipate her own state in the next moment as one of comfort, rather than fear. She described a new interactive expectation: with me she felt she had found a place to "rest." Her rhythms became more flexible and variable, no longer frozen in a steady state of fear. This process illustrates Sander's (1977, 1995) concept that the interactive regulation may facilitate (or constrain) the person's access to and awareness of her own states, and her ability to use her states in organizing her behavior. Moreover, this vignette illustrates that expectancies can be reorganized in the implicit, procedural domain of action knowledge without necessarily reaching conscious awareness (see Lyons-Ruth, 1999).

For therapists and adult patients, as well as mothers and infants, what is at stake in the procedural expectancies of self- and interactive contingency is the organization of intimate relating. This process entails how each individual comes to know, and be known by, the partner's mind, as well as how each comes to know his own mind. Alongside verbal forms of intimacy, expectancies of implicit procedural forms of intimacy are co-created, generally out of awareness. Lyons-Ruth (1998b, 1999) argues that, because relatively little of the implicit procedural domain becomes translated into the symbolic domain, the implicit is more pervasive and potentially more organizing in adult treatment.

The pay-off from infant research lies in a greater awareness of the power of patterns of implicit, procedural communication in ourselves, and in our patients. Moment-by-moment shifts in the degree of stability in each person's bodily rhythms, and in each person's degree of coordination with the other, powerfully affect the emotional climate of the dyad.

It is easier to learn to observe the patient's behavior than one's own. Our ability as therapists to sense and *not to inhibit* our own bodily arousal, attention patterns, affective reactions, orientation shifts, and touch patterns is key. This is the therapist's *action knowledge* of her own bodily communication. Although it is largely out of awareness, we can teach ourselves to be somewhat more aware. It is our own bodily visceral feedback that feeds our ability at the linguistic, narrative level to become more aware of parallel or analogous experiences in our own lives that help us empathize with the dilemmas of our patients (see Hennelenlotter et al., 2008; Slavin, 2012).

The implicit, procedural process viewed through our dyadic systems view of the co-creation of self- and interactive contingency changes the entire context in which we ply our trade. We are at the epicenter of information from far more sources than ever recognized. This fine-tunes our ability to function therapeutically. But it places more demand on our ability to notice, to juggle, and to organize these sources of information. We are called upon to be more accountable. We can increasingly recognize the power of nonverbal as well as verbal gestures, and we can become more viscerally aware of self- and interactive contingency patterns and the dyadic "fit." As sensitivity to these processes is absorbed by therapists into the way they ply their trade, their humanity is freed.

Using the Statistical Analyses to Learn to View Mother–Infant Interactions

Our data analysis predicting attachment outcomes from 4-month mother–infant communication provided an essential guide with which to view the videotaped interactions. Prior to the data analysis, I (Beebe) saw various kinds of potentially disturbing patterns, particularly in the disorganized dyads. But it was not possible to identify which patterns might actually be more prevalent in dyads on the way to disorganized or resistant attachment, compared to secure. For example, mothers of both future disorganized and future secure infants at times loomed into the infant's face. Without the statistical analyses we could not have figured out that mothers of future disorganized infants were more likely to loom than mothers of future secure infants.

Once we had the statistically significant findings, I (Beebe) used them to view the videotapes. I learned to look in more precise ways. With the help of my research assistants, I located the moments of chase and dodge, maternal gaze aversion, infant simultaneous discrepant smile and whimper, or maternal over-stabilized faces, like temporary "still-faces." With the help of my study groups I watched dyads with high and low levels of interactive contingency, for example maternal lowered coordination with infant facial-visual engagement, characteristic of disorganized dyads, to see what this pattern might look like. By creating frame-by-frame analyses of the videotapes, we were able to study the various patterns of disturbance to see how they unfolded, moment-by-moment. This visual grounding gave the work a visceral, intuitive, and immediate form of comprehension. I was able to translate the abstract statistical findings into concrete interactions. Our effort in this book was to use our conceptual framework to translate into language the procedural forms of interactive disturbance identified by the data analyses. But the most immediate and intuitive way of understanding this research is to view the videotapes.

This dyadic systems framework illuminated the origins of resistant and disorganized attachment at 4 months, as well as the origins of insecure attachment in general.

We have known since the groundbreaking work of Ainsworth et al. (1978) that disturbances in maternal sensitivity predict insecure attachment at 12 months.

Nevertheless maternal insensitivity does not predict disorganized attachment. There is little work specifically predicting disorganized attachment from interactions in the early months of life (as exceptions see for example Carlson, 1998; Jaffe et al., 2001; Tomlinson et al., 2005). Thus we have known very little about the specific kinds of mother–infant interactions that set the stage for disorganized attachment, and its outcome of dissociation in young adulthood. We have known for the past decade that the approach–avoid pattern of disorganized attachment at 1 year sets the stage for dissociative outcomes. But we have not known its early relational origin.

What is new in our work is the remarkable degree of specificity and differentiation in the pictures of future resistant and disorganized dyads at 4 months. We documented that aspects of resistant and disorganized attachment at 12 months are *already in place at 4 months*. Moreover many new forms of relational disturbance were identified, such as inter-modal discrepancies, described next. By examining the infant, not just the mother; attention, orientation, and touch, not just affect; self-contingency as well as interactive contingency; and behavioral qualities, we were able to see far more of the details and complexity of these early disturbances.

Discrepant Communication

One of the most interesting aspects of our work is the documentation of confusing discrepancies between different communication modalities. For example, in the origins of disorganized attachment, infants smile and whimper in the same second, as if they are simultaneously saying "yes" and "no." In the origins of resistant attachment, infants vigilantly coordinate their facial-visual engagement with maternal facial affect, but they inhibit their engagement coordination with maternal touch, which becomes progressively less affectionate. It is as if the infants have "one foot on the gas" and "one foot on the brake." They resist being organized by mother's touch, but meanwhile they vigilantly follow and join her emotional state. These are complex discordant adaptations that we would hardly imagine 4-month infants being capable of making. They teach us anew about the extraordinary communicative capacity of infants at this young age.

In the origins of disorganized attachment, mothers also showed discrepant forms of communication, such as tending to loom at times into the infant's face, coming too close; while at other times tending to look away, becoming too distant. In addition the dyad showed discrepancies in communication. For example, when the infant showed distressed faces and vocalizations, these were greeted by maternal surprise expressions or smiling faces. These moments are profoundly painful to watch.

Our conceptual framework is a general one, not specific to attachment. In the past decade we have used it to illuminate other kinds of mother–infant communication disturbances. Moreover, discrepant communication is not limited to the origins of attachment insecurity; it was associated with maternal depression, anxiety and self-criticism (Beebe et al., 2007, 2008, 2011; Beebe, Lachmann, Jaffe et al., 2012; Beebe, Lachmann, Markese, & Bahrick, 2012; Beebe, Lachmann, Markese, Buck et al., 2012). For this reason we believe that discrepant forms of communication are important in the origins of psychopathology.

Discrepant forms of communication are also important in adult treatment (see Bateson, Jackson, Haley, & Weakland, 1962; Watzlawick et al., 1967). They can alert us to moments of conflict in the patient or the therapist, as noted in the case vignette of Sandra in Chapter 4.

The Origins of Resistant and Disorganized Attachment at 4 Months

Future resistant mothers were more likely to show the spatial intrusion pattern of "chase and dodge," accompanied by a relatively unpredictable form of orientation as they moved in to chase. These mothers were also more likely to show tactile intrusion, in patterns of increasingly less affectionate touch. We interpreted this pattern as the maternal wish for infants to stay with them, in the context of maternal preoccupation with the infant's attention and emotional presence. We proposed that future resistant infants will represent the experience of moving away from mother by "dodging" as she moves in with spatial and tactile intrusion. They will represent responding to mother by going in opposite directions as they vigilantly coordinate with maternal engagement while they tune out maternal touch. And they will have difficulty communicating what they "like" or do not "like" in relation to maternal touch, a confusion in sensing their own state, and ultimately a difficulty in coming to know what they feel.

However, two key arenas were intact in the origins of resistant attachment. Because mothers showed no dysregulation in interactive contingency, infant interactive agency in this realm was not disturbed. And there were no difficulties in maternal facial mirroring or the more general arena of maternal affective correspondences. Thus considerable social capacity remains visible in these dyads.

We argued that the difficulties of future disorganized dyads are at a fundamentally deeper level than those of future resistant dyads. *Infants have difficulty feeling sensed, known, and recognized* as mothers greet intense infant distress with smiles and surprise faces, or show closed-up, inscrutable faces; as mothers withdraw from following the infant's attentional and emotional ups and downs; as mothers lower their touch coordination, compromising infant expectancies that their own more agitated forms of touching will be met by tender and affectionate maternal touch; as mothers look away extensively and unpredictably, generating a feeling of not being seen; as mothers loom relatively unpredictably into the infant's face, generating alarm, or threat. These same patterns reciprocally disturb the infant's capacity to *know the mother's mind* as well. The future disorganized infant will have *difficulty knowing himself* in his moments of discrepant affect, for example smiling and whimpering in the same second; as he lowers his engagement self-contingency, so that it is more difficult to anticipate his own next move"; and as he has difficulty touching, getting stuck in states of "no touch," disturbing his visceral feedback through touch and disturbing his own agency in regulating distress through touch.

Future disorganized infants are confused about their own basic emotional organization, their mothers' emotional organization, and their mothers' response to their distress. They do not experience Sander's (1995) "moment of meeting," a match between two partners such that the way one is known by oneself is matched by the way one is known by the other. They come to expect that their distress states are not shareable. At moments infants look alarmed, and show frantic forms of distress. These experiences compromise infant interactive agency, sense of safety, and emotional coherence. They set a trajectory in development which may disturb the fundamental integration of the person. It is for this reason that our findings on the 4-month origins of disorganized attachment fit so well into the literature predicting dissociation in young adulthood from disorganized attachment at one year, which we discuss below.

Because there is so much emphasis on disturbances in affect regulation in the origins of attachment insecurity, it is important to note that all communication modalities studied showed dysregulations in the origins of disorganized attachment. All communication modalities except gaze showed dysregulations in the origins of resistant attachment. Examination of different modalities of communication unpacks the more general term of *affect regulation*. This approach gave us much greater specificity in identifying mother–infant communication disturbances and potentially gives us more specificity in looking at parallels in the adult treatment dyad. In short, our research suggests that we broaden our perspective from *affect regulation* to *dyadic communication*. We should study all of these communication modalities in adult treatment (for example, for the role of the face, see Eigen, 1993; for orientation, see Davis & Hadiks, 1990; for gaze, see Lieberman, 2000; for touch, see Fosshage, 2005).

Implicit, Procedural Communication in Adult Treatment

In the implicit, procedural mode of action knowledge, much of our communication is too rapid and complex for central cognitive control (Bernstein, 1967; Newtson, 1990). Thus much of it is out of awareness. Moreover, in real time it is often extremely difficult to discern exactly what happens. A good example is the facial mirroring film presented in Chapter 1. Watching in real time, my students often insist that the infant broke eye-contact and looked down at the moment he did because the mother had moved her finger in toward the infant's belly, about to poke. But the microanalysis reveals the opposite order: the infant broke eye-contact and looked down first, the mother reacted with some facial tensing, and then she lightly poked the infant's belly, as if to say, "Come back."

Because nonverbal communication is remarkably similar across the lifespan, adult face-to-face communication is informed by mother–infant communication. The complexity and range of nuance in mother–infant communication patterns alert us to the similar extraordinary richness and nuance present in the implicit, procedural dimension of adult communication. Once language develops, language is in the foreground, and the procedural dimension recedes into the background. Nevertheless, the procedural dimension remains extremely powerful in the co-creation of relatedness across the lifespan. It is a pivotal context for the ways that language is understood and received. For example, if the therapist's rhythm of speaking is out of synch with that of the patient, or if therapist is too fast or too slow on the uptake as she takes her turn, the therapist's words may not be "useable." In adult treatment the narrative dynamic issues and the moment-by-moment procedural negotiation of relatedness fluctuate in a foreground-background manner.

In our usual ways of working in adult treatment, we assume that the symbolized narrative (conscious and unconscious) guides social behavior. This approach has yielded a rich understanding of human behavior across the history of psychoanalysis. The procedural view in contrast argues that the control of social behavior is largely out of awareness, and lies in ways that the individual and the partner co-create action patterns (Fogel, 1992; Newtson, 1990; Thelen & Smith, 1994). In other words, the organization of meaning is implicit in the action sequences of the relational dialogue and does not require reflective thought or verbalization to be known (see Beebe, 2004; Lyons-Ruth, 1998b, 1999). It is at this level that social behavior is coordinated on a split-second, moment-by-moment basis, largely out of awareness.

It is increasingly understood that we need both modes of understanding in adult treatment: the symbolized, explicit mode, and the procedural, implicit mode (see for example Anderson, 2008; Bucci, 2011; Downing, 2004; Heller, 2012; Knoblauch, 2000; Lyons-Ruth, 1999; Ogden, Minton, & Pain, 2006; Rustin, 2013; Schore, 1994; Tronick, 2007; The Boston Change Process Study Group, 2007). In our case studies, and in the cases of the discussants (see Part III), both modes are integrated. The adult treatment cases of Dolores and Sandra, by Beebe, illustrate the therapeutic value of an attempt to translate into words aspects of the procedural action knowledge. Lachmann's case illustrates a process of therapeutic action that took place largely in the procedural mode. In fact, Lachmann spoke very little during the treatment. We see the symbolized and procedural modes as continuously affecting each other. Indeed Bucci (1997, 2011) argues that the effort to symbolize the procedural action-sequence mode can be seen as one of the major goals of psychoanalysis.

It is often assumed that the implicit aspects of the communication are most evident in adult treatments of highly disturbed patients, or in moments of disruption. We do not agree with this, although certainly the implicit mode of communication is very important is these contexts. In moments of disruption, perhaps the therapist is more aware of the implicit, procedural mode because she is activated by the disruption. With more disturbed patients, perhaps the therapist's need to be more alert to her own processes, and how she is affecting the patient, makes her more aware of the implicit mode.

Our position is that the implicit, procedural mode of action knowledge is fundamentally organizing as the constant out-of-awareness fabric of the exchange. For example, I (Beebe) am having a telephone conversation with a friend in which I am trying to explain what the implicit level of communication might mean for adult treatment. My friend is arguing that the implicit level is more relevant in the disturbed patient, or in moments of disruption. But I say I disagree. I hesitate, trying to think it through. The rhythm of my words becomes less predictable; I have a staccato stop–start rhythm (momentarily my self-contingency becomes lower). My friend interrupts me, and tries to finish my sentence as I hesitate. I say, "Maybe, I'm not sure." My friend now pauses longer; he follows me (he has a higher degree of interactive contingency). His pause gives me more time to think. He senses my attempt to figure it out. My rhythm slows down and I think better. At this moment I realize that what has just happened in the past few seconds between us is a good example of what I was trying to explain. So I re-play the process in my mind's eye and describe it to him. And he says, "I get it. I see why." We then shift back into our more usual self- and interactive rhythms. Although this moment was not a "disruption," it does illustrate the negotiation of a moment of difference between us.

The Dyadic Systems View

Various traditions, each with its own methods and literature, spanning development across the lifespan, have tended to focus either on the organization of the individual, and self-regulation; or the organization of the relational field, and interactive regulation. Each focus tends to exclude the other (Beebe et al., 1992). Instead our dyadic systems view of face-to-face communication between two people integrates both self- and interactive processes and helps us conceptualize the relation of the individual to the dyad. Our view grew out of psychoanalysis, but has developed within the context of infant research. It holds the potential to enrich psychoanalysis.

Our dyadic systems view was influenced by Sullivan's (1940) interpersonal theory, particularly his view that "a personality can never be isolated from the complex of interpersonal relations in which the person lives and has his being" (p. 90). He suggested that "the only way ... personality can be known is through the medium of interpersonal interactions" (Greenberg & Mitchell, 1983, p. 90). Sullivan was a contemporary of Winnicott. They shared the concept that a person can only be understood in the context of the relational field (see also Bowlby, 1969; Fairbairn, 1941/1952; Ferenczi, 1930; Spitz, 1963).

Winnicott's (1965) famous statement that "there is no such thing as an infant" (p. 39) is paralleled by Sullivan's (1964) similarly famous phrase, "the illusion of personal individuality." This assumption of the centrality of the relational field contrasts sharply with an alternative, influential twentieth century view that the individual is fundamentally alone and is drawn into interactions and relationships. Stolorow and Atwood (1992) termed this view "the myth of the isolated mind" (see also Kohut, 1971; Overton, 1994).

Instead, our dyadic systems approach begins with the relational matrix as a system in which each partner affects and is affected by the other. Louis Sander was a seminal figure in infant research who grasped the power of the dyadic systems approach in the 1960s and has influenced infant researchers ever since. He was the central translator between systems views of theoretical biology and infant research and he has influenced psychoanalysis (Beebe, 1998; Nahum, 1994; Sander, 1995, 2002; Seligman & Harrison, 2011; Stern et al., 1998). One of Sander's (1977) most important concepts was that the organization of behavior is an emergent property of the dyadic system, not the property of the individual. The dyad is the fundamental unit of analysis. He argued that both partners generate complexly organized behavior that must be coordinated in a bi-directional process of mutual modification. This is a beautiful description of interactive contingency as we use it in this book. Thus in a two-person face-to-face encounter, each person's experience is in part dependent on what the other is doing and saying.

Moreover, the mutual modification in a bi-directional process provides a theory of therapeutic action in the procedural mode. Bi-directional coordinations between components of a system (such as two partners) generate emergent properties which provide one critical "engine" of development (Gottlieb, Wahlsten, & Lickliter, 1998; Lewkowicz, 2000). Thus, as two people interact, each individual may modify the partner's behavior, and each may shift her own degree of self-predictability. In this process each may come to re-organize their expectancies of "how things go," facilitating the re-organization of experience.

Jaffe and Feldstein (1970), working in parallel to Sander, developed their dyadic systems view of rhythms of dialogue in the 1960s at the William Alanson White Institute. Influenced by Sullivan, Jaffe and Feldstein (see also Feldstein, 1998) documented the interpersonal, pragmatic features of the rhythms of adult dialogue timing that were relevant to the communication of mood, the phenomenon of empathy, and the breakdown of effective dialogue.

A key tenet of our systems view proposes an intimate association between self- and interactive regulation. Fogel (1992) described it this way: at each moment, all behavior is unfolding in the individual, while at the same time it is modifying and being modified by the changing behavior of the partner. Although such a connection between self- and interactive regulation is assumed by systems models, for the first time we can empirically document it.

In a recent study we analyzed all the mothers and infants discussed in this book, irrespective of attachment classification. We showed that for both mothers and infants, an individual's self-contingency process is itself influenced by the way the individual coordinates with the partner (Beebe, Messinger et al., 2012). Thus the process of regulating oneself via self-contingency is dependent upon the way one responds to the partner via interactive contingency; and vice versa.

This finding helps us understand how self- and interactive processes are *co-created.* The implication is that an individual's self-contingency is not solely a process contained within the self; it is bound up with coordination with the partner. Reciprocally, an individual's interactive contingency is not solely a property of the dyad; it is bound up with a process within the self.

Let's imagine that this finding could be replicated in adult treatment dyads. In that case, the therapist's response to her patient (therapist's interactive contingency) would be in part a function of how stable or predictable her own ongoing rhythms are (therapist's self-contingency). And the degree of stability of her own ongoing rhythms would be in part a function of how highly coordinated she is with her patient. The same process would apply to the patient.

The implications are startling. What we experience as *our own behavior* is actually an emergent property of the dyad. To understand ourselves dyadically is to see ourselves as more porous and vulnerable to the state and behavior of the other than we would often like to think.

Knowing and Being Known: Entering the Distressed State of the Other

In Chapter 4 we discussed modes of entering the state of the other through nonconscious procedural dimensions of face-to-face communication in adult treatment. Although these modes are broadly relevant to positive as well as distressed states, they can be used to refine our understanding of entering distressed states in particular. Distressed states are at the center of adult treatment. The therapist's ability to reach her distressed patient is dependent on her ability to comprehend both the narrative of distress, and procedural bodily forms of distress, both in her patient and in herself. The outcome of this process generates one critical dimension of the experience of recognition in adult treatment.

Here we address modes of entering the distressed state of the other largely at the nonconscious level. A facial expression produced by one person tends to evoke a similar expression in the partner, out of awareness (Dimberg et al., 2000), a powerful way of participating in, or "entering," the state of the other. This is such a robust phenomenon that some researchers dub it an "automatic" facial mimicry (Hatfield et al., 1993; Hodges & Wegner, 1997). Perhaps mirror neurons, an "action-recognition" mechanism in which the actor's actions are reproduced in the premotor cortex of the observer, help explain why this is such a robust phenomenon. Most likely this is a ubiquitous process in adult treatment.

Paulina, a mid-40s married professor, began her face-to-face treatment with me (Beebe) in a silent state (see Beebe & McCrorie, 2010). She asked me not to talk. She felt that a previous long treatment had not helped her very much. She barely looked at me. After I had tolerated her silence for several weeks, she gradually began to cry. Only when she was crying did she feel "genuine." I could grasp only that she was desperately unhappy with her devoted but rather remote and self-preoccupied husband of 15 years. Any direct questions or comments on my part disturbed her ability to cry. The focus was on her ability, and mine, to go into and tolerate agonizing levels of distress. I began a form of vocal rhythm coordination with her distress sounds, a loose matching or elaboration on the rhythm and the cadence of her sounds. My face also was sad as I echoed some of her cry sounds. Only after a number of months did I become aware of this behavior on my part. In retrospect, I realized that I had learned to do this when attempting to interact with distressed infants. Particularly when infants do not look, joining their sounds is often an effective way to reach them. With Paulina I made my sounds briefly and somewhat infrequently, since more activity disrupted her crying. My vocal rhythm coordination and her crying soon constituted a bi-directional exchange. My sounds facilitated her crying, and her sounds in turn influenced the timing, cadence, and intensity of my vocal rhythms. In this process we both felt close to each other, and we tolerated her intense distress, which so often verged on being intolerable. She told me how understood she felt in little notes that she would enclose with her check.

This vignette illustrates a form of entering the distress state of the patient, not only through vocal rhythm coordination, but also through an approximate matching of the vocal affect cadences of her distressed sounds, and through my own facial sadness. I had never before been asked to be completely silent in an adult treatment. Out of awareness I began to draw on what I ordinarily do with distressed infants. More than with infants, however, with Paulina I viscerally entered her sadness. At times I felt myself tearing up. I made a bodily "decision," only vaguely in awareness, not to inhibit my tears. In this process I came to feel her distress acutely, and to feel closer to her. The ways that I found to join her distress proved to be very powerful for Paulina. They highlight the importance of finding different ways of joining distress states of the patient.

Maternal difficulties in being able to enter and join infant distress are pivotal in our findings on the origins of disorganized attachment. As we have seen, mothers of future disorganized infants do not "match" or join the distress of their infants, despite the fact that this process is so robust that it is often termed an "automatic" facial mimicry. Perhaps Paulina had this kind of childhood; but this is something we will never know for sure. Our findings identify many ways in which mothers may fail to enter the state of the infant. We suggested that the mother's own distress is so disturbing that she cannot afford to allow the infant's painful affect to be evoked in her own body. The mother's inhibition of her own visceral response of distress disturbs her ability to enter into, and to empathize with, the infant's distress.

In our framework, the analysis of the interactive contingency of facial affect, which we refer to as "facial mirroring," includes following and entering both positive and negative facial affect shifts. We analyze vocal affect in the same way. In the origins of disorganized attachment at 4 months, mothers show dampened ability to follow and join the infant's facial-visual-vocal engagement. Thus they have difficulty following the infant's distressed moments, as well as the infant's more positive moments. With Paulina, as I entered her distressed sounds, I also entered her facial distress, even though she hardly ever looked at me. Thus two central procedural modes of entering the patient's distress are following and joining increments of facial distress, and joining and elaborating rhythms and cadences of vocal distress. This process may allow the patient to sense her distress more acutely, and at times to verbalize her distress.

In addition to having difficulty in acknowledging and joining the infant's distress through coordinating with the infant's patterns of facial-visual-vocal engagement, mothers of future disorganized infants showed many other kinds of difficulty in joining the infant's distress, such as greeting the infant's distress with smiles or surprise faces; or with inscrutable, closed up faces; or with looking away repeatedly and unpredictably; or with failing to coordinate with the infant's touch pattern by failing to read a high frequency of infant touching as a cue of infant vulnerability which requires more tender, affectionate touching. The details of these different patterns "unpack" the more general concept of failures of maternal recognition.

I (Beebe) often ask my students or psychoanalytic audiences to role-play the patterns in which the mother cannot join the infant's distress. I ask the "infant" partner to look into the "mother" partner's eyes with the most distressed face possible. I ask the "mother" partner to then smile brightly, looking directly into the "infant" partner's eyes. Then I ask the partners to switch roles, and this time as the "infant" partner looks at the mother with a very distressed face, the "mother" partner looks back with a completely still, inscrutable face (or shows a surprise face, or looks away).

This role-play is very powerful. My students tell me that reading about the patterns of the origins of disorganized attachment is upsetting. Seeing the films is even more upsetting. But enacting the patterns in their own bodies, with a partner, is the most upsetting. Many people laugh anxiously. The role-play provides them with an immediate, visceral understanding of the impossible position the infant is in. The pretend role-play suddenly becomes unexpectedly "real."

In describing their experiences of playing out the "infant" role, the students say for example that they felt unsafe, at a loss, unable to figure out what was happening. Some express a sense of disbelief. Some say it was hateful, intolerable, or like falling into an abyss. They had to look away. Some felt, "how do I stop this; this can't be happening." Some students also remark on understanding something more about the mother's own trauma when they play out the mother's role. They sense the mother's dissociation as they look at the "infant" partner with an inscrutable face, for example. Some people simply refuse to play the mother's role; it feels sadistic. Some people sense the mother's desperation. We then role-play more optimal forms of distress regulation, such as the maternal empathic "woe-face" and woe vocalization to infant distress. Everyone is visibly relieved.

When we enter aspects of the action-sequences of the partner's distress, we understand something with our bodies that goes beyond what we understand through language. This is *action knowledge*. Theories of embodied simulation discussed in Chapter 4 explain the process of entering aspects of the actions (expressions, gestures, postures) of the partner, which they term *mimicry*. Mimicry is seen as an internal simulation of the perceived action, which facilitates an understanding of its meaning. In the action mode, such as the individual's failure to enter the partner's distress, the partner can feel violated in ways that go beyond verbal forms of aggression. And in the action mode, such as the individual's show-ing a "woe-face," the partner can feel understood and recognized in ways that go beyond linguistic forms of empathy and understanding.

As another example, in analyzing the initial videotape of my face (Beebe) as I interacted with Dolores, I saw that, although my face was relatively quiet while soft and visually intent, with each sentence I slightly changed the pattern of the way my hand was self-soothing my face. My hand and head movements registered my own efforts to regulate my own intense feelings with Dolores. Thus another way that I followed and joined her distress was through my own self-soothing efforts. Although these movements were out of my awareness at the time, in view-ing the videotape Dolores and I both noted my own efforts to self-soothe. We used it to try to understand more about the soothing that she needed.

However, the therapist's ability flexibly to follow the patient *out of distress* is also important in this process. The ability to follow the partner out of distressed moments into increasing increments of positive engagement was illustrated in our description of the secure disruption and repair dyad in Chapter 1. As another example, in our Project for Mothers, Infants and Young Children of September 11, 2001, many of the infants were frequently distressed as we assessed mother–infant interactions at 4 months (Beebe, Cohen, Sossin, & Markese, 2012). One of our most talented mothers had the knack of briefly entering her infant's distress, and then rather quickly being able to engage him in a process in which they both gradually shifted into a bit lighter mood.

Another example: In a videotaped session with Dolores (treated by Beebe), Dolores shifted at one moment into a more playful state, saying, "Your face jumped into my eyes, for one little second." I greeted her playfully with, "Really? [pause] Well, that's good." My eyebrows went up, and I had a big smile. The phrase "Well, that's good" had a "sinusoidal" contour, known as a "greeting" contour.

Moreover, there are times when it is important *not* to enter the patient's distress so fully. Daniel, a college student treated by Beebe, entered the treatment unsure of his own reality. His father, the main attachment figure, had seemed to keep "double books," changing the story of whatever had happened to suit his own needs. After a number of years of finding ways to describe this puzzling situation, an underlying fear in Daniel began to emerge. He began to be afraid that he had various diseases. At this point in the treatment my ongoing ways of relating to Daniel had to change. When I joined various aspects of his distress, he became more panicked. His fears seemed more real. I realized that my usual level of facial coordination escalated him. I learned to dampen my facial responsivity. As he vigilantly searched my face for my reaction, I learned to hold my face relatively steady, in a soft, accepting way. Thus joining the state of the partner can be both optimal and nonoptimal, as a function of the specific dyadic context (see Beebe et al., 2005).

Our findings on the origins of disorganized attachment at 4 months taught us a great deal about potential maternal difficulties in entering the distressed state of the infant. Based most likely on her own traumatic history, these maternal difficulties disturbed the infant's process of coming to know and be known by the mother's mind, as well as coming to know himself. We suggested that these findings can be useful to the adult clinician in understanding the earliest infant experiences which set a developmental trajectory toward dissociative outcomes in young adulthood. As we discussed in chapter 4, disorganized attachment at one year predicts dissociation in young adulthood.

Young Adult Dissociation: Relevance of Our Findings on the 4-Month Origins of Disorganized Attachment

Dissociation can be seen as a self-alteration to withdraw from contradictory input that cannot be integrated (Spiegel & Cardeña, 1991). It can be seen as an effort to protect oneself from inescapable threat (Bucci, 2011; Porges et al., 1994; Schore, 2011; Siegel, 1999, 2012). In the reunion phase of the Ainsworth attachment assessment, the Strange Situation, the very parent that the infant needs for comfort is the parent who alarms him, for infants who will be classified as disorganized attachment (Main & Solomon, 1990). Dissociation in adults may also have its roots in a trauma of non-recognition (Bromberg, 2011; Lyons-Ruth et al., 2006). For Bromberg (2011), the developmental trauma of non-recognition is so enormous that it is continually dreaded, like the shadow of a tsunami.

Fear without resolution, failure of integration, and non-recognition are important theories of the origins of dissociation. Nevertheless they remain rather global. Many examples of each of these theories can be found in our findings on the 4-month origins of disorganized attachment. By recasting our findings along these lines, we can "unpack" and further specify these theories of the origins of dissociation.

Maternal threat, for example, is evident in our data in many patterns, such as maternal positive faces or surprise faces greeting infant distress, or looming into the infant's face. *Infant signs of alarm* are visible in many patterns, such as frantic levels of vocal and facial distress, moving the hands up and back into a "don't touch me" pose as mothers loom; or in moments of "freeze" as mothers loom.

Failures of integration are evident through intermodal discrepancies, for example infant simultaneous smile plus whimper, which disturbs the infant's confidence in the coherence of his experience; maternal contradictory patterns of being both too far away visually (more looking away) and too close in spatially (more loom), generating an infant confusion of, "are you coming or are you going?"

Forms of maternal non-recognition are evident in our data in many patterns, and tended to occur in the context of infant distress. These patterns include, for example, maternal inscrutable, unmoving faces (infant loses maternal responsivity); maternal unpredictable looking away (infant feels unseen); maternal smile or surprise face response to infant distress (which disturbs infant confidence in the validity of his experience).

Forms of disturbance in predictability were also identified, which are not obviously contained within these theories of dissociation. Disturbances in

155

predictability are evident, for example, in unstable infant engagement self-predictability, disturbing the temporal coherence of infant experience; overly stable infant states of no-touch, disturbing infant access to touch; lowered maternal self-predictability of looking and looking away, disturbing the "attentional frame."

By detailing these various patterns relevant to the major theories of dissociation, each theory becomes more experience-near and clinically useful. Our hope is to call attention to potential parallel processes in adult treatment (see Chapter 4). Such expanded awareness by the clinician may facilitate their repair in adult treatment.

In conclusion, how does the dyadic systems view change the look of adult treatment? Our systems approach, and specifically our emphasis on the co-creation of relatedness, provides both expansion and constraint in the therapist's role. The concept of the co-creation of experience implicates the therapist in every aspect of the treatment. As Lachmann (2000) notes, no moment can be written off as purely the patient's transferences or projections, or as purely the therapist's counter-transferences, or as projective identifications. Furthermore, at every moment there is the potential to re-organize (or not re-organize) expectations of intimacy, trust, mutuality, repair of disruptions, as well as to disconfirm (or not disconfirm) rigid archaic expectations.

Both therapist and patient contribute to this process in the implicit, procedural mode of action knowledge, largely out of awareness, as well as in the explicit linguistic mode. However, at times one can notice one's bodily experiences, so that some glimmers of this action–dialogue can become more conscious. As the therapist understands more of the power of the nonverbal dialogue, and does not inhibit its emergence, therapeutic action is facilitated. The therapist's use of the nonverbal action–dialogue occurs implicitly through her own bodily arousal, somatic sensations, and affective reactions. These are the processes that allow the therapist to *change with* her patient's action sequences, to *enter into* her patient's experiences.

This book is offered as a proposal to clinicians about how the research we present could be used in adult treatment. However, the bridges from the new data of this book to adult treatment have just begun to be constructed.

In Part III of the book we have invited discussants to comment on the research findings. They will offer other ways of building bridges. We invite you, our readers, to build many more.

Part III

DISCUSSANTS
Relevance of the Research to Child and Adult Treatment

Carolyn S. Clement
Malcolm Owen Slavin and E. Joyce Klein
Estelle Shane
Alexandra Harrison
Stephen Seligman

RONALD FAIRBAIRN'S THEORY OF OBJECT RELATIONS AND THE MICROANALYSIS OF MOTHER–INFANT INTERACTION

A Mutual Enrichment

Carolyn S. Clement

"... if, at a later date, the infant should come into analysis."
D.W. Winnicott (1965, p. 55)

Beatrice Beebe and her colleagues provide us with rich, provocative data from their microanalysis of mother–infant interaction at 4 months, unpacking, I believe for the first time, detailed qualities of communication that contribute to resistant and disorganized attachment styles between mother and infant at 12 months.

This study enriches what has now become a substantive body of research on the mother–infant relationship, showing us the nearly unimaginable complexity of interaction and communication, much of it taking place out of our awareness and in "good enough" pairs, involving a synchronization for which we are biologically primed.

There is a moment between a father and his 8-day-old infant described by Louis Sander (1984), focusing on the specificity of joint coordination, that I have always found especially beautiful. This example comes from a paper by Lyons-Ruth (2000) who provides the context: apparently the infant became fussy while being held by the mother and was handed over to the father; then fell asleep. When the event was viewed frame by frame:

> It can be seen that the father glances down momentarily at the baby's face. Strangely enough, in the same frames, the infant looked up at the father's face. Then the infant's left arm, which had been hanging down over the father's left arm, began to move upward. Miraculously, in the same frame, the father's right arm, which had been hanging down at his side, began moving upward. Frame by frame the baby's hand and

the father's hand moved upward simultaneously. Finally they met over the baby's tummy. The baby's left hand grasped the little finger of the father's right hand. At that moment the infant's eyes closed and she fell asleep, while the father continued talking, apparently totally unaware of the little miracle of specificity in time, place, and movement that had taken place in his arms.

(Sander, 1984, p. 155)

In contrast to this beautiful series of micro-moments of interpersonal synchrony, in the findings on the origins of disorganized attachment in this book we are presented with multiform disjunctions, including many expressions of maternal withdrawal or frightening intrusion, contradictory instances of simultaneous smile and rough handling, and a striking ambivalence regarding intimate connection, e.g., via mutual gaze, touch, or sustained efforts to repair disruptions. It is postulated that given the traumatic histories of these mothers, they come to the experience of mothering with profound anxiety, vulnerability to being triggered by their baby's distress, and a need to self-monitor or self-regulate, placing a barrier between mother and child.

In broadest theoretical terms there is traumatic disruption of the ongoing experiences necessary for the consolidation of a basic sense of self and of a fundamental connectedness to others. In addition to Winnicott's work as a psychoanalytic pediatrician, most meaningfully incorporated in Louis Sander's work, I have found the writings of Fairbairn to be poetically synchronous with specific findings in the current study and with the body of mother–infant research as a whole. Fairbairn, the father of object relations theory, challenged, somewhat unsuccessfully at the time, Freud's ego psychological structure of the mind with his "endopsychic structure" based on the internalization of conflictual object relations. While Fairbairn's formulation of an original, unitary ego subsequently split into a triad of libidinal, central, and antilibidinal egos no longer fits with our constructivist, intersubjective paradigms, Fairbairn, writing in the 1950s, was especially attuned to the early and profound dependency on the mother and the traumatic experience of needing yet fearing that mother, along with the absolute devastation of her rejection. I cannot resist a passage from one of his last papers:

. . . it also becomes a dangerous procedure for the child to express his libidinal need, i.e. his nascent love, of his mother in face of rejection at her hands; for it is equivalent to discharging his libido into an emotional vacuum. Such a discharge is accompanied by an affective experience which is singularly devastating. In the older child this experience is one of intense humiliation over the depreciation of his love, which seems to be involved. At a somewhat deeper level (or earlier stage) the experience is one of shame over the display of needs which are disregarded or belittled. In virtue of these experiences of humiliation and shame he feels reduced to a state of worthlessness, destitution or beggardom. His sense of his own value is threatened; and he feels bad in the sense of "inferior." The intensity of these experiences is, of course, proportionate to the intensity of his need; and intensity of need itself increases his sense of badness by contributing to it the quality of 'demanding too much.' At the same time his sense of badness is further complicated by the sense of utter impotence which he also experiences. At a still deeper level (or a still earlier stage) the child's experience is one of, so to speak, exploding ineffectively and being completely emptied of libido. It is thus an experience of disintegration and imminent psychical death.

(Fairbairn, 1952, p. 113)

This terror of psychic annihilation is strikingly captured in a dream reported by my patient, Ann, who had struggled to find a life-sustaining bond with a rejecting, explosive and depressed mother.

> I was clinging to two rocky protuberances emerging out of a stony sheer rock face. It was vertical, rising above me, extending below me. I saw my mother above me, to my left, in a tower—standing at a window. And I was straining to climb. Suddenly in horror I realized that my feet were dangling free, with no support, and there was no footing. I wouldn't be able to hold on much longer. A voice erupts onto the scene: "But the good news is . . ." She then awakes. The denouement will come later.

Fairbairn's relational discussion of attachment to "bad objects" has stood the test of time in psychoanalytic discourse. Specific contingencies described in the current study vividly portray the registration not only of confusion and resultant disorganization of behavior but the simultaneous registration of conflictual affects that speak to an early organization of conflict and defense or the incipient formation of internal working models. First, let us look at the conflict-inducing details. Two of the most compelling moments are the mother's response of smile/surprise to the infant's distress and the infant's simultaneous, contradictory expressions of smile and vocal distress. It is important to keep in mind that these are heightened affective moments embedded within an ongoing backdrop of infant helplessness and confusion and of maternal unpredictability, as described above. Fairbairn coins the term "static internal situation" which dramatically captures what we might term a potential internal working model much akin to the classic double bind.

The double bind, first introduced as a theory of pathogenic communication by Bateson et al. (1962), was initially applied to a theory of schizophrenia but ultimately to family systems. In essence, the child is punished for expressing his love and also punished if he does not. The mother says with a smile "Come here darling," then pulls back in anxiety when the child approaches. If the child does not respond to his mother's request, she will also become anxious and angry, his behavior suggesting that she is not a good mother. "There is never a 'message' singly, but in actual communication always two or more related messages, of different levels and often conveyed by different channels—voice, tone, movement, context . . . These messages may be widely incongruent and thus exert very different and conflicting influences" (p. 56). Ironically, this important research group was antagonistic to the ego psychological psychoanalytic thinking of the day, unaware of the parallels in British object relations theory or, of course, not privy to the subsequent mother–infant research detailing the formative effects of communication.

In Fairbairn's static internal situation the child's life is likewise defined by an insoluble dilemma inherent in the bond to the life-sustaining mother. Fairbairn describes a patient's dream in which he is standing beside his mother with a bowl of pudding on the table. He is starving and there is no other food available; yet he knows that the pudding is poisoned. He knows that if he does not eat the pudding he will die of starvation, yet if he does eat it he will certainly die. The poignancy of the infant's simultaneous smile and whimper comes to mind here, as I interpret the smile as a plea for love and protection while the whimper expresses the "knowledge" that love and protection are absent. Fairbairn asked his patient what action he thought he would have taken if action had been part of the dream. The patient said that he would have eaten the pudding.

Here we have Fairbairn's "moral defense," best summed up by his infamous declaration: "It is better to be a sinner in a world ruled by God that to live in a world ruled by the devil." The child cannot consciously acknowledge the mother's fragility or destructiveness as she is the source of survival. What follows is a lifetime of self-blame, sense of destructiveness and alienation, including the sense of not feeling fully human, and self-doubt regarding the legitimacy of one's perceptions and affects.

Many of our patients have eaten the poisoned pudding and approach us with a smile and a whimper. As Fairbairn suggested, we offer them the possibility of a new object relationship, that ultimately allows the patient who is able to take the risk, an opportunity to discover an autonomous self, entitled to life.

My patient, Ann, took this risk as we worked together weathering painful ruptures often triggered by her experience of a momentary withdrawal or absence of my full affective presence. In another dream near the end of treatment, the fear of falling forever has not completely disappeared . As Lyons-Ruth (2000) points out, "One can never fully unregister one's experience . . ." (p. 96). Nevertheless, our bond has become real. This time, she has climbed a mountain and knows that she must come down, but there is a gap—a dangerous, unchartable space on the descent. She looks for me to help her, but I am nowhere to be found. Nevertheless, along with a sense of danger, there is a sense of her own strength and equanimity as she faces the descent. She said, "I couldn't find you, but I knew you were there."

10

PROBING TO KNOW AND BE KNOWN

Existential and Evolutionary Perspectives on the "Disorganized" Patient's Relationship with the Analyst

Malcolm Owen Slavin and E. Joyce Klein

Re-narrating the "D" Attachment Scenario in Development and Treatment

Our comments focus on broadening the picture of what is at stake in Dr. Beebe's exquisitely detailed picture of very early, disorganized attachment interactions between mother and infant and then, by extension, between therapist and patient.

First, we re-narrate the generic attachment scenario—from its secure to its disorganized versions—using a vantage point rooted in both existential and evolutionary-adaptive perspectives. This perspective recognizes what is aberrant and pathogenic in disorganized attachment interactions. Yet, at the same time, it keeps us focused on what may be the *universal* dimensions of *relational conflict, multiplicity, deception, and self-deception* that, while often painfully heightened in disorganized interactions, are also part of *all human relating.*

We focus on the "disorganized" patient's desperate effort to *know* the therapist's capacity to bear the patient's, as well as the therapist's own, experience of *existential terror and conflict.* Thus we hope to bring into even greater clinical relevance Beebe and Lachman's depiction of the crucial processes of "knowing and being known" in the earliest human interactions.

Existential Dread, Multiplicity, and Probing for Realness and Reciprocity

We'll start with a developmental narrative from a highly articulate mother–child pair. Not because they represent a disorganized style interaction—they don't—but because, in their capacity to articulate certain crucial issues, they illustrate what we see as the larger universal human issues at stake in all developmental negotiations (Slavin, 2011).

Noah, the 6-year-old son of a patient named Sarah, had become terrified to go to sleep. During the day he seemed obsessed with all the dangerous and violent things he would see in the news. At night, Noah worried that people, creatures, might come into his room, maybe steal him away. Maybe he will die. We knew of no particular identifiable, significant trauma in his history.

Sarah listens as Noah expresses his mortal fears. She tries to show him she understands his fear of somehow losing his connection with her and his dad. She tries to reassure him that his world is *not* such a dangerous place. He listens to her, and his fears continue.

In analysis, we start to realize that maybe, in part, Noah is seeing an aspect of our world and its dangers that is barely tolerable to us all: to Sarah, to her husband, to her analyst. Yes, of course he wants and needs some reassurance about his relative safety. But also, perhaps, more acknowledgment of what he too clearly sees.

Sarah goes back and shares with him her sense that maybe he wants her and his dad to admit just how much scariness there is in the stuff he sees and hears on TV, Internet, and newspapers. That maybe he is aware of this scary stuff in ways that she and his dad have gotten so used to they don't have to feel it, or see it any more. Yet he does. Noah then seems a little bit calmer. Still scared, but much more interested in talking to her and in what she has to say.

Soon, in fact, the following conversation emerges at another bedtime:

Mom: I know it can be scary going to sleep. But you can count on us being here and we'll protect you.

Noah: But, mom, I think . . . maybe you're not strong enough to protect me.

Mom: We're, ah, pretty strong grown-ups. You're safe in here with us and we love you very much.

Noah: But, mom, you love *yourself* more than me.

Mom: Well, ah, not really . . . I, ah, parents . . . love their children just as much as themselves.

Noah: But, mom, I think I love *myself* more than you.

Mom: Well, that's probably how it should be for kids. You need to love yourself a whole lot, probably *should* love yourself *best*.

Noah continues to be very frightened of going to sleep.

During our next several analytic hours, Sarah continues to talk about how she handled Noah's fears—feeling pushed beyond the limits of her understanding by his assertiveness, unable to think, overwhelmingly emotionally challenged. The analyst felt some of this, too—though greatly appreciating Noah's verbally disarming candor.

Sarah and his dad's more open recognition that there was some very real basis to Noah's perception of the scariness in the world seemed to begin to open up his ability to bear what we'll call his basic *existential anxiety*. Now he was broaching highly related, even thornier, *relational-existential-moral questions:* How we navigate the tensions between our love for ourselves and our connections with loved others; the self–other tensions that intertwine with our whole sense of meaning, faith, and love, in the face of *everyone's multiple agendas,* as well as shared, background existential terror. He candidly confronts the everyday, taken for granted, *deceptions and self-deceptions* that inevitably intertwine with these realms of experience.

Sarah slowly came to feel that, maybe, she could somehow acknowledge that while she loved Noah very much, she was also very involved in things in her own life, including her work. Yes, sometimes this might pull her thoughts away from him, pull her to things and people apart from him. She contemplated the possibility of acknowledging, in words he might grasp, that such a tension—such multiplicity, actually—existed inside her. It seemed unquestionably to be a tension that Noah intuitively sensed.

A few nights later, Sarah told Noah: "You were probably seeing something more clearly about me and you than I had realized . . . you saw that I love you as much as I can imagine loving anyone. And there are also other things I love, and love to do—things that sometimes take me into my own mind, sometimes away from you."

Noah looks at her for a while. He nods his head, seeming to signal that he hears her. He seems much calmer, nestles in, body relaxing, and soon falls asleep. Things settle down.

Sources of Danger and Safety in the Family: Shared Existential Anxiety, Differing Agendas, Multiplicity, Deception, and Self-Deception

So what is Sarah and Noah's interaction about? A narrative of Noah's struggle for attachment security in face of darkness, aloneness, dangers in fantasy and in the larger, outside world. Yes. But there are many other dimensions to this story. Listen to several that we hear.

We hear the story of Noah and Sarah as illustrating the larger relational context in which all meaning is made: how we create a sense of living with hope in a secure-enough, knowable, trustable, meaningful world. Each time that secure existential envelope emerges, it will often be lost—tested in face of all life events, including aberrant, traumatic ones, to be sure. As we see in the frame-by-frame illustrations, these early negotiations between the mother–infant pairs, the future disorganized infants' internal working models, for example, are "characterized by expectancies of emotional distress and emotional incoherence" (Beebe et al, 2010, p. 7), challenging the capacity to create a meaningful, trustable world.

In the face of this haunting, existential abyss, the crucial, sustaining power of human interaction (such as simply a mother's animated face) is apparent. As seen in the Tronick (1989) still face demonstration, deprived for even 2 minutes of any response (even a mis-cued, unrecognizing, intrusive response) infants seem immediately, innately, desperately, to miss the sense of connection to, and impact on, the world that mother's facial animation and vocalizations represent.

Yet, for a *human* infant this overt need may not be all there is to it. It may, in fact, be only half the story. The human infant's response may also signal the nascent emergence of that ever-present, ready to appear, sense of absence—the empty void, the nothingness—that undergirds human annihilation anxiety. An anxiety in face of which mother's responsive presence can, indeed must, serve not only as an innate, interactional need, but, as such, as a vital, innate *antidote*. Not simply because the infant innately needs her presence as a protector from *outside* dangers—the core evolutionary insight of Bowlby's (1969) whole paradigm. But, also (as Bowlby and even contemporary evolutionists tend to ignore) because her presence imbues him with something he must potentially experience in his gut: that there is something between him and the abyss—the inner/outer abyss that does *not* derive from her absence, but is overwhelmingly terrifying without her *presence* (Slavin, 2011). In this sense, we see Noah's attachment to his mother, beneath and beyond any observable interactions, as an attachment to a meaning-making *semi-deity*. To, as Hoffman (1998) says, one of the parental "gods of infancy and childhood."

Note the emphasis here on the way this experience is partly magical, essentially *sacred*—far beyond the rational (or even affective)—dimensions of parenting. "Semi-deity" parents provide the intimate yet authoritative experiences, idealizations, and recognitions needed by the child to create a subjective foundation on which to build a fundamental experience of hope—a basic trust in the very existence of a meaningful, trustable world that is safe enough to live in, and inevitably, to die in.

Most importantly, Beebe notes, "maternal withdrawal *from distressed infants* compromises infant interactive agency and emotional coherence in future disorganized (vs. secure) infants. We characterized these infants as 'frantic,' not sensed or 'known' in their distress, and relatively helpless to influence mothers with their distress" (Beebe et al., 2010, p. 109).

These patently damaging interactions will certainly shape and distort the disorganized infant's experience of the world—and often impede the creation of a good-enough transitional space in which the buffering, parental semi-deity function operates. Yet we should not let this environmentally induced damage obscure the fact that disorganized interactions themselves do not generate the universal human proclivity to experience a haunting, existential dread. A dread to which we, like Noah, are all exposed by our basic human capacity for an awareness of the existential realities of transience, loss, and the Otherness of even the most intimate loving relationships.

Indeed, the awareness of these universal realities may in fact be painfully heightened for those who have been disorganized infants. Heightened in a way that, while skewing and "distorting" their experience in the narrow, normative sense, actually attunes them painfully and powerfully to an arena of human experience with which we must all grapple. Disorganized children, in our terms, have lost the reliable, vital, god-like parental function—the near-miraculous creation of a sense of meaning in face of its inevitable transience and loss. Their trauma saddles them with a raw, direct awareness of aspects of life and relating that cries out for our recognition—not only as aberrant and non-normative. But, in addition, as with Noah and Sarah, evokes sometimes deeply dissociated levels of our own anxiety as well as the often painfully uncomfortable multiplicity of our needs and motives.

Providing the antidote, as we called it, to that ultimate aloneness, the parental semi-deity functions entail a parent's revisiting her version of that same human existential anxiety that is in the process of taking form in the child. Illuminated through Noah's words and Sarah's analytic conversations, but present in maternal gestures from the beginning, parents are always facing their own versions of their child's anxieties. And they are doing this in the very complex matrix of differing, potentially conflicting, agendas in the human family. With the disorganized infants, Beebe and Lachmann repeatedly note that the traumas in the mothers' histories greatly affect their ability to empathically respond to their infants.

Negotiating the Otherness of a Semi-Deity

Noah's verbal challenges demand that Sarah open her own struggle to sustain a working, good-enough illusion of security in a potentially insecure world. It turned out that Sarah (and her husband) needed to peel away a layer of self-deception about the existence of violence in the world and to re-open an older, taken-for-granted edge of illusory certainty about her familiar, subjectively safe world. She needed to re-open and revisit—and in an important sense re-create—her subjective sense of her own strength and power to protect.

Like every mother who, as Winnicott (1965) says, "hates her baby from the word go"—meaning not the affect of hate but the inevitable clash between her subjective experience and that of her child—Sarah struggled with re-opening herself to Noah's challenges—especially some of her reflexive, established notions about how she valued and balanced her own needs as they differed and conflicted with his.

Beebe's data (Beebe et al., 2010) often show us more extreme versions of what she calls the "dyadic affective conflicts" that occur when whatever mother's needs and agendas move in ways that are particularly at variance with an infant's distressed affect state. Mothers of disorganized infants often seem to be trying to hold tenaciously onto their own state, and perhaps induce an alteration in the child's state, by simply displaying their own contradictory affect—such as showing surprise or smiling as the child is distressed. Perhaps followed by verbalizations such as "don't be that way," or "no fussing, you should be happy." The mother may communicate her need state by excessively looking away and/or swooping down and looming in.

Such poorly matched behavior seems likely to be pathogenic. Yet in other extraordinarily interesting research Jaffe, Beebe, and colleagues show that overly close behavioral matching (of vocal rhythms) predict insecure attachment (Beebe et al., 2000; Jaffe et al., 2001). For us the idea that there is a normative mid-range between a close matching of states and their relative lack of coordination fits our expectation that conflict (internal and intersubjective) is a universal relational challenge. Disorganized attachment interactions certainly do not reflect normative (in the sense of average, expectable) ways of communicating conflicts entailed in our human otherness. However, the underlying existential-relational conflicts—to which they represent aberrant responses—(the background sense of transience and the constructed sense of all our meanings) are, in our view, a universal, indeed essential, part of even the most intimate, human relating.

Thus, in Sarah's inner dividedness around attunement to herself and her beloved son we see a mother's natural multiplicity, her complex subjectivity—even, at times, utterly normal state of dissociation, if you will, between competing, hard-to-reconcile aspects of her being (Benjamin, 1995). Her multiplicity is thus a critical background dimension of the ordinary, good-enough devoted environment (Slavin, 2010; Slavin & Kriegman, 1992). Combined with her natural struggle to sustain meaning in the face of existential anxiety, these "moral" (my needs versus yours) conflicts and a mother's inevitably somewhat deceptive and self-deceptive strategies for dealing with them set the larger stage on which all mothers and children, including the disorganized infant and her mother, encounter each other. However, for the disorganized mother–infant pair, the experience may be even more extreme, more complex than the so-called normative range of conflict. Given the mother's earlier unresolved losses, her experience of the existential realities may be too fraught and may make it even more difficult to negotiate the inherit conflicts of interest with her child.

The Capacity to Probe the Other: The Child's Agency in the Attachment Process

From a contemporary evolutionary perspective, human children have unquestionably evolved a highly complex inner capacity: the ability to both anticipate and navigate the multiple existential challenges of making and sustaining meaning in relationship to others who are simultaneously regulating their own annihilation anxiety, and their existential awareness of their own multiplicity and often complex competing agendas (Hrdy, 2010; Slavin, 2010; Slavin and Kriegman, 1992).

Noah is actively working to build his transitional space—the space where, in these moments, a personally meaningful connection to the world is made: largely, mom's divided heart as well as her need for illusion. He pushes for a kind of spontaneous, "personally expressive deviation" (Hoffman, 1998) from what will usually be hidden from the child in the language, rituals and roles, values, and worldview of the ordinary adult environment: "Oh, parents love children more than themselves . . . ." Noah seemed to probe actively, trying, in our view, to know through interaction—as this book teaches us over and over—the less accessible sides of his mother. He probes for *her capacity* to know the less accessible sides of *herself.*

This testing, evaluating, seeing, and knowing the nature of parental otherness, parental multiplicity, and self-deceptiveness is what we're calling "probing." It is a capacity that will be strained to its limits when parents are struggling, like the disorganized mothers, to maintain self-deceptively fixed (yet highly brittle) perceptions of themselves and their child.

Probing the Therapist's Existential Anxieties, Multiplicity and Self-Deception

So, what is the basic *clinical* value of laying out the complex existential and adaptive backdrop of attachments in these broad, universal terms? The value lies ultimately in one basic observation. In our experience, patients who have had to grapple with the challenges of trying to probe for the elusive grains of trustworthiness in a disorganized attachment parent have often become extremely attuned to precisely the most challenging universal dimensions of human experience—the dilemmas that, in some fashion, we all suffer and share. Our disorganized attachment (perhaps, so-called borderline) patients have not simply suffered the distorting and dis-regulating effects of adapting to the disordered behavior of a dissociated, highly self-deceptive parent. They have. They have also experienced—up close, directly— *the undisguised underside, the existentially precarious and conflictual context of all attachments.* They have seen and known the existential void, the precarious and illusory dimension of all meaning, the potential loss of self that is always a background feature in human experience.

The former disorganized attachment child, however, often knows this facet of life in a far more raw, direct, unmediated way. They have known, usually in some inchoate sense, the dangers that originate in the existential realities we all share, yet that we are often able to keep adaptively dissociated—self-protectively at bay. For the disorganized attachment patient, the trauma they have experienced has, in its way, laid these truths bare. Mother's behavior represents a trauma that will not substantially abate before the messages it carries are heard—the messages about *both* one's unique, painfully aberrant experience *and* the larger redeeming message about the universal truths and haunting dangers to which a disorganized childhood may uniquely equip one to see.

Which is, for one thing, the resonances of both themselves and their disorganized mother in the therapist. Not in the simple sense of repeating the traumatic disorganized mother–child experience in the transference. The "dread to repeat" here (Ornstein, 1974) is, in our view, a far larger, stronger aim than any "compulsion to repeat."

To allow the traumatic past to speak, as it were, the disorganized child must invite and open up the therapist's own struggles with annihilation terrors (around loss and mortality) and moral conflicts (over self vs. other love) by, first of all, usually challenging the therapist's inevitable self-deceptions. Will she begin to get to see, to know, who this analyst really is? Will she come to know, viscerally, the therapist in comparison to the mother who—struggling with her own version of these existential dilemmas—became too overwhelmed to provide the kind of semi-deity strength and genuine recognition of her child's needs, despite what may have been the years of probing mother to engage in precisely this same way?

Yes, much of what, defensively, we're often tempted to see and call manipulative, such as asking for changes in the therapeutic frame, asking for personal information, testing the analyst's limits in other ways is, indeed, a search in all the hardest places for a more secure attachment. A search for another whose inner narrative, if you will, is somehow secure enough to not repeat the behavior of the disorganized mother.

The illusion of an idealized self-object, or a consistently mirroring therapist, who transcends these struggles may, for a time, serve as useful demi-god. But, in the face of the probing of the disorganized patient, if the mirroring, twinning, and idealization do not open in a far more vulnerable, reciprocal fashion, the patient is apt to feel once again very alone. The therapist may be felt as hiding herself—the ultimate form of mis-recognition and emotional withdrawal.

Is there a single stance or analytic perspective that is broad enough to embrace this larger existential dialectic? Not as far as we know. Yet, thinking about the larger existential context helps to frame some of the potential strengths and pitfalls in all analytic perspectives.

A *classical, neutral stance* will ultimately represent a confirmation of one's badness in face of an absent, withdrawing other. The neutral "still face" and opacity can be devastating. Yet, sometimes disorganized patients turn out to be deeply grateful for the authoritativeness, the *seeming* invulnerability, toughness, stalwart consistency of the classical analyst who, in this way, becomes the needed, missing semi-deity. In our experience, this idealization usually changes in face of what the disorganized patient comes to feel is the increasingly apparent fear and defensiveness in the classical therapist wearing the mask of so-called analytic authority. Especially in the face of what often becomes an increasingly angry, perhaps desperate, probing by the—now often increasingly pathologized—patient.

An *empathic stance,* informed by self-psychological and intersubjective systems perspectives, serves as a crucial antidote to the earlier, badly mis-attuned, failing disorganized attachment environment. Yet, in our view, a true empathic connectedness must be understood as a stance that is *relationally achieved* (versus applied as a technique). In our experience, vital as it is, a consistent and carefully practiced empathic immersion can, in itself, begin to represent a relational retreat, a hiding, a backing off from what the patient senses is at stake for the therapist: namely, the therapist's fuller, personal, emotional participation in grappling with what is essentially *her own version* of the patient's issues.

While *relational analysts* aim to address and incorporate a sense of the analyst's subjectivity, we find that, unfortunately this emphasis on the analyst's experience often comes at the cost of a deeply grasped understanding of the centrality of empathy. Sometimes relational analysts tend to experience an empathic immersion in the patient's experience as inherently incompatible with the analyst's own realness and presence (Slavin, 2010). Sometimes, too it is as if, in this perspective, the analyst is assumed to be far more capable of an awareness of her own multiplicity and struggle to create meaning than is likely to be the case. As if a profoundly mutual, reciprocal process of change can be achieved simply through a technical emphasis on the analyst's openness to being known. The openness is very useful, but it must not fall short of the analyst's gradual re-opening and re-encountering her own (often dissociated) existential struggle.

Dr. Beebe's beautifully detailed descriptions attune us powerfully to the disorganized attachment infant's (and then the adult patient's) relentless striving to evoke, provoke, and compel a fuller and more recognizing responsiveness in any potentially caretaking relationship. Our commentary represents perhaps a starker version of what Lyons-Ruth (1999, 2008) proposes as "the process of coming to know and be known by another's mind" that depends upon "whether the partner is capable of a collaborative dialogue." Aware of this universal existential background, we hope to allow our especially challenging, probing patients to evoke our own deeper annihilation fears and conflicts around the inevitably clashing needs and agendas that also pervade our relationships with them. Failing this we intensify what is the worst aspect of their trauma: The way it separates them continuously from the world, because very few, if any of us, can bear the existential truths of what they've seen.

11

ON KNOWING AND BEING KNOWN

The Case of Oliver

Estelle Shane

I formulated my understanding of Oliver as described in the case illustration below based on reading the research findings in this book on the 4-month origins of 12-month disorganized attachment. My appreciation of these findings was deepened following my experience of listening to Beatrice Beebe introduce her work on future disorganized vs. secure dyads at a workshop offered in the 2012 Relational Conference in New York City (Beebe, Orfanos, & Sandberg, 2012). In her moving presentation, the implications for a mature adult of having experienced infancy on the way to disorganized attachment emerged full blown into my imagination: my patient, Oliver, stood before me *in vivo*.

Beebe had begun her 6-hour workshop putting forward an array of impressive data on qualities of future disorganized attachment dyads, with findings in the domains of attention, affect, spatial orientation and touch. Self- and interactive contingencies in the future disorganized dyads were compared with those of future secure dyads, with a picture emerging of what one might speculate would be the theory of mind of such an infant at 4 months of age, the working models of self and other.

Oliver has been in a four times a week analysis with me for a several years. He is a successful professional in an (apparently) happy marriage of ten years. He has two young daughters whom he adores, and on the whole, the family is regarded as ideal by their neighbors and friends, as well as by the teachers from their girls' school.

In the office with me, Oliver sits with his chair facing mine, but with his body turned slightly away from me and his face persistently averted, rarely meeting my eyes. Whole sessions go by with his not ever looking at me, and even entering and leaving the office, he is turned away.

We've discussed this issue from the beginnings of our analytic work. When we were first exploring the prospect of his choosing to do analysis with me, he looked directly at me and spoke with great confidence, but as our relationship deepened, so too did his refusal to make eye-contact. The best Oliver could do at first to explain his "hiding from me," as he phrased it, was to acknowledge that he often felt shame in my presence. Further exploration evoked the sense that he was afraid of what he, or I, might find in one another if we exchanged glances, much less if we were to indulge in a lingering visual exchange. He wondered if we would we find a mutuality of anger or hostility, on the one hand, or a mutuality of desire, or lust, on the other. Would his mistrust of me be validated by what he saw in me? Would he discover distressing confirmation of the emotional mis-attunement he all too often experienced with me? He could only conclude that looking at me, or having me look at him, was risky business.

Despite this, at those times when our work is going well, we've successfully explored many issues together to our mutual satisfaction, and he would say, perhaps grudgingly, that some of his problems have diminished in the time we've been together. He is minimally better, he concedes. But yet Oliver remains a deeply unhappy man, with his eruptive states of rage (Lachmann, 2000) openly expressed with me but kept a dark, humiliating secret from others. Indeed, his outbursts of anger are a source of profound shame for him.

His bitter refrain is, no one really knows him, including, and especially, me. "You think you know me; you all think you know me," Oliver sneers one day, "but you don't. You see me as angry, yes, but," turning to the pen in the ink well on my desk, "it's like you see the ink in this pen and think that's all the ink there is . . . you don't see, because it's hidden from your eyes and you have zero imagination, the vast amount of ink in the well. That's how you understand my anger, only the surface, not the depths. How can you help me when you don't know me!! You don't know me at all!" The fact that he won't let me look at him is not lost on him.

At times, in more kindly moods, he commiserates with my not-knowing. On one occasion he said to me: "It isn't *all* your stupidity; it's not *all* your lack of imagination. I don't know myself. I never know how I'm going to be, or feel, or what I am going to do, from one moment to the next. I go to sleep at peace and wake up minutes later in a rage. I get in the car and suddenly find myself driving like a mad man. I end up going somewhere I haven't planned to drive. I can't, and never could, predict my own behavior. My car is a mass of dents from collisions that I don't even remember making. How can I expect *you* to do better with me than I do?" Also in these moods he can remind me that I'm not alone in my lack of understanding: no one, not his mother, not his father, not his brother, not his wife, not even his beloved daughters, has ever gotten him, has ever understood him, has ever been sufficiently interested in what he thinks, feels, believes, experiences. He is alone and has always been alone.

As further evidence of his own inability to know or predict his mood changes, he tells me that on occasion he finds himself, weirdly, crying, tears running down his face, for no reason that he knows about. He can be feeling happy, watching his girls swimming in the pool, for example, and then, out of nowhere, his face is wet with tears. He is in much better control when others are around, but sometime, even laughing at someone's joke, he finds himself crying.

Oliver has another significant complaint; he never feels safe with me. He knows, of course, that he has also never felt safe with anyone. His father, who travelled around the world on business a good deal of the year, was rarely available when at home either. Once, weeping about his loneliness, he accused his father of forgetting about him altogether. His father responded remorsefully, first showing

173

Oliver where Oliver might find pictures of him when he was gone, as if a picture might substitute for his physical presence, and then admitting that he often felt bad leaving him at home alone with his mother because she was not well mentally. When Oliver looked surprised and pressed him further, his father told him that his mother was schizophrenic.

As a matter of course, Oliver tearfully defended his mother against that accusation, but he had to admit to me, telling me about this central incident with his father, that his mother *was* scary to be with. She was so peculiar, so unpredictable, crying without control at some moments, making jokes with him the next. She could be cruel, too. She'd done things to him that he can't forgive her for even now, like washing his mouth out with soap for saying a bad word, like raging at him once when he was a child, and then, suddenly, picking up a knife, pointing it to her chest, and threatening to stab herself with it. "What do you want me to do?" she screamed on that occasion, "Do you want me to kill myself? Will that satisfy you?"

She could be close and loving, too, when he was small, and she would love to confide in him, to tell him intimate things about sex, about how to masturbate, about how to touch a girl. Talking about these things with me, telling me about these conversations with his mother, Oliver would suddenly become very angry: "How could he trust her?" he demanded of me once. "How could I have been left alone with her?" But still, it was confusing because his mother was a very successful woman, respected in the community for her good works and her efficient engagement in business and social affairs. She had many friends who were devoted to her. He still didn't know how to think about this.

I think it might be understandable, based on my experience in relating with Oliver as outlined here, that I often thought of Oliver as reflecting aspects of disorganized attachment. Attending Beatrice Beebe's workshop both revised and further clarified my thinking and my speculations on this patient's early history, listening especially to her presentation of the basic issue of ". . . how the infant comes to know his mind, and [to] be known, by another's mind." Mind is conceptualized by Beebe, Orfanos, and Sandberg (2012) from the infant's perspective in terms of how the infant construes "expectancies of procedurally organized action sequences." . . . "[T]he infant's perception of correspondences between his own behavior and that of the partner provides the infant with a means of sensing the state of the partner . . . and whether this state is shared or not . . . These correspondences facilitate the development of infant agency, coherence, and identity."

On the basis of their research findings, Beebe and colleagues describe how these capacities can be disturbed, how the "future disorganized infant" will have difficulty feeling known by his mother when he is distressed. I paraphrase the Beebe et al. (2010; Beebe, Orfanos, & Sandberg 2012) findings on the origins of disorganized attachment below (see also Chapter 7). I speculate that these findings relate to experiences akin to those of the infant Oliver in interaction with his mother; they delineate precisely my own subjective experience of Oliver as well as what emerges in the intersubjective system we form between us.

The future disorganized infant will have difficulty feeling known by his mother in moments when he is distressed, and she shows smile or surprise expressions, that is, his distress states are not shareable (e.g., Oliver's fear that if he looks at me he will feel affirmed in his dread of my lack of attunement); in moments when the mother looks away repeatedly and unpredictably, so he does not feel seen (e.g., Oliver's fear that were he to look at me, he'd see I had turned away from him). The future disorganized infant will have difficulty knowing his mother's mind (e.g., when Oliver's mother is loving one minute and aggressive the next).

The future disorganized infant will have difficulty knowing himself in his moments of discrepant affect, for example smiling and whimpering in the same second (e.g., Oliver's complaint that he cannot predict his own moods or behaviors and finds himself weeping without understanding why); as his own engagement self-contingency is lowered, making it more difficult to sense his own facial-visual action tendencies from moment-to-moment (e.g., Oliver has no idea what he will do next, where he will drive, what he will feel). The future disorganized infant's experience of agency with regard to his own states is disturbed (e.g., Oliver does not feel he knows himself. He can't trust what he will do next. He does not understand his rapidly shifting states). For the infant to come to know and be known by another's mind, the partner must be capable of a collaborative dialogue. Overall, the mother of the future disorganized infant does not generate collaborative dialogues (e.g., the child, latency, and young adolescent Oliver had repeated experiences of conversations with his mother that were impossible for him to understand because of the disruptive nature of her style with him).

The expectancies of the future disorganized infant include intense emotional distress and the inability to obtain comfort; difficulty in predicting what will happen, both within the self and within the partner; difficulty in knowing what the self feels and what the partner feels; not feeling sensed or known, particularly when distressed; the presence of intrapersonal and dyadic contradictory communications, conflict, and remarkable intermodal discrepancies (Beebe et al., 2010; Beebe, Orfanos, & Sandberg, 2012).

These disturbances characterizing future disorganized infants are, I believe, fully visible now in Oliver who, as an adult, manifests similar disturbances in his relations with others in his surround, with himself, and with me in the transference.

Just recently, however, we've experienced a breakthrough emerging through an enactment that had gone on between us for many months. It concerns the core issues of his feeling unknown by me and of not able to trust me. The enactment began during one session when, in an extraordinary rage, even for him, Oliver had made a new accusation: "You are not afraid of me," he shouted, "because you are incapable of knowing what I feel! Do you even know that I am angry enough to murder you? Do you realize that I want to destroy you? To attack you? To do you real bodily harm? Here we are, alone in the office, behind closed doors," he charged, continuing to escalate his wrath. "I'm obviously in a fury, and you're not afraid!!! It's just because you don't really get it that I could kill you! That I want to kill you!!!"

By this time he is really screaming. And I'm of course horrified. My heart is pounding. I'm shaking. I feel intensely disrupted, indignant, and on the verge of the outrage I'm attempting to stifle. Still, I am trying to control my breathing, keeping my feet planted solidly on the floor in order to stabilize myself. But with it all, with all of his feelings and my own, Oliver is basically right. I'm not *afraid* of him. I know that he *wants* to hurt me. But I also know he won't. I confess as much. I tell him that I can't imagine how it could be otherwise, how I could sit in an office with someone and ask him to tell me all of what he feels, all of his thoughts and fantasies, which have so often included, in his case, I remind him, hostile, aggressive, rapacious ideas and intentions, announcements of wanting to rape me, to rip me to shreds, to tear off my breasts.

How could I sit with him, with all of these feelings, and not, at bottom, trust him implicitly. I tell him that I *do* know him; I know that he has never hurt anyone, and that while he may want desperately to hurt me now, as he has often wanted to in the past, he has always managed to keep to words, or, at the most, to stalk around the room, loom into me in my chair threateningly (and here I can see in my mind's eye the image of the mother of the future disorganized infant in Beebe's films looming into the face of her infant), and even throw a Kleenex box or two at me, always managing to miss. I don't mean to challenge him and his anger, I tell him. And I don't mean to say that I don't feel disrupted, even angry myself, in the face of it. That it isn't hard to keep my cool. I just want to be honest about my feelings, even if it enrages him, and even if he sees me differently than I see myself: "I want you to be able to experience *all* of this rage bodily, and to express *all* of it in words, because it's the only way I know of that will help you begin to integrate these terrifying feelings and somatic and somaticized horrific emotions. And it's the only way for us, for both of us, to find out what they're about. I think it's imperative if you are, ultimately, going to be able to feel better. No, I don't enjoy it; yes it does upset me greatly, but I am not scared, and I do, with it all, and despite my own sense of disruption, value the experience for both of us."

What he was finally able to make clear to me, what we were finally able to come to together, emotionally, is that my not knowing that he was capable of killing meant that I didn't know him, who and what he was, and that if I didn't know him, who and what he was, it meant he couldn't trust me to take care of him in his intense emotional states. And if he couldn't trust me to take care of him, he couldn't allow me, or him, to know him deeply, from the inside. It was, indeed, a vicious circle, but real, and important.

Finally we arrived at some resolution: I could know that he *could* kill me, while at the same time I could know that he *wouldn't* kill me. That was how each of us could know and understand subjectively our respective feelings in the intersubjective mix between us, how we could mutually recognize and accept one another, and, perhaps, move on to a place where he felt less alone and more known to himself and to me. At least for that moment things had calmed between us, and I, at least, felt the relief and soothing pleasure of renewed connection.

12

IMAGINING CHLOE IN INFANCY

Alexandra Harrison

This chapter relates my psychoanalytic psychotherapy of 4- to 6-year old Chloe to what I imagine about Chloe's experience in infancy. I use Beebe et al.'s (2010) research findings on the origins of disorganized attachment to imagine Chloe's interactions with her mother during infancy. I focus on the "intrapersonal and interpersonal discordance or conflict in the context of intensely distressed infants" which Beebe et al. (2010, p. 7) consider the central feature of future disorganized dyads at 4 months.

When I met her, Chloe suffered from severe temper tantrums, sleep disturbance, and tactile hypersensitivity. Her family relationships—especially with her mother—were characterized by conflict and over-control. In the psychoanalytic treatment Chloe and I were able to identify and elaborate symbolic themes related to conflicts about dependent and sexual longings and destructive aggression. Additionally, Chloe's dysregulation in the domains that Beebe et al. (2010) describe—attention, emotion, body orientation, and touch—had a profound effect on me and contributed in important ways to my intersubjective experience. Chloe's dysregulation appeared to arise from a different—presymbolic—level of experience; one can imagine an infant with a positive expectation of mother's comforting her, followed by an awareness that mother will not help.

There was a corresponding dysynchrony in the therapeutic process. I routinely videotape my treatment sessions with young children in an effort to better understand the interactional dynamics. Microanalysis of Chloe's play sessions revealed two unusual patterns: Chloe interrupting my speech and Chloe making bursts of brief vocalizations, sometimes with simultaneous actions like stamping her feet. Here, one can recognize the infant's urgent demand for attention that is not satisfied. These patterns, along with dysregulation of attention, emotion, orientation, and touch, helped me make sense of the transference and my intersubjective responses. They guided me in constructing the metaphors I used to understand the painful mismatch between Chloe and her mother at 3 to 4 years old, and—through my knowledge of infant research—what happened at the beginning of her life.

I first briefly recount her history and the beginning of the treatment. Then I describe the process of one individual session, including a microanalysis of the videotape. I relate the microanalysis of the clinical session to the research findings on the origins of disorganized attachment. Finally, I describe how my interpretive interventions are informed by infant research.

Each partner—infant and mother, patient and therapist—contributes a unique constellation of experiences to the interactive process of development. Thus it is impossible to draw a direct line from trauma in infancy, parental reaction to this trauma, parents' experiences of caregiving in their own backgrounds, etc. to a psychopathological outcome. Neither would I attempt to assign Chloe to an attachment category. Nonetheless, information from the research in this book proved useful to me in my formulation of the case of Chloe and in my clinical interventions.

Clinical History

Chloe's parents brought their 4-year-old daughter for a consultation because of severe, intractable tantrums. During the tantrums, Chloe seemed unable to calm herself, nor could she be comforted by her parents. Chloe had been evaluated at a major teaching hospital, where she was given a diagnosis of mood disorder, and Risperdal had been recommended. Her parents were alarmed at the serious diagnosis and sought a second opinion.

Chloe's mother's pregnancy was normal, as was the delivery, except for a drop in fetal heart rate that resulted in a forceps delivery. Chloe's birth weight was 8 lb. She was hospitalized at 3 days for a high fever diagnosed as due to a urinary tract infection. During this 2-week hospitalization, Chloe received multiple painful medical procedures. In one, a voiding cystourethrogram (VCUG), she was catheterized and dye was injected into her bladder. She had intravenous antibiotics and blood tests, often from less experienced technicians when the one main technician was not available. Chloe's parents were asked to wait outside the room during these protracted procedures. They vividly remember hearing Chloe screaming, feeling agonized and helpless to protect her.

For 3 months after discharge from the hospital, Chloe had what her parents called "classic colic," crying every day from 6:00 pm to midnight. This got better after 3 months. Chloe's mother nursed her for 4 months until she went back to work. The parents hired a motherly and affectionate nanny.

At 6 months Chloe's maternal grandmother, a nurse, observed staring spells and worried Chloe was having seizures. The spells would last for a few seconds, during which Chloe would not respond to her name, although she would always respond to touch. Her parents say that these "staring spells" persisted, though EEG results at age 2 years were not consistent with a seizure disorder.

Chloe remained on antibiotics for one year for her urinary tract infection. A VCUG was repeated, determining that there was no reflux into her kidneys. However, the procedure was invasive, painful, and frightening.

At 18 months, Chloe became ill with Henoch-Schonlein purpura. This condition—with purple blotches on the skin and abdominal and joint pain—spontaneously resolved after 2 weeks. Around this time Chloe began to have the screaming tantrums she had at the time of consultation, in which she would scream for hours and wet herself. Her pediatrician told her parents that she was "just spoiled." As she got older, she began to complain of leg and foot pain during the tantrums and to demand to be carried. When Chloe was age 2 years, 4 months, her brother, Liam, was born.

At age 3, Chloe developed a gastro-intestinal illness, to which her mother dates a "downward spiral" of her temper tantrums, sleep disturbance, and tactile sensitivity. The dehydration resulting from the illness required intravenous hydration in the emergency room. Chloe screamed frantically. After this illness Chloe developed trouble going to sleep. She would wake several times during the night and scream, insisting that her mother sleep on the floor of her room. Chloe's sensitivity to touch grew worse. She would refuse to wear all but a few clothes. A meltdown could be triggered by something as innocuous as Chloe bumping herself gently.

Family History

When Chloe was 2 years old, shortly after her brother Liam was born, the family said goodbye to the nanny and moved to another city. Chloe's father found a job that would give him more time with his family. This was a sacrifice for Chloe's mother, since she was highly successful at her job in the first city and had a supportive work environment. It was hard for them all to leave the nanny, with whom they remain close.

After the move, Chloe's mother worked at home, in a less satisfying position and without the social support of her previous job. The strain caused by Chloe's problems, and by the move, contributed to her mother's emerging depression. Chloe's mother also experienced a major rupture in the relationship with her own mother, resulting in an extended period of little contact. Chloe's mother had always been preoccupied with managing her own mother's emotional state. Chloe's grandmother had always been "labile," but her moods would usually blow over until this period.

Chloe started at a new daycare center. Her teachers described her as shy but well behaved with friends. Her main difficulty was separating from and reuniting with her mother. Her teacher said that Chloe would get very mad, yell at her mother and hit her. During the day, however, Chloe responded well to the classroom routine and played well with other children.

Clinical Picture

Chloe's most disturbing symptom was her severe tantrums. These meltdowns could be provoked by not getting her own way, becoming frustrated with an activity, or observing her mother paying attention to someone else. At times she screamed and physically attacked her parents if they embraced each other. Sometimes when she had a tantrum, her parents would ask her to go to her room, and other times she would go by herself. In her room she would scream and cry inconsolably, often screaming, "Mommy, come!" "Mommy, help!" But when her mother would come, she would then scream, "No! Mommy go!" If her mother tried to comfort her, she would scream louder, "Mommy, go!" but if her mother did leave the room,

Chloe would instantly scream, "Mommy, come!" This excruciating cycle would continue until she and her mother—and the rest of the family—were exhausted.

When I began to see Chloe at age 4, I asked her parents to place a video camera in her bedroom. In the video one can observe Chloe screaming for her mother and writhing on the bed. When her father came to help, she screamed, "No! Mommy!" But when her mother came, she screamed, "Mommy, go!" While alone, there were periods of 1 to 2 minutes when she was quiet. At these times she attempted to soothe herself by rubbing the bridge of her nose or her genital area, while staring off in an unfocused way, looking dissociated.

Treatment

Beginning of Psychotherapy

The treatment began with Chloe, mother, me, and sometimes Liam in the playroom, Chloe dominating the sessions. Later I held individual sessions with Chloe. Chloe introduced play themes but could not elaborate them. In retrospect, it is likely that Chloe's fear of her own easily escalating over-arousal, her tenuous regulatory capacity when she was excited, and her fear of the destructive effects of her aggression, were factors in constraining her creative activity.

One of the key play themes was that of a baby who was sick. Chloe would get the doctor kit and ask her mother's help in examining the baby doll. Chloe said that the baby was sick, and she told her mother to cry for the baby. She and her mother tried all sorts of things to comfort the baby, but no matter what they did, they could not make the baby better. Chloe would disappear into the playroom, adjacent to the office where her mother and I were sitting, and return with one toy after another. We would ask, "Will this make the baby better?" and Chloe would shake her head silently, no. Needless to say, we never found a remedy for the baby's distress.

I connected Chloe's current distress to her rocky neonatal period and the mother's inability to comfort her sick newborn and protect her from the painful needles. In a slow, repetitive way, corresponding to the repetition of the play theme, I would point out how sad it was that no matter what this mommy tried to do, she could not help her baby feel better. This intervention, of course, also addressed the mother, who was present in the room.

After several months of the treatment, I received an email from Chloe's mother. Her parents had been discussing the father's routine blood test, when Chloe remarked, "I remember having a needle and I cried and I could not stop crying. Mommy was there trying to comfort me but Daddy was not there. *When you are a baby you don't know that mommies are trying to comfort you and you don't stop crying. I could not stop crying.*" It seemed that Chloe, and indeed her whole family, was reflecting on her experience in infancy and wondering if it could be related to her 4-year-old unhappiness.

Once Chloe came with her father to her session. When he left her at the door of my office, she proceeded to have a tantrum, climbing under one of the chairs in my office and screaming for her father. It had been our custom to accommodate Chloe's demand that her mother accompany her into the session. But since her father had brought her, I suggested that he wait in the waiting room. I spoke to Chloe about how awful it felt when no one came to comfort her. She screamed for me to be quiet. I told her that at home she screams for her mommy—"Mommy, come!"—but then when her mommy comes she screams, "Mommy, go!" I said it must be terrible to scream for your *nice mommy* to help you and then have your *mean mommy* come instead. ("Nice" and "mean" were the words Chloe used to label people who were or were not in her good graces.) I told her that right now I must be the "mean Dr. H" to her, and that makes her feel so much worse! She must worry that I am going to be really, really mean. Maybe she is even scared of me! After the time was over, Chloe crawled out from under the chair, and without a word to me, joined her father in the waiting room. On returning home, her mother emailed me that she had spent a peaceful evening at home.

This intervention was designed to help Chloe make sense of her polarized images of her mother, and of me in the transference, and to appreciate how they related to her anger and panic. I thought that if she could begin to appreciate how her own projected anger frightened her, she and I could start to explore her anger and aggression. I also had in mind infant research showing the infant's sensitivity to angry facial expressions. I thought that the trauma of Chloe's newborn illness for her mother, and also her mother's experiences with her own mother, might have interfered with her mother's capacity to tolerate Chloe's distress states. In that case, using the findings in this book on the origins of disorganized attachment, and specifically the maternal difficulty in empathizing with infant distress states, I imagined that her mother might have responded to Chloe's distress by not being able to "follow" or empathically join her distress. Or the mother might have responded with angry or aggressive facial expressions, with smiles or surprise faces, with closed-up inscrutable faces, or by looking away from her distressed infant. During Chloe's first 3 years, she and her mother created a pattern of anger and fear that bound them together in a way that mutual comfort could not. The exclusivity, interdependence, and control characterizing their relationship were rigidly repeated.

Detailed Process from an Individual Session

Summary of the Session

After many months Chloe was willing to come into the office with me alone. I videotaped one of the early sessions. It was unusual in that her father had brought her. Although she fussed about her daddy leaving, she was cheerful in the office. She told me about her daddy's phone; it ran out of batteries. I admired her description of her Daddy's equipment. She asked me to help her open the dolls' house, but then opened it herself. She then wanted the second dolls' house, declined my offer to get it, and went to get it herself. Chloe declared that the house was "kind of dirty," the "paint got off" the house, and it "lost its stickers too."

She explained that the house was "old." She sat on a toy, and exclaimed, "Ow, ow, ow!" but without distress. She then told me that, "You have to tighten things when they get loose. That happened to my bike, and I kept falling off and getting boo boo's." She tried to fit a doll into the baby cradle but it was too big. She looked for a baby doll to fit into the cradle and found one; it fit. Then she found the policemen. Suddenly, she got up and said that she had to go to the bathroom, though she added that she "already went to the bathroom." After returning from the bathroom she told me that she didn't have to go to the bathroom after all, "But if you think you have to go, you should try because otherwise you might pee pee in your pants, and that's OK for a baby . . ." She then picked up a bottle cap and said that it looked like a toilet. She played with the top, putting it various places, including on top of her nose.

She then moved to the garage and put figures in the elevator, where they got stuck. She took everybody out of the elevator and said, "Daddy loves basketball. I don't. It's boring." I said that she has been thinking a lot about her daddy lately. She put a rubber band on her nose and then stuck her tongue out. Looking through the baskets, she found the broken-off leg of a giraffe and suggested that I glue the leg on. We found the giraffe belonging to the broken piece and another identical giraffe that was intact. She said of the first giraffe, "She lost a leg," and tried without success to make it stand up. Then she pushed the broken piece of the giraffe's leg into the broken part of the leg and said, "Aha!" standing the giraffe up against the house and declaring, "Now he is old because his leg fell off." She compared the two giraffes, calling the intact one the "baby one" and the broken one "the fixed one." Then she told me that she "accidentally licked (her) chin" and made a little car careen along the rug.

Comment

Chloe entered the session after having enjoyed her daddy's iPhone games, clearly feeling enhanced by her connection with him. She started to tell me about all her daddy's wonderful equipment. Interestingly, her narrative is rather incoherent, something that is not always the case. In the play that follows, several themes emerge: the strong, older person versus the dirty, weak baby (carrying the toy into the room herself, going to the bathroom though she had just gone); the defective body (giraffe with broken leg, house that is old and dirty with paint off, bikes that have to be tightened so parts don't fall off, sitting on a toy—"ow, ow"); and the beginning of the threat of aggression or sexuality on the integrity of one's body or a relationship (licking her chin, little car that careens out of control).

Video-Based Observations and My Subjective Experience

The following four sequences are consecutive, 20-second video episodes, beginning after she and I enter the office together.

Sequence 1: 0–20 Seconds

Chloe paces a little and then stands still, facing me, as I sit on the floor. I affirm Chloe's ability to figure out how to open the house. Chloe speaks immediately after I stop, declaring, "Hey, daddy, daddy have one of those." I do not know what she is referring to, so I ask, taking my turn right after she stops speaking, "Daddy does?" I am feeling slightly lost, trying to find a way of joining her. She comes in immediately, "Yeah, but it's white." I respond, again immediately, "Oh, that's interesting." She interrupts me, saying, "And daddy, . . . and it's way bigger than." I ask, "Yeah?" and she responds, "Yeah." Then after a short pause, "It's not black." I respond in a long turn corresponding to hers, "Well, your daddy has some cool things, doesn't he?" She interrupts me again and says, "Yeah." After a short pause, I remark, "He has that little thing that has games on it . . ."

Comment, Sequence 1: In this sequence I am trying to make a connection with Chloe. I try to match her pause pattern, but she interrupts my third vocal turn, and then she makes two short consecutive vocalizations without waiting for me to take a turn. When I try to match her vocal turn pattern by repeating the duration of her previous long turn, she interrupts me again.

The tight coordination of Chloe's vocal responses, often beginning to speak immediately when I finish speaking, followed by her interruptions, begins to call to my mind a pattern of "Mommy, come, mommy, go." The tight coordination communicates urgency, as in the "Mommy come!" and when I "come" by trying to match her pattern, she interrupts me in what I might—although I actually do not—experience as a rejection. In the interruptions, it is as if she is not fully aware of my presence.

Considering the videotape material through the lens of the research findings regarding attention, affect, orientation, and touch, we can make some interesting observations. Chloe begins speaking about her father's cell phone without negotiating a shift in the focus of attention with me, from the dolls' house to the cell phone. The orientation of her body is not coordinated with mine: after I sit down by the toys, ready to play, she paces and then continues to stand in front of me as she speaks. Although Chloe's pacing and the intensity of her speech indicate high arousal, her facial and vocal affective expression is rather blank, and she seems almost closed down, an intermodal discrepancy. Her closed affective quality contrasts with my animated face and voice. In these domains of potential coordination, Chloe and I are poorly coordinated.

Sequence 2: 20–40 Seconds

After a brief pause, Chloe says, "No, it's his phone." She is still standing, facing me, and fingering the hem of her shirt. I match the duration of her pause before saying, "Oh, that's his phone—his phone you can play games on?" She interrupts me; I match her pause and begin to take a turn, and she cuts me off. When I attempt to affirm her communication about the apps on her daddy's phone, playfully declaring, "No, I don't believe that!" she interrupts me again. In response to Chloe's lack of acknowledgement, I repeat playfully, "Really!?" This time she acknowledges my communication and says, "Yeah. I counted them." But again there is a major disconnect between my positive affect and her solemn but intense affect.

Comment Sequence 2: It seems as if Chloe is not taking in my communications in the manner of typical discourse. One time she doesn't acknowledge my remark about "games" and immediately moves to "apps;" another time she is still thinking about how many apps her daddy has and doesn't seem to take in my admiring remark. Considering the research domains of attention, affect, orientation, and touch, we notice some relevant patterns. Constraints on Chloe's capacity to focus attention are illustrated by her failure to acknowledge my playful initiatives. She remains standing, and touches her shirt in a self-regulatory manner. There is a lack of coordination between my positive, animated affect and Chloe's solemn affect.

Sequence 3: 40–60 Seconds

I say, "My gosh!" She responds immediately, "I counted them!" I say, "Your daddy has so many cool things!" She then interrupts me, making a long speech, "Those are not games. They're just . . . they help, help daddy get games. I counted the games. I counted them altogether." She adds, "But it's not the same as your phone. You can only—you can't press the buttons. You can only do it." I sense her internal lack of coordination in her speech and actions, and the discrepancy between her intensity and her blank facial expression.

Sequence 4: 60–80 Seconds

Chloe continues, "It's that kind of phone. It's an iPhone." She stamps her feet as she speaks, declaring, "But it's a boring color. It's black!" I ask, "What color would you like?" Chloe responds, stamping as she speaks, "Pink, pink, pink, pink!" I laugh, interrupting her last "pink," saying, "You think pink is a much prettier color?" and she repeats, "pink." I repeat, "A much prettier color . . ."

Observations on the Micro-Process

In these four 20-second sequences, there are characteristic patterns of Chloe's *interrupting me,* and taking *repetitive brief turns.* It is a struggle for me to achieve a state of shared attention with her, since her verbal communications are somewhat incoherent and her vocal rhythms unpredictable. In the sequence 60–80 seconds, the meaning of Chloe's stamping her feet is not entirely clear. It emphasizes her words, but the quality of repetitive bursts suggests an attempt to regulate a high arousal state, and also perhaps an ambivalent and aggressive reaction related to her meaning of the color "pink."

Yet, the video offers more clues to Chloe's inner world. She remains solemn and a little petulant in her facial expression and voice, despite her dramatic and somewhat playful stamping. This affective discrepancy between her facial expression and her stamping reminded me of her mixed speech pattern of tight coordination and interruption: a "Mommy come, mommy go!" pattern. Although this discrepancy between positive and negative is consistent with the psychoanalytic meaning of ambivalence, its sequential rhythm conveys an additional aspect. I imagine this pattern arising from her presymbolic experience as an infant, with a positive expectation of mother's comfort, followed by an awareness that mother will not help.

Video observation of the remainder of the session reveals Chloe's repetition of the two unusual patterns of interruptive turn taking and sequences of brief vocalizations, sometimes with simultaneous actions. The interruptions seem to indicate unmanaged high arousal—either negative or positive. Chloe's interruptions have a dysregulating effect on me. They interfere with reciprocity by obstructing my initiatives. They insist on the dominance of her intentions. Also unusual are Chloe's orientation, pacing and standing above me, as I remain seated waiting for us to play. The unpredictability of her standing position recalls the unpredictable maternal "loom" of the research. I do not know when or whether she will join me in the play space; our spatial relationship is unstable.

Chloe does not interrupt me in the middle of my vocal turn, but rather just at the end of my vocalization. In some ways, that has a greater subjective disruptive effect on me. In my efforts to join her, I realize that, out of awareness, I attempted to match my vocal turns to hers; for example, I try to match the duration of her previous vocalization. If she cuts me off just before the end of my turn, I cannot match her previous turn; mine is shorter.

The repetitive bursts of her vocal and action turns suggest unmanaged arousal. One effect is to commandeer my attention. It is impossible to organize one's own thoughts in the presence of this kind of insistent behavior in one's partner. The subjective effect on me is fatigue, confusion, and sometimes helplessness. I feel that it is so difficult to take my own turn, and respond to her.

Chloe is in profound conflict. She must absolutely control me—get me to pay attention, know her intention, know her distress. But she must also be able to make me go, interrupt me, not allow me to find her. In her fantasy, she fears that the mother who comes might be the "mean mother" who hurts her. This symbolic level of meaning is powerfully contextualized by the implicit level. In attention, affect, orientation, and coordination of rhythms, Chloe seems to be creating a pattern of approach and avoid; "Mommy come, mommy go."

Conclusion

As I play with Chloe, I attend to her symbolic communications in language and play and I struggle to stay connected with her. These two domains of analytic activity can be captured in metaphors derived from psychoanalytic theory and from the infant research findings.

185

In creating symbolic meaning, psychoanalytic theory helps me make sense of her fear of aggression and sexuality. Her ambivalence toward her mother and Oedipal excitement about her father are represented in her transference reactions to me and in her fascination with her father's equipment. Her sense of herself as defective and bad is revealed in her interest in the old and broken toys and her story of falling off her bicycle. The scratching of her nose and rubbing her genitals is likely related to erotic fantasies. These behaviors suggest intense conflicts about dependent longings, emerging romantic love, and aggressive wishes. Whereas "Mommy come, mommy go!" characterized the relationship with her mother at the beginning of the treatment, this pattern has now developed into a more complex set of feelings and fantasies which include both her father and mother.

Yet, there is more going on in the sessions than the symbolic narrative. Her disjointed rhythms, fragmented attention, and discrepant affect are dysregulating and implicitly confusing to me. My experience is that of being pulled in toward her, straining for a connection, analogous to "Mommy come!" and then being cut off by her interruptions or shifting attention, analogous to "Mommy go!" As she commandeers my attention with insistent, unpredictable behavior, I become fatigued, confused, sometimes helpless. On the other hand, Chloe's delicate beauty and charm, and her intense interest in me, sometimes hidden by ostentatious rejections, draw me toward her.

Metaphors from infant research help make sense of what is going on below the level of the symbolic narrative. The dysregulation began in the neonatal hospitalization during which mother and infant were unable to establish facilitating rhythms. In the hospital, some people approached her to comfort, and others approached her to cause her pain. Chloe seems to have had difficulty distinguishing which partner would help her, and which would hurt her. After the hospitalization, continuing stress in the family, including Chloe's colic, made it hard to repair these patterns. The further disruptions of the mother's second pregnancy and Liam's birth, the move to another city, and the loss of the nanny and many other family supports, followed.

The mother of course has a corresponding experience. She feels that when she tries to comfort her baby, the baby continues to cry. In the hospital the mother was asked to stay out of the room during the painful procedures. In addition, the mother carried within her a pattern of taking responsibility for her own mother's moods and the belief that if she were not successful in making her mother happy, she was a failure. Chloe's mother would try not to withdraw from her child when she screamed unrelentingly, but her emotional withdrawal as a reaction to her helplessness was apparent. When Chloe looked to her mother's face for comfort, using the research findings presented in this book, she might have seen a scared or angry face, a blank face, or a discrepant surprised or smiling face. In any case, we know that she was not comforted.

Chloe and her mother both came to anticipate negativity and disappointment, what her parents called "walking on eggshells." The mother felt trapped in the cycle of coming when called, only to be turned away. The child felt trapped in calling the mother to come help, but knowing that she cannot help. Chloe struggled with distress that escalates out of control. Mother struggled with depression. Both mother and child used withdrawal to self-comfort. Chloe also used dissociation.

In this discussion I used Beebe et al.'s (2010) research findings on the origins of disorganized attachment to illuminate the infancy history of Chloe's disturbance. I tried to imagine what might have occurred between Chloe and the hospital technicians, and between Chloe and her mother. Beebe's research domains of attention, emotion, orientation and touch drew my attention to analogous patterns of dysregulation as I studied the videotapes and observed Chloe interact with her mother and with me.

Patterns of attention dysregulation were observed in Chloe's pattern of interrupting my verbal turns. Patterns of emotion dysregulation were observed in discrepant affect within Chloe in Mommy come, Mommy go; in Chloe's excitement but neutral face; dyadic discrepant affect was observed between my positive affect and her neutral affect during her excited play. Patterns of orientation dysregulation were observed in her "looming" stance above me, as if wanting my attention, discrepant with her inability to use my attention. Patterns of touch dysregulation were observed in Chloe's extreme sensitivity to tactile sensations, from early infancy associated with expectations of pain and danger.

In summary, the analytic treatment of Chloe can best be understood in two domains of therapeutic activity. The first concerns the communication of symbolic meaning in language and play. In this domain, Chloe and I engage meanings from her private, inner world about her defectiveness and her destructiveness in intimate relationships. In play about a baby whose mommy cannot comfort her, for example, we begin to question what is hurting the baby and why the mommy cannot help. But, when we analyze the video micro-process and use insights from infant research to inform our thinking, we see that a great deal of the therapy takes place in a domain of therapeutic action below the level of speech and symbolic play. In my efforts to "match" Chloe's vocal turn pattern I am also attempting to "comfort the baby." My study of the vocal and action turn patterns alerted me to the disjunctions in the rhythms. Instead of feeling stressed by them, I can feel free to allow the disturbances to happen and to experiment with different ways of finding a "match." The findings of this book gave me a new lens with which to identify dimensions of therapeutic action in the implicit domain.

13

FROM MICROSECONDS TO PSYCHIC STRUCTURE

Stephen Seligman

This volume presents very important work with significant implications for both researchers and clinicians. In showing how details of mother–infant interactions at 4 months predict attachment classifications at 12 months, Beebe, Jaffe, and their colleagues have empirically confirmed what most infant observers, especially infant clinicians, have taken for granted, namely that very early interactive patterns are reflected in later patterns of relating and of experiencing oneself and others. Although previous research found correlations between general descriptions of maternal sensitivity and attachment security, the current focus on the details of the moment-to-moment interactions adds further precision and dimension.

That 4-month mother–infant interaction patterns predict attachment classification suggests that they may also predict a number of other significant markers. Attachment classification at 12 months predicts the infant's internal working model of attachment in adulthood (measured with the Adult Attachment Interview [AAI]), as well as the 12-month attachment classification of the infant's own infant with her, once she becomes a parent (Main et al., 2008). Thus, mother–infant interaction patterns at 4 months may predict the infant's later style of organizing attachment security in adulthood and also her ability to be a responsive and sensitive parent. In any case, that the finding that 4-month interaction patterns predict attachment classification at one year takes a place alongside previous findings that attachment classification at one year predicts both adult attachment status and the attachment status of offspring in the next generation.

These are all remarkable correlations, with few parallels in the developmental psychological literature. Apart from the domain of attachment, there are very few adult psychological characteristics with clear-cut developmental antecedents or indications of intergenerational transmission *of any sort* that can be predicted so strongly, especially from social-emotional factors. Moreover, the findings from the field of attachment have led to equally remarkable findings. For example, 12-month disorganized attachment classification correlates with differences in adult brain anatomy related to emotion regulation, predicts borderline psychopathology, and is correlated with infant relational trauma (Gabbard, Miller, & Martinez, 2008).

Since these predictions are now closely tethered, subsequent researchers will be able to proceed with broader scope, and clinicians will be able to work with more confidence in principles on which they have already relied. Overall, we now have substantial empirical support for the view that early parental care has an important influence on subsequent personality organization (see Seligman, 2012).

The new findings are important at the level of *developmental theory*, since they support an increasingly comprehensive model of early development and its longer-term effects that integrates several levels of observation, from the microanalytic to the global. Previous research has shown that more macro phenomena such as maternal sensitivity and attachment classification are both significant and interre-lated. The addition of prediction from microanalytic data now expands the empiri-cal support for an already well-established dynamic nonlinear complex systems model. This model integrates different dimensions of development and personal-ity, ranging from neurological and endocrinological, to microanalytic observation of very early parent-baby interaction, to such broad psychological measures as attachment, AAI classification, reflective functioning, and psychopathology.

In the breakthrough decades of the 1970s and 1980s, the core strands of attach-ment theory and microanalytic infant–parent interaction research developed at some distance from one another, albeit with an implicit conviction that their obvi-ous synergies might be empirically delineated eventually. This work marks a clear watershed in that project, as Beebe, Jaffe, and colleagues have brought their long-standing microanalytic project in direct predictive correlation with the attachment classifications. As affective and cognitive neuroscience and psychoanalysis—both clinical and theoretical—have also developed along similar lines, there are now multidimensional consiliences among these various fields.

We can now think more clearly and with empirical support about how infancy affects how adults feel and interact with others and themselves. Our models describe how psychological development is a complex system with continu-ity over time and over different situations. Much of this, though not all, can be translated into clinical work. In a sense, this is what psychodynamic clinicians have always done—interpret the developmental literature in a way that gener-ates clinical hypotheses—but we can now go forward with greater clarity and force.

Working clinicians now have greater empirical legitimacy behind the clinical imagination,[1] one that both finds and creates workable coherences across a wide range of observations and speculations, whether about someone's expectations of intimate partners, her ongoing sense of personal security, her relationship with her own parents, her interest in offering a communicative account of herself, her way of regulating emotions, the details of how she responds to her baby, her char-acteristic facial expressions, what may well be going on in certain regions of her brain and so on. These become part of an expanded array of observational frames by which the therapist gets to know the patient, frames that she tries to bring together to make helpful models of what is going on. There are many ways that these orientations can work, including generating diagnostic frameworks, orient-ing behavior, organizing and stabilizing the therapist's own internal experience, and shaping interventions.

189

Issues in the Clinical Application of Developmental Research

Translating a study like this for its clinical value can take place on different levels. One level involves a more or less direct transposition of its measures and descriptors to the psychotherapeutic arena. For example, an adult therapist might become more sensitive to her patient's expectations about interactive contingency: Does the patient check often for a response that fits? Is she especially ready to detach in the face of a slightly misplaced emotional gesture? But before we examine the clinical application of specific findings, I want to discuss another, more general dimension: How to think about linkages between different conceptual levels and between processes occurring in different time frames vis-à-vis the therapeutic enterprise. Beebe and her colleagues are remarkable observers of dyadic interactions occurring in very short time frames. They work with 1-second intervals, briefer than a therapist can keep explicit track of, and in examining the video sequences they take us into even finer-grained sequences.

Attachment researchers, psychoanalysts, and other psychologists typically work with much longer timespans—minutes, hours, months, years, decades, and lifetimes. How do we mediate among these? What links them? These are important questions for developmentally oriented therapists (as well as researchers). Throughout the book, Beebe and colleagues elaborate an array of mediating concepts and higher-level hypotheses that link the different observational frames, relying on a broad and deep array of contributions from other infancy researchers.

The overall approach looks something like this: The basic phenomena of interest are the intertwined, if not simultaneous, regulations of emotion, behavior and meaning in dyadic interactions, including the bi-directionality of such regulatory processes, with infants and mothers influencing one another's behavior and state of mind almost continuously and at a very rapid pace. These lead to the development of more generalized expectancies and dispositions, along with procedural representations of interpersonal relationships and senses of self, internal working models of attachment, the sense of personal felt security, attachment classification, and the like. Nonverbal forms of psychic organization are central, especially those pertaining to affectively organized interpersonal expectancies. The potentially enduring effects of dysregulation are also stressed. Typically, the authors follow an intersubjective direction, proposing that interpersonal recognition is a key for the development of an adequate sense of self and felt security. For example, they propose:

> . . . that the future D [disorganized] infant represents *not being sensed and known* by the mother, particularly in states of distress. We proposed that the emerging internal working model of future D infants includes confusion about their own basic emotional organization, about their mothers' emotional organization, and about their mothers' response to their distress, setting a trajectory in development which may disturb the fundamental integration of the person.
>
> (Beebe et al., 2010, p. 7)

This readily translates into a picture of an ordinary two-person interaction gone awry that can be made experience-near for psychotherapists: People pay attention to those who are interested in, protect, and also threaten them; they hope to be paid attention to in return. It can also be said more abstractly: Emotions and meanings are created in social interaction which in turn supports the development of individual patterns of regulation, equilibrium, and experience with other people. The experience of negative emotions such as fear and other forms of distress usually amplifies the search for an attentive person who can be protective. Adequate caregiver responsiveness under such conditions supports individual feelings of coherence, effectiveness, interest, and security; poor responsiveness leads instead to more conflicted, relatively disorganized, and insecure experiences. Those who apply current developmental models to psychotherapy start from the view that such dynamics are also central in everyday psychotherapeutic process.

Adult therapists who are interested in infancy will be intrigued by how the baby's world seems to embody the same directness and immediacy that they seek in their clinical practice; the data of this study capture the "this is just how it is"-ness of everyday relating. The data also reflect a very striking quality of the infant's experience, namely that it is often reasonably well organized in nonverbal, sensorimotor emotional patterns, manifest in dyadic interactions which are meaningful, coherent, recognizable, and communicable. In one sense, these conceptualizations can be seen as the developmentalists' evolving response to the psychoanalysts' problematic of "psychic structure," which attempts to account for and model personal continuity and coherence over time and space.[2] Since psychodynamic psychotherapists are eager to establish continuities between early development and later life, they will find such models especially appealing, since they call attention to these dimensions that can be observed in infancy and also in adulthood.

The emphasis on nonverbal, non-reflective organizations in many developmental accounts has been of special interest to psychotherapists. Psychodynamic therapies depend on hypotheses about which enduring patterns structure the patient's approach to the world, so as to construct interventions to alter them. Therapists of different persuasions seek to communicate with the patient about these patterns in various ways, whether in words or through other inventive pathways, like direct emotional contact or a focus on the body. Although not all these therapies invoke developmental findings, the explanatory hypotheses they do employ typically rely on accounts of the continuity between experience early in life and later in development. Thus contemporary developmental ideas about "expectancies," "internal working models," and "implicit relational knowing" offer very useful conceptual envelopes for working therapists of different orientations.

Linking the Microanalytic with the Macroanalytic: Implications for Psychotherapy Practice

With this background, some specific implications for clinical assessment and technique come into clearer relief. Among others, Beebe and her colleagues assert that direct observation of and intervention with rapid interactive micro-processes similar to those described in this volume can be very helpful in psychotherapies. In one extraordinary case report, for example, Beebe (2004) describes how she observed a patient's dramatic gaze aversion as part of her effort to understand how frightened the patient was of emotional contact, and she subsequently provided video images of her own face to her patient when the patient felt emotionally unable to tolerate in-person contact. This eventually led to the recovery and repair of memories of childhood traumatic separations (see Fraiberg's [1982] seminal work on gaze aversion as one precursor of defense in infancy).

In introducing a more mundane example, Harrison and I have declared that:

> ... nonverbal communication of psychic states ... in adult psycho-therapy ... is often overlooked. Patient and therapist are constantly communicating in facial expressions, physical gestures, vocal rhythms, and pauses and silences as well as even more subtle gestures such as the rustling of their clothes or a change of position. For example, a throat-clearing may communicate stress whereas leaning forward may commu-nicate intensified interest: In a rather ordinary encounter, the therapist greeted her patient, a divorced middle-aged man, in the waiting room and walked with him into the office. The patient had not yet spoken, and his facial expression was unremarkable, but the therapist detected a change. "Something's up! Something good," she remarked. The patient's face relaxed into a grin. "I've met someone," he said. He told the story of his new romance, and the therapist wondered, but could not clarify, what alerted her to the presence of "something good." As the patient turned to say goodbye at the session's end, however, he made an almost-unnotice-able flourish with his head and shoulders. The therapist suddenly recog-nized that he had made the same gesture as he had stood aside for her to enter the office at the beginning of the session. The affectively charged gesture, which she had not consciously noted before, had communicated his good news (Seligman & Harrison, 2011, p. 245).

What is remarkable about such "affectively charged gesture(s)" is not only their evocative power, but the extent to which they are the basic stuff of the ongoing flux of everyday human contact. Usually, much of this goes on outside of explicit awareness. Brain responses to the observation of another's emotion displays may occur in time intervals much briefer than a second after the display is presented, too fast for the usual reflective processes to come into play. This is generally adap-tive, since it allows for more complex, efficient communication and for urgent responsiveness at times of distress or emerging danger. At other times, however, overly intense and/or contradictory social-affective inputs overwhelm the capaci-ties of one or both members of the dyad. This may be especially likely in intimate, emotionally laden relationships like romances, domestic partnerships, parent-ing—and psychotherapy.

Even a few glances at the "split-screen" illustrations of the interactions presented in Chapter 1 evoke a powerful internal sense of the emotional impact of these brief dyadic exchanges. That these frames reflect just a few seconds of interaction, at most, is a compelling demonstration of how the infant–parent matrix can induce the strongest emotions in those who take the time to observe it. It offers an experiential window into understanding how such interactions can be so definitive in forming enduring structures of experience and behavior. Imagine watching one of the videos of the disorganized dyads for say, 40 minutes, or spending 90 minutes with such a mother and her baby, as many infant clinicians routinely do, or for that matter, watching them for 3 minutes in the supermarket aisle. Even more poignantly, imagine being the baby—lost, out-of-sync, frightened with the very person that you expect to protect you, the one that comprises your world more than anything else.

If we assume that these interaction patterns are characteristic of the observed dyads, then both our common intuition and clinical sense tell us that they will lead to habits of thinking and feeling that will be generalized elsewhere. Where nonrecognition and failure to comfort are typical, it would be reasonable to assume that the baby's biobehavioral systems will be primed for disruption, distress, and danger elsewhere, and indeed this is what the research about disorganized attachment, trauma, and borderline psychopathology indicates.

In this context, this study does two remarkable things at once: It provides empirical evidence that dyadic interaction patterns are influential in the formation of subsequent psychic structure, *and* it describes the details of such interactions as it does so. This is especially valuable in light of the extent to which the very short interaction processes are not immediately available to ordinary observation.

The accounts in this book may not adequately convey the power of the time-series analyses, buttressed by data analysis, that its authors undertook. For each dyad they studied the sequence of 250 consecutive 1-second intervals, and after discerning robust features through statistical examination, they were able to look at the slowed-down video of these interactions and thereby see things that would utterly escape the naïve observer in real-time. The drawings suggest a bit of the power of watching these in a series of unfolding freeze-frames, but when the movement and temporal dynamics are added, as in one of their videos, the effects are even more striking.

Exposure to this material, in whatever form, sensitizes the therapist to similar processes in the consulting room. Although we can't expect to keep up with a second-to-second flow, keeping the nonverbal, microanalytic dimension in mind draws the therapist's attention to meaningful gestures and moments that she might not otherwise realize were occurring.

For example, I am now more likely to notice whether my patient looks at or away from me at the beginning of sessions, especially after a vacation or other similar disruption. I notice vocal rhythms and tones, variations in skin tone, movement synchronies and asynchronies, and so on. Sometimes this leads to an explicit comment on what I have observed; at other times, I privately try to make sense of what I have noticed. I make implicit use of an assumption that these micro-moments are indicative of more general individual patterns of meaning-making, relating, defense, affect regulation, and the like.

These observations are helpful in thinking through my own emotional reactions to the patient, since they help me become aware of some of the specific pathways by which I have been influenced to feel whatever I am feeling. In fact, I have come to make a kind of countertransference–transference intervention in which I try to tell the patient as specifically as possible about what she did that led to my talk-ing about a particular idea or reacting in a particular way. For example, I recently told a superficially curious patient that the way he drops his voice at the end of his questions gives me the feeling that he may mean something less cooperative than the apparent interest in hearing what I think that he communicates verbally. This kind of intervention presents the usual danger of the therapist projecting his own concerns into the patient even when he is aware of the intersubjective complexi-ties, but I have found that a reflective and judicious use of this "technique" can be quite helpful, including in some tight countertransference–transference binds. Patients have often heard these kinds of accounts before, and when they can be offered in the relatively non-punitive atmosphere of the therapeutic relationship, creative work is sometimes potentiated.

One of the strongest contributions of this study for clinicians, then, is its excep-tionally rich, detailed descriptions of dyadic interaction systems and their func-tion and evolution. Page after page delineates specific details of what is going on. Take, for example, the following introductory account of what they looked at in terms of "modalities of communication," which is notable for its attention to distinct details:

> We refine the study of the origins of attachment by examining separate modalities of communication: attention, affect, orientation and touch. Face-to-face communication generates multiple simultaneous emotional signals in numerous modalities. Infants are sensitive to all modalities and are capable of coordinating them to apprehend affective states . . . . Redundancy and overlap facilitate selective attention, learning and memory. However, with disturbed communication, different modalities can convey discordant infor-mation, difficult to integrate into a coherent percept . . . .
>
> (Beebe et al., 2010, p. 28)

Thus, rather than focus only on visual coordination between mother and baby, the authors analyzed several different communication modalities, in several different combinations, such as "(1) infant gaze–mother gaze, (2) infant facial affect–mother facial affect." The experience-nearness of this scheme captures what occurs in ordinary interaction between mothers and 4-month infants—and in conversa-tion between adults. This expands and refines the observational field, makes the research more meaningful on its face, and implicitly suggests a more elaborate and complete map of the nonverbal dimensions of therapist–patient interaction.

Beebe and her colleagues also call attention to how these processes are occurring over time. The temporal dimension of relating and meaning-making has not been sufficiently explored, and yet it is crucial to the development of the sense that the world is a predictable place where one's efforts can have an effect (Seligman, 2011, in press; Stern, 2010). Interpersonal interaction always take place over time, even when the time frames are very short. Descriptors which are already quite specific, such as "disruption and repair," "chase and dodge," and of course, the central conceptual variable here, "contingency," become all the more vivid in light of the temporal orientation of the detailed accounts offered here, which, after all, are presentations of lived experience in time.

These temporal process descriptors can be adapted for the working clinician's mindset. As do other colleagues influenced by infancy research, I often observe patterns of patient–therapist interaction that follow these interactive contours, as when, following an interpretation, I notice a sequence that seems like a chase-and-dodge (a description that sometimes seems more helpful and experience-near than the term "resistance"), or when the sense of a contingent call-and-response seems to suddenly give way to a choppy, incoherent set of monological gestures. In this second circumstance, I try to recall, as precisely as possible, when the disruption began. While this might lead me to an effort to repair the break, it might well lead to an exploration of the discordant affect or meaning; it might also lead to a non-reparative, further development of the non-contingent rhythm.

At one time, Beebe, Jaffe and their colleagues expected that the highest levels of contingency in infant-mother vocal interactions would be associated with secure attachment. Instead, they found much more complex patterns: high contingency is not in itself necessarily a desirable state of affairs (Jaffe et al., 2001). In addition to being very important in itself, this finding suggests the possibility that there may be a number of different ways of negotiating the vicissitudes of the therapeutic relationship. Finding harmony might not be the most important task for the therapist and patient; indeed, experiencing incoherence together might be a necessary step in some instances. Thus integrating infant research findings into psychotherapy practice might need to be less prescriptive than some might think.

The importance of affect regulation in the caregiving interaction is stressed throughout this book. Moreover, the special place of the management of negative affect and heightened affect in the mother–infant relationship suggests parallels to psychotherapy, since therapists are typically most interested in the patient's intense, negative experiences, past or present. Following psychoanalysis, attachment theorists since Bowlby have seen both interpersonal and intrapersonal processes as oriented by attention to negative affects, especially fear-anxiety (see Slade, in press); they suggest that this is a bias of the human biopsychosocial system essential to species survival. With such an abundance of empirical, observational, and conceptual riches, Beebe and her colleagues do not overlook the extent to which affect is at the center of what is at issue in both the 4-month mother–infant interactions and the attachment classifications themselves.

This study is a very important contribution in support of the current intuition that effective, coherent coordination of individual and of infant–parent dyadic regulation of attention and affect, as well as of orientation and touch, provides for the most flexible and positive functioning in emotional relationships throughout the rest of the lifespan. Its synthesis of microanalytic infant–parent interaction research, emerging models of personality development and psychopathogenesis, and attachment theory and research is extraordinary, especially in such an elegant and experience-near empirical study. Respecting complexity, it does not abandon clarity or immediacy. It provides robust support for the creative application of developmental research to the theory and practice of psychodynamic psychotherapies.

Notes

1 With regard to the special issues and controversies about the place of empirical scientific methods in relation to psychoanalysis, the short version of my own view is that the risks of dialogue with empiricism are worth taking when the analytic discourse method remains at the center of whatever syntheses may emerge.
2 They also include a view of unconsciousness, but one which relies on a more general conception of intrapersonal and interpersonal awareness than the traditional psychoanalytic one with its emphasis on repression.

Appendix A

CODING OF ORDINALIZED BEHAVIORAL SCALES

Modality			Definition	
Mother Facial Affect[a]	*Mouth widen (MW)*	*Mouth open (MO)*	*Other*	
90 mock surprise	MW 0 (1)	MO 3 (4)	eyebrows raised	
85 smile 3	MW 2	MO 3 (4)		
80 smile 2	MW 2	MO 2		
70 smile 1	MW 1	MO1 (2)		
67 oh face ⎫	MW 0	MO 1 (2)		
60 positive ⎬ Interest	MW 0	MO 1 (0)		
attention ⎭	MW 1	MO 0	[kiss/ purse]	
50 neutral	MW 0	MO 0		
45 2 = woe face			empathic pout	
40 1 = negative face	grimace and/or compressed lips		and/or frown	

Infant Facial Affect[b]	*MW*	*MO*	*Other*	
5 medium high/ high positive	2	3 (4)		
4 low/medium positive	1	1 (2)		
3 interest/neutral	0 (1)	0		
2 mild negative	Grimace	0 (1)	[and/or frown]	
1 negative	squared anger mouth/pre-cry/ cry-face (partial/full display)	2 (3)	[and/or frown]	

Mother/Infant Gaze

1 = on partner's face

0 = off partner's face

Infant Vocal Affect[c]

6	high positive	rising intonations, peals, laughter
5	neutral/positive	includes gurgles, coos, neutral sounds
4	None	

3   fuss/whimper
2   angry protest   distinct angry quality
1   Cry   full-blown cry

For data analysis, codes were combined:
4   positive/neutral
3   None
2   fuss/whimper
1   angry protest/cry

Infant Head Orientation[d]   **Infant Touch**[e]
6   en face   0   None
5   enface/head down   1   touch/suck own skin
4   30–60 degree minor avert   2   touch/suck own clothing, strap, chair
3   30–60 avert + head down   3   touch/suck mother's skin, clothing
2   60–90 degree major avert   *For data analysis, codes were ordinalized:*
1   Arch   3   more than one code within one sec

                                                2   any one code
                                                1   None

Mother Spatial Orientation[f]
3   upright   torso/shoulders perpendicular to floor
2   forward   torso bent 45 degrees, minimum 12
                                                inches from infant's face
1   loom   torso bent 80 degrees, within 12 inches
                                                of infant's face

---

Dyadic Mother "Chase"–Infant "Dodge" [f] **Coding Rules**

1.   The infant may initiate the chase and dodge sequence with a "dodge" that consists of at
     least a 30-degree lateral head aversion from the vis-à-vis orientation with the mother.
2.   A maternal "chase" requires that mother is already in a forward or loom spatial ori-
     entation, and that she alters the position of her head or body in the direction of the
     infant's head aversion. The mother must begin chasing within 1 sec of the infant's
     head aversion.
3.   If more than 1 second elapses between the infant's head aversion and the mother's
     movement, then the chase and dodge sequence is said to be initiated by the mother's
     movement.
4.   Chase and dodge movement focuses only on lateral movement. This refers to move-
     ment away from the vis-à-vis position toward the side from which the infant has just
     moved.
5.   Chase and dodge is present as long as movement by at least one partner continues
     within 2 seconds (e.g., the infant turns his head from side to side). Even if the infant's
     head is averted or the mother is in a "chasing" position, chase and dodge is not consid-
     ered present if there is no movement for 2 seconds or more.
6.   Chase and dodge is no longer coded when either the mother or the infant are in the
     vis-à-vis position for 1 second.
7.   A minimum of 2 seconds duration is required to code chase and dodge.

Note. Codes within each modality coding scheme are mutually exclusive. Coding rules for multiple
codes within the same second follow Tronick and Weinberg (1990). If two codes occur in the same

second, the code occurring in the first half of the second is attached to that second; the code occurring in the second half of the second is attached to the following second. For vocalization, this coding rule was adapted as follows: if two vocalizations occur in the same second, code the most intense one; if they are of equal intensity, code the second one. Vocalizations are scored in the second they occur even if they occur in the second half of the second (consistent with Tronick & Weinberg, 1990).

a Mother Facial Affect coding follows Beebe and Gerstman (1980). Two degrees of mouth widen (MW) were distinguished: MW1 = sideways lip stretch (without zygomaticus retraction); MW2 = lip-corner raise (zygomaticus retraction). Four degrees of mouth open (MO) were distinguished, from lips slightly parted to maximal display of mouth open ("gape"). Reliability was evaluated based on configurations (levels 40–90).

b Infant Facial Affect coding follows Koulomzin et al. (2002) and Marquette (1999). Two degrees of mouth widen and four degrees of mouth open were distinguished, definitions identical to that of *mother facial affect*.Reliability was evaluated based on configurations (levels 1–5).

c Infant Vocal Affect coding follows Demetri Friedman, Beebe, Jaffe, Ross, & Triggs (2005), adapted from Tronick and Weinberg (1990).

d Infant Head orientation coding follows Koulomzin et al. (2002) and Marquette (1999).

e Infant Touch coding follows Koulomzin et al. (2002); see also Hentel, Beebe, & Jaffe (2000); Marquette (1999).

f Mother Spatial Behavior coding follows Kushnick (2002) and Demetriades (2003); Mother Chase–Infant Dodge coding follows Kushnick (2002).

Appendix B

ORDINALIZED MATERNAL TOUCH SCALE

From Affectionate to Intrusive

The Mother Touch Scale (overleaf) comprises 11 ordinalized categories of 21 types of touch behaviors, defined below in Appendix C (Stepakoff, 1999; Stepakoff, Beebe, & Jaffe, 2000). Each category describes the type of maternal touch, intensity, and location of maternal touch in relation to the infant's body.

The most intuitively positive mode of touch is "affectionate touch," which occurs less frequently in depressed mothers (Stepakoff, 1999). "Static touch" refers to holding or gently squeezing (legs/feet or arms/hands), resting mother's hand or palm on infant (legs/feet or arms/hands), or providing the mother's hand or finger for the infant to hold (arms/hands). This category of touch is intuitively gentle. "Playful touch" refers to tap/graze, tickle, rub, or flex/extend or lift/circle (legs/feet or arms/hands). This form of touch is more active, and overtly "playful," often involving games. All three of these categories occur exclusively in the location of arms/hands or feet/legs. We followed Stepakoff's hypothesis that touch to the periphery of the body was less stimulating than touch to the center of the body. These three categories account for approximately one-third of the data. The category of "no touch", which accounts for 38.9% of the data, is next in the ordinalization. At this point of the scale, almost 72% of the data is accounted for.

The next two categories, "Caregiving", which accounts for very little data, and "Jiggle/Bounce," a substantial category (8%), both occur exclusively in the location of arms/hands or feet/legs. They differ from the first three categories in that they are more active. "Oral touch", a relatively rare code (1.3% of the data), is defined as mother putting her finger in the infant's mouth. "Object mediated touch" (2.7%) involves mother touching the infant with an object in between her body and the infant's body, such as mother dangles toy on infant's chest. Depressed mothers use more "object mediated touch" (Stepakoff et al., 2000). "Centripetal touch" (9%) is defined both by central body location (face, body, head and neck, excluding hands, arms, feet, and legs) and by mild intensity. Touch to the central body was considered more stimulating (Stepakoff et al., 2000). The final two categories can be considered intrusive. "Rough touch" (3%) includes scratch, pull, push, constrain, force, or control infant movement (such as force infant's foot into infant's face, or force infant's hand down), pinch or poke/jab, in any location on the infant's body. The final category "high intensity touch" (3.9%) was by definition intrusive, involving "rapid, abrupt or intrusive touch," irrespective of the type of touch.

201

	Scale Category	Type	Location	Intensity (intense)	%	Cat%
11	Affectionate Touch	(3) stroke, caress (6) kiss, nuzzle (21) pat	(4) hands, arms, (5) feet, legs	(1) mild or moderate	0.8	
10	Static Touch	(1) hold, (2) provide hand or finger for infant to hold	(4) hands, arms, (5) feet, legs	(1) mild or moderate	24.6	
9	Playful Touch	(4) tap, (8) tickle, (9) rub, (11) large movements with arms or legs	(4) hands, arms, (5) feet, legs	(1) mild or moderate	7.5	32.9
8	No Touch	(0) no touch	n.a.	n.a.	38.9	38.9
7	Caregiving	(5) caregiving	(4) hands, arms, (5) feet, legs	(1) mild or moderate	0.4	
6	Jiggle / Bounce	(13) jiggle, bounce	(4) hands, arms, (5) feet, legs	(1) mild or moderate	8.0	8.4
5	Oral Touch	(14) infant-directed oral touch	(1) face, (4) hands, arms, (5) feet, legs	(1) mild or moderate	1.3	1.3
4	Object Mediated	(19) object-mediated Touch	(1) face, (2) body, (3) head, neck, (4) hands, arms, (5) feet, legs	(1) mild or moderate	2.7	2.7
3	Centripetal Touch	(1) hold, (3) stroke, (4) tap, (5) caregiving, (6) kiss, nuzzle, (8) tickle, (21) pat	(1) face, (2) body, (3) head, neck	(1) mild or moderate	9.0	9.0
2	Rough Touch	(10) scratch, (15) pull, (16) push, (17) pinch, 18 (poke)	(1) face, (2) body, (3) head, neck, (4) hands, arms, (5) feet, legs	(1) mild or moderate	3.0	
1	High Intensity Touch (Intrusive)	Any	(1) face, (2) body, (3) head, neck, (4) hands, arms, (5) feet, legs	(2) high intensity	3.9	6.9

Note: Category = Categories of the scale, from affectionate touch to high intensity intrusive touch; Type = Numeric entries refer to specific types of touch (see Appendix C, Mother Touch Codes) defining the category; Location = Location on Infant's Body: (1) face, (2) body, (3) head, neck, (4) hands, arms, (5) feet, legs; Intensity = 1 = mild or moderate; 2 = high rapid, abrupt, intrusive.

Appendix C

MOTHER TOUCH CODES

00   no touch
01   hold or gently squeezed, rest hand or palm on infant
02   provide hand of finger for infant to hold
03   stroke, caress
04   tap (using one or more fingers), graze
05   caregiving (e.g., reposition infant in infant seat; wipe infant's mouth; adjust infant's clothing; adjust strap in infant seat; etc.). (Code only if caregiving is appropriate; if mother initiates caregiving for no apparent reason, for example pulls infant's socks up and down repeatedly or continuously rubs infant's face with a cloth, code as 'object-mediated touch')
06   kiss, nuzzle
07   self-directed oral touch (e.g., suck on infant's toes or fingers, nibble on part of infant)
08   tickle
09   rub (can be unidirectional or bidirectional, one finger or many)
10   scratch
11   flexion, extension, lift arms or legs, circling motions, and similar large movements
12   rock
13   jiggle, bounce, shake, wiggle
14   infant-directed oral touch (e.g., offer finger for infant to suck, put finger in infant's mouth, put infant's hand in infant's mouth, put infant's toes in infant's mouth)
15   Pull
16   push, inhibit/constrain movement, force or control infant's movement (e.g., force infant's foot into infant's face, force infant's hand down)
17   pinch
18   poke, jab (pressing one or more fingers into the infant's skin) (include maternal use of infant's foot or toe to press into infant's skin if there is a poking-type effect)

19   object-mediated touch (e.g., waves cloth in infant's face, dangles toy on infant's chest, manipulates clothing for non-caregiving purpose) (also code if mother mediates her touch with a part of the infant's body, for example mother tap infant's hand against infant's face)
20   other (e.g., sniffs, chews, knocks with knuckles)
21   pat (implies use of whole hand, if only with finger, code as "tap")
99   uncodable (e.g., due to changes of position, camera errors, etc.)

Intensity Code: Each code was given an intensity rating (i) mild/moderate, (ii) high intensity (rough, abrupt, intrusive).
These codes were used to construct the ordinalized mother scale (see above)

Note. Mother Touch coding follows Stepakoff (1999; Stepakoff et al., 2000) elaborating on Tronick and Weinberg (1990). (a) *Type of touch behavior:* Only one type of touch behavior (of the 21 codes) can be coded in any one second. Only those segments of data in which infants were sitting in the infant seat were analyzed (although infants could at times be held on table, on mother's lap, to mother's chest, or in transition). (b) *"Primary" touch behavior:* Because mother touch can occur with both hands, occasionally two forms of touch occurred, one with each hand. In this case, one form of touch was coded as "primary" and the other as "secondary." For the purpose of this study only primary touch was used for data analysis. (c) Location on infant's body was coded as (1) face, (2) body, (3), head, neck, (4) hands, arms, (5) feet, legs.

Appendix D

MOTHER AND INFANT ENGAGEMENT SCALES

Beebe and Gerstman (1980) developed an ordinal scale of degree of infant and mother facial-visual engagement. By 3–4 months, an extensive range of interpersonal affective play is present in the infant. Observations of infants sustaining or disrupting the face-to-face play encounter led to the development of an infant engagement scale describing the various ways that infants combine their orientation to the mother, their visual attention to her, and subtle variations in their facial expressiveness (Beebe and Gerstman, 1980, 1984; Beebe and Stern, 1977). This scale was influenced by the concept that nuances of affective quality occur on a continuum of gradations, rather than only as discrete on-or-off categories.

Although our previous versions of the infant engagement scale used infant gaze, facial affect, and head orientation, in this study we also integrated infant vocal affect into the ordinalization of the multimodal infant engagement scale. Thus the construction of the infant engagement scale underwent extensive revision. The mother engagement scale was not changed. The mother engagement scale is ordinalized consistent with the mother facial affect scale (see Appendix A). Mock surprise is the highest mother engagement level based on ordinalizing by degree of mouth opening; as such it carries the fullest degree of display of the positive expressions.

The entire data set was run through a series of successive versions of the engagement scale, and frequency analyses were performed to see what percentage of the total seconds of data was accounted for by the engagement categories in each of the versions of the scale. Any engagement levels that accounted for less than 2% of the data were regrouped with other similar levels. Any large proportion of seconds unaccounted for by the existing categories led to the creation of new levels, until 92% (infant) and 94% (mother) of the data set was included in each engagement scale, and no single level of engagement represented less than 2% of the entire data set (with the exception of two levels of infant distress). These percentages can be found in the final column of the engagement scales.

Table D1 Infant Engagement Scale

Eng	Gaze (On/Off)	Head Orientation	Facial Affect	Vocal Affect	Description	%
Positive On						
18	ON (1)	En Face (6)	Hi Positive (85)	Hi(6) / Neut (5) / No Voc(4)	Hi Positive Engagement	3.7
17	ON (1)	En Face (6)	Mild Positive (70)	Hi(6) / Neut (5) / No Voc(4)	Mild Positive Engagement	6.2
16	ON (1)	En Face (6)	Neutral (55)	Hi(6) / Neut (5)	Positive/Neutral Engagement	2.1
15	ON (1)	En Face (6)	Neutral (55)	No Voc (4)	Neutral / Interest	19.9
Negative On						
14	ON (1)	En Face (6)	Neutral (55)	Fuss (3)	Negative Engagement (Voc)	3.4
14	ON (1)	En Face (6)	Negative (40)	Neut(5)/No Voc(4)/ Fuss(3)	Negative Engagement	
Look Angled-escape						
13	ON (1)	Any except En Face (1–5)	Any except Cry (40–85)	Any except Protest or Cry (3–6)	Look Angled for Escape	2.2
Positive Off						
12	OFF(0)	Any	Hi Pos (85)/ Mld Pos(70)	Hi(6) / Neut (5) / No Voc(4)	Neutral Face / No Voc	2.2
11	OFF (0)	Any	Neutral (55)	Hi Pos (6) / Neut Pos (5)	Neutral Face / Pos Voc	3.2
Neutral Off						
10	OFF (0)	En Face (6)	Neutral (55)	No Voc (4)	En Face	16.5
9	OFF (0)	Head Down, vis a vis (5)	Neutral (55)	No Voc (4)	Head Down, vis a vis	3.5
8	OFF (0)	30–60 Avert (4)	Neutral (55)	No Voc (4)	30–60 Avert	7.8
7	OFF (0)	30–60 + Head Down (3)	Neutral (55)	No Voc (4)	30–60 + Head Down	4.6
6	OFF (0)	60–90 (1) / Hd Up & Back (2)	Neutral (55)	No Voc (4)	60–90/Head Up & Back	3.0
Inf Gaze At Object						
5	Look at Object	Any	Any	Any	Object Engagement	6.2
Neg Off/ En Face						
4	OFF (0)	En Face (6)	Neutral (55)	Fuss (3)	Off En Face – Negative	2.9

	OFF (0)	En Face (6)	Negative (40)	No Voc (4) / Fuss (3)	Off En Face – Negative	
4	OFF (0)	En Face (6)	Negative (40)	No Voc (4) / Fuss (3)	Off En Face – Negative	
Neg Off/Avert						
3	OFF (0)	Any (except En Face) (1–5)	Neutral (55)	Fuss (3)	Gaze Avert	2.2
3	OFF (0)	Any (except En Face) (1–5)	Negative (40)	No Voc (4) / Fuss (3)	Gaze Avert	
Distress						
Cry Face						
2	ON/OFF	Any	Cry Face (20)	No Voc (4) / Fuss (3)	Cry Face	
Angry Protest						
2	ON/OFF	Any	Neutral (55) Neg (40) / Cry Face (20)	Angry Protest (2)	Angry Protest	
Discrepant Affect						1.6
2	ON/OFF	Any	Negative (40)	Neutral Positive (5)	Low Discrepancy	
2	ON/OFF	Any	Mild Positive (70)	Fuss (3)		
2	ON/OFF	Any	Negative (40)	Hi Positive (6)	Medium Discrepancy	
2	ON/OFF	Any	Hi Positive (85)	Fuss (3)		
2	ON/OFF	Any	Cry Face (20)	Hi Positive(6) / Neut Pos (5)	High Discrepancy	
2	ON/OFF	Any	Hi Pos(85)/ Mild Pos(70)	Angry Protest (2)		
2	ON/OFF	Any	Hi Pos(85)/ Mild Pos(70)	Cry (1)		
Cry						
1	ON/OFF	Any	Neutral (55) Neg (40) / Cry Face (20)	Cry (1)	Cry	1.0

Note. We required that data were available for all component variables (gaze, facial affect, vocal affect, and head orientation) in order to calculate infant engagement level.

Table D2 Mother Engagement Scale

	Gaze (On/Off)	Facial Affect	%
	Gaze at Infant		
9	On	Mock Surprise (90)	2.0
8	On	Smile 3 (hi) (85)	3.2
7	On	Smile 2 (med) (80)	15.5
6	On	Smile 1 (lo) (70)	22.7
5	On	Oh Face (67)	1.1
4	On	Positive Attention (60)	38.0
3	On	Neutral (50) / Woe (45) / Negative Attention (40)	2.2
	Gaze Off Infant		
	Positive Off		
2	Off	Oh(67)/Sm1(70)/Sm 2(80)/Sm3(85)/Mock(90)	3.8
	Neutral / Negative Off		
1	Off	Neg Attn(40)/Woe(45)/Neut(50)/Pos Attn (60)	6.9

Note: For details of Mother facial affect coding and ordinalization, see Appendix A. "Oh Face" = Mouth open midway, no smile; "Positive Attention" = Gaze on with slight mouth widening and / or opening without smile; "Woe Face" = Slight down-turned corners of mouth with pursed out lips; "Negative Attention" = Gaze on, with mouth corners turned down in grimace and / or frown and / or mouth drawn in tightly in "compressed lips".

Appendix E

DEFINITIONS OF BEHAVIORAL EXTREMES

(Derived from Behavioral Qualities of Ordinalized Behavioral Scales)

Ordinalized Behavioral Scale		Definitions of Behavioral Extremes	
Infant	Gaze	Gaze Away	Look away from mother's face
	Facial Affect	Negative Facial Affect	Frown, grimace, pre-cry, and cry face
	Vocal Affect	Negative Vocal Affect	Fuss, whimper, angry protest, cry
		Distress (Facial or Vocal)	Either negative facial affect or negative vocal affect
		Discrepant Affect	Simultaneous (within the same sec) positive affect in one modality (either facial or vocal) and negative affect in the other
	Touch	No Touch	No infant-initiated touch
		Touch own skin	Touch/suck own skin
	Head Orientation	60°-90° Avert	Avert head 60°–90°
		Arch	Arching back
		% Avert or Arch	Either 60°–90°avert or arch
Mother	Gaze	Gaze Away	Look away from infant's face (20% + time)
	Facial Affect	Positive Facial Affect	Smile 2, smile 3, mock surprise
		Negative Facial Affect	Frown and/or grimace and/or compressed lips
	Touch	Intrusive Touch	Rough (scratch, push, pinch)/ high intensity aggressive touch
		Interruptive Touch	Maternal touch "push, constrain movement, force or control infant movement" (e.g., force of infant's hand down)
	Spatial Orientation	Loom	Mother head "loom" in toward infant's face (20% + time)
Dyadic	Infant Facial/ Vocal Affect, M Facial Affect	M Positive Facial Affect while I Distressed	Infant distress episodes initiated by sec in which infants showed negative vocal/facial affect; Mother positive face smile 2 or higher
		Chase and Dodge	2 consecutive sec in which mother moves head toward infant's face while infant (in same or following sec) orients head away

209

Note. See Appendix A for all definitions of behaviors. If the means of the behavioral scales did not differ by attachment classification, the behavioral extreme was tested (20% or more time in that behavior, across the 2½ minutes coded per dyad).

REFERENCES

Ainsworth, M., Blehar, M., Waters, E., & Wall, S. (1978). *Patterns of attachment: A psychological study of the strange situation.* Hillsdale, NJ: Lawrence Erlbaum Associates.

Anderson, F. (Ed.). (2008). *Bodies in treatment.* New York: The Analytic Press.

Aron, L. (1996). *A meeting of minds.* Hillsdale, NJ: The Analytic Press.

Badalamenti, A., & Langs, R. (1992). Stochastic analysis of the duration of the speaker role in the psychotherapy of an AIDS patient. *American Journal of Psychotherapy, 46,* 207–225.

Bahrick, L., & Lickliter, R. (2002). Intersensory redundancy guides early perceptual and cognitive development. *Advances in Child Development and Behavior, 30,* 153–187.

Balint, M. (1992). *The basic fault.* Evanston, IL: Northwestern University Press.

Bateson, G., Jackson, D. Haley, J., & Weakland, J. (1962). A note on the double-bind. In: D. Jackson (Ed.), *Communications, family and marriage: Human communication,* Vol. 1 (pp. 55–61). Palo Alto, CA: Science and Behavior Books.

Beebe, B. (1982). Micro-timing in mother–infant communication. In M. R. Key (Ed.), *Nonverbal communication today.* Series Edited by Joshua Fishman, *Contributions to the sociology of language.* Volume 33. New York: Mouton.

Beebe, B. (1998). A procedural theory of therapeutic action: Commentary on the symposium, "Interventions that effect change in psychotherapy" by L. Sander, K. Lyons-Ruth, E. Tronick, D. Stern, A. Harrison, N. Bruschweiler Stern, J. Nahum, & A. Morgan. *Infant Mental Health Journal, 19*(3), 333–340.

Beebe, B. (2004). Symposium on intersubjectivity in infant research and its implications for adult treatment. IV. Faces-in-relation: A case study. *Psychoanalytic Dialogues, 14*(1), 1–51.

Beebe, B. (2005). Mother–infant research informs mother–infant treatment. *Psychoanalytic Study of the Child, 60,* 7–46.

Beebe, B., & Gerstman, L. (1980). The "packaging" of maternal stimulation in relation to infant facial-visual engagement: A case study at four months. *Merrill-Palmer Quarterly, 26,* 321–339.

Beebe, B., Cohen, P., Sossin, K., & Markese, S. (2012). *Mothers, infant, and young children of September 11, 2001: A primary prevention project.* New York: Routledge Press.

Beebe, B., & Gerstman, L. (1984). A method of defining "packages" of maternal stimulation and their functional significance for the infant. *International Journal of Behavioral Development, 7,* 423–440.

Beebe, B., Jaffe, J., Buck, K., Chen, H., Cohen, P., Blatt, S., Kaminer, T., Feldstein, S., & Andrews, H. (2007). Six-week postpartum maternal self-criticism and dependency and

4-month mother–infant self- and interactive contingencies. *Developmental Psychology*, *43*(6), 1360–1376.

Beebe, B., Jaffe, J., Chen, H., Buck, K., Cohen, P., Feldstein, S., & Andrews, H. (2008). Six-week postpartum depressive symptoms and 4-month mother–infant self- and interactive contingency. *Infant Mental Health Journal*, *29*(5), 442–471.

Beebe, B., Jaffe, J., & Lachmann, F. (1992). A dyadic systems view of communication. In N. Skolnick & S. Warshaw (Eds.), *Relational perspectives in psychoanalysis* (pp. 61–81). Hillsdale, NJ: Analytic Press.

Beebe, B., Jaffe, J., Lachmann, F., Feldstein, S., Crown, C., & Jasnow, J. (2000). Systems models in development and psychoanalysis: The case of vocal rhythm coordination and attachment. *Infant Mental Health Journal*, *21*, 99–122.

Beebe, B., Jaffe, J., Markese, S., Buck, K., Chen, H., Cohen, P., Bahrick, L., Andrews, H., & Feldstein, S. (2010). The origins of 12-month attachment: A microanalysis of 4-month mother–infant interaction. *Attachment & Human Development*, *12*(1–2), 3–141.

Beebe, B., Knoblauch, S., Rustin, J., & Sorter, D. (2005). *Forms of intersubjectivity in infant research and adult treatment*. New York: Other Press.

Beebe, B., & Lachmann, F. (1988). The contribution of mother–infant mutual influence to the origins of self- and object representations. *Psychoanalytic Psychology*, *5*, 305–337.

Beebe, B., & Lachmann, F. (1994). Representation and internalization in infancy: Three principles of salience. *Psychoanalytic Psychology*, *11*, 127–165.

Beebe, B., & Lachmann, F. (1998). Co-constructing inner and relational processes: Self and mutual regulation in infant research and adult treatment. *Psychoanalytic Psychology*, *15*(4), 1–37.

Beebe, B., & Lachmann, F. (2002). *Infant research and adult treatment: Co-constructing interactions*. Hillsdale, NJ: The Analytic Press.

Beebe, B. & Lachmann, F. (2003). The relational turn in psychoanalysis: A dyadic systems view from infant research. *Contemporary Psychoanalysis*, *39*(3), 379–409.

Beebe, B., Lachmann, F., Jaffe, J., Markese, S., Buck, K., Chen, H., Cohen, P, Feldstein, S., & Andrews, H. (2012). Maternal depressive symptoms and 4-month mother–infant interaction. *Psychoanalytic Psychology*, *29*, 383–407.

Beebe, B., Lachmann, F., Markese, S., & Bahrick, L. (2012). On the origins of disorganized attachment and internal working models: Paper I. A dyadic systems approach. *Psychoanalytic Dialogues*, *2*(2), 253–272.

Beebe, B., Lachmann, F., Markese, S., Buck, K., Bahrick, L., Chen, H., Cohen, P., Andrews, H., Feldstein, S., & Jaffe, J. (2012). On the origins of disorganized attachment and internal working models: Paper II. An empirical microanalysis of 4-month mother–infant interaction. *Psychoanalytic Dialogues*, *22*, 352–374.

Beebe, B., Margolis, A., Hane, A. A., Bahrick, L., Buck, K., Chen, H., et al. (2009). Mother–infant face-to-face self and interactive contingency across modalities: A dyadic systems view. Manuscript, NYSPI.

Beebe, B. & McCrorie, E. (2010). The optimum midrange: Infant research, literature, and romantic attachment. *Attachment: New Directions in Psychotherapy and Relational Psychoanalysis*, *4*, 39–58.

Beebe, B., Messinger, D., Bahrick, L., Margolis, A., Buck, K., Chen, H., Cohen, P., Andrews, H., & Jaffe, J. (2013). A dyadic, dynamic systems view of mother–infant face-to-face communication. Manuscript, New York State Psychiatric Institute.

Beebe, B., Messinger, D., Bahrick, L., Margolis, A., Buck, K., & Jaffe, J. (2012). Self-regulation is dependent on partner influence, and vice-versa: A dyadic systems view of mother–infant communication. Paper presented at *International Conference Infant Studies,* Minnesota, June 9.

Beebe, B., Orfanos, S., & Sandberg, L. (2012). Organizing principles of face-to-face communication in infant research & adult treatment. *International Association for Relational Psychoanalysis & Psychotherapy,* 10th Anniversary Conference, March 1, New York City. Part I: Beebe, B. Origins of disorganized attachment; Part II: Beebe, B. & Sandberg, L. Videotaping the analyst's face: Video feedback consultation with a patient who does not look, with discussion by Dr. Larry Sandberg.

Beebe, B., Steele, M., Jaffe, J., Buck, K., Chen, H., Cohen, P., Kaitz, M., Markese, S., Andrews, H., Margolis, A., & Feldstein, S. (2011). Maternal anxiety and 4-month mother–infant self- and interactive contingency. *Infant Mental Health Journal, 32*(2), 174–206.

Beebe, B., & Stern, D. (1977). Engagement–disengagement and early object experiences. In N. Freedman & S. Grand (Eds.), *Communicative structures and psychic structures* (pp. 35–55). New York: Plenum Press.

Belsky, J. (1997). Theory testing, effect-size evaluation, and differential susceptibility to rearing influence: The case of mothering and attachment. *Child Development, 68,* 598–601.

Benjamin, J. (1995). *Like Subjects, Love Objects.* New Haven, CT: Yale University Press.

Berlyne, D. (1966). Curiosity and exploration. *Science, 153,* 25–33.

Bernstein, E., & Putnam, F. (1986). Development, reliability, and validity of a dissociation scale. *Journal of Nervous and Mental Disease, 174*(12), 727–735.

Bernstein, N. (1967). *Coordination and regulation of movements.* New York: Pergamon Press.

Blehar, M., Lieberman, A., & Ainsworth, M. (1977). Early face-to-face interaction and its relation to later infant–mother attachment. *Child Development, 48,* 182–194.

Bloom, L. (1993). *The transition from infancy to language.* New York: Cambridge University Press.

Bornstein, M. (1985). Infant into adult: Unity to diversity in the development of visual categorization. In J. Mehler & R. Fox (Eds.), *Neonate cognition* (pp. 115–138). Hillsdale, NJ: Lawrence Erlbaum Associates, Inc.

Boston Change Process Study Group (2005). The something more than interpretation revisited: Sloppiness and co-creativity in the psychoanalytic encounter. *Journal of the American Psychoanalytic Association, 53* (3), 693–729.

Boston Change Process Study Group (2007). The foundational level of psychodynamic meaning: Implicit process in relation to conflict, defense and the dynamic unconscious. *International Journal Psychoanalysis, 88,* 843–860.

Bower, T., Broughton, J., & Moore, M. (1970). Infant responses to approaching objects. *Perception and Psychophysics, 9,* 193–196.

Bowlby, J. (1969). *Attachment and loss, Vol. I: Attachment.* New York: Basic Books.

Bowlby, J. (1973). *Attachment and loss, Vol. II: Separation.* New York: Basic Books.

Brazelton, T., Koslowski, B., & Main, M. (1974). The origins of reciprocity. In M. Lewis & L. Rosenblum (Eds.), *The effects of the infant on its caregiver* (pp. 137–154). New York: Wiley-Interscience.

Bretherton, I. (1980). Young children in stressful situations: The supporting role of attachment figures and unfamiliar caregivers. In G. Coelho & P. Ahmed (Eds.), *Uprooting attachment* (pp. 179–210). New York: Plenum.

Bretherton, I., & Munholland, K. (1999). Internal working models in attachment: A construct revisited. In *Handbook of attachment theory* (pp. 89–111). New York: Guilford.

Bromberg, P. (2011). *The shadow of the tsunami and the growth of the relational mind.* London/New York: Routledge, 2011.

Bucci, W. (1985). Dual coding: A cognitive model for psychoanalytic research. *Journal of the American Psychoanalytic Association, 33,* 571–608.

Bucci, W. (1997). *Psychoanalysis and cognitive science: A multiple code theory.* New York: The Guilford Press.

Bucci, W. (2011). The role of subjectivity and intersubjectivity in the reconstruction of dissociated schemas: Converging perspectives from psychoanalysis, cognitive science and affective neuroscience. *Psychoanalytic Psychology, 28,* 247–266.

Carey, W. (1970). A simplified method for measuring infant temperament. *The Journal of Pediatrics, 77,* 188–194.

Carlson, E. (1998). A prospective longitudinal study of attachment disorganization/isorientation. *Child Development,* 69(4), 1107–1128.

Carlson, E., & Putnam, F. (1993). An update on the Dissociative Experiences Scale. *Dissociation, 6,* 16–27.

Carlson, E., & Sroufe, L. A. (1995). The contribution of attachment theory to developmental psychopathology. In D. Cicchetti & D. Cohen (Eds.), *Developmental processes and psychopathology: Vol. 1. Theoretical perspectives and methodological approaches* (pp. 581–617). New York: Cambridge University Press.

Carr, L., Iacoboni, M., Dubeau, M., Mazziotta, J., & Lenzi, G. (2003). Neural mechanisms of empathy in humans: A relay from neural systems for imitation to limbic areas. *Proceedings of the National Academy of Sciences USA, 100*(9), 5497–5502.

Cassidy, J. (1994). Emotion regulation: Influences of attachment relationships. *Monographs of the Society for Research in Child Development, 59*(2–3, Serial No. 240), 2228–2249.

Cassidy, J., & Berlin, L. (1994). The insecure/ambivalent pattern of attachment: Theory and research. *Child Development, 65,* 971–991.

Chartrand, T., & Bargh, A. (1999). The chameleon effect: The perception–behavior link and social interaction. *Journal of Personality and Social Psychology, 76,* 893–910.

Davis, M., & Hadiks, D. (1990). Nonverbal behavior and client state changes during psychotherapy. *Journal of Clinical Psychology, 46,* 340–351.

De Wolff, M., & van Ijzendoorn, M. (1997). Sensitivity and attachment: A meta-analysis on parental antecedents of infant attachment. *Child Development, 68,* 571–591.

DeCasper, A., & Carstens, A. (1980). Contingencies of stimulation: Effects on learning and emotion in neonates. *Infant Behavior and Development, 9,* 19–36.

Demetri Friedman, D., Beebe, B., Jaffe, J., Ross, D., & Triggs, S. (2010). Microanalysis of 4-month infant vocal affect qualities and maternal postpartum depression. *Clinical Social Work Journal, 38,* 8–16.

Demetriades, H. (2003). Maternal anxiety and maternal spatial proximity in 4-month mother–infant face-to-face interaction. Doctoral Dissertation, L. I. U., C. W. Post Campus, Brookville, NY.

Dickstein, S., Thomson, R., Estes, D., Malkin, C., & Lamb, M. (1984). Social referencing and the security of attachment. *Infant Behavior and Development, 7,* 507–516.

Dimberg, U., Thunberg, M., & Elmehed, K. (2000). Unconscious facial reactions to emotional facial expressions. *American Psychological Society, 11,* 86–89.

Downing, G. (2004). Emotion, body and parent–infant interaction. In J. Nadel & D. Muir

(Eds.), *Emotional development: Recent research advances* (pp. 429–449). Oxford: Oxford University Press.

Downing, G. (2011). Uneasy beginnings: getting psychotherapy underway with the difficult patient. *Self psychology: European Journal for Psychoanalytic Therapy and Research, 44/45*, 207–233.

Dutra, L., Bureau, J., Holmes, B., Lyubchik, A., & Lyons-Ruth, K. (2009). Quality of early care and childhood trauma: A prospective study of developmental pathways to dissociation. *Journal of Nervous and Mental Disease, 197*(6), 383–390.

Eibl-Eibesfeldt, I. (1971). *Love and hate: A natural history of behavior patterns.* New York: Holt, Rinehart and Winston, Inc.

Eigen, M. (1993), *The Electrified Tightrope.* Northvale, NJ: Aronson.

Eisenberg, N., & Fabes, R. (1992). Emotion, regulation, and the development of social competence. In M. Clark (Ed.), *Emotion and social behavior: Review of personality and social psychology* (pp. 119–150). Thousand Oaks, CA: Sage.

Ekman, P., Levenson, R., & Friesen, W. (1983). Autonomic nervous system activity distinguishes among emotions. *Science, 221*, 1208–1210.

Emde, R., Birengen, Z., Clyman, R. B., & Oppenheim, D. (1991). The moral self of infancy: Affective core and procedural knowledge. *Developmental Review, 11*, 251–270.

Fagen, J., Morrongiello, B., Rovee-Collier, C., & Gekoski, M. (1984). Expectancies and memory retrieval in three-month-old infants. *Child Development, 55*, 936–943.

Fairbairn, R. (1952). Endopsychic structure considered in terms of object relationships. *Psychoanalytic Studies of the Personality* (pp. 82–132). London: Tavistock.

Fairbairn, R. W. D. (1958). On the nature and aims of psycho-analyticl treatment. *International Journal of Psychoanalysis, 39*: 374–385.

Feldman, R. (2007). Parent–infant synchrony and the construction of shared timing; physiological precursors, developmental outcomes and risk conditions. *Journal of Child Psychology and Psychiatry, 48*(3,4), 329–354.

Feldstein, S. (1998). Some nonobvious consequences of monitoring time in conversations. In G. Barnett (Series Ed.) & M. Palmer (Vol. Ed.), *Progress in Communication Sciences,* Vol. XIV (pp. 163–190). Norwood, NJ: Ablex.

Ferenczi, S. (1930). The principle of relaxation and neocatharsis. *The International Journal of Psychoanalysis, 11*, 428–443. Reprinted in *Final contributions to the problems and methods of psychoanalysis* (pp. 126–142). New York: Basic Books, 1955.

Field, T. (1981). Infant gaze aversion and heart rate during face-to-face interactions. *Infant Behavior and Development, 4*, 307–315.

Field, T. (1995). Infants of depressed mothers. *Infant Behavior and Development, 18*, 1–13.

Fogel, A. (1992). Co-regulation, perception and action. *Human Movement Science, 11*, 505–523.

Fonagy, P., Gergely, G., Jurist, E., & Target, M. (2002). *Affect regulation, mentalization and the development of the self.* New York: Other Press.

Fosshage, J. (2005). The explicit and implicit domains in psychoanalytic change. *Psychoanalytic Inquiry, 25*(4), 516–539.

Fraiberg, S. (1982). Pathological defenses in infancy. *Psychoanalytic Quarterly. 51*, 612–635.

Fraley, R. C. (2002). Attachment stability from infancy to adulthood: Meta-analysis and dynamic modeling of developmental mechanisms. *Personality and Social Psychology Review, 6*(2), 123–151.

Freedman, N., Barroso, F., Bucci, W., & Grand, S. (1978). The bodily manifestations of listening. *Psychoanalysis and Contemporary Thought, 1*, 156–194.

Gabbard, G. Miller, L., & Martinez, M. (2008). A neurobiological perspective on mental-izing and internal object relations in traumatized borderline patients. In E. L. Jurist, A. Slade, & S. Bergner (Eds.), *Mind to Mind: Infant Research, Neuroscience, and psycho-analysis*. New York: Other Press.

Gazzaniga, M., & LeDoux, J. (1978). *The integrated mind*. New York: Plenum.

Gergely, G., & Watson, J. (1996). The social biofeedback model of parental affect-mirroring. *International Journal of Psychoanalysis, 11*, 1181–1212.

Ghent, E. (1990). Masochism, submission, surrender – masochism as a perversion of surrender. *Contemporary Psychoanalysis, 26*, 108–136.

Gianino, A., & Tronick, E. (1988). The mutual regulation model: The infant's self and interactive regulation coping and defense. In T. Field, P. McCabe, & N. Schneiderman (Eds.), *Stress and coping* (pp. 47–68). Hillsdale, NJ: Lawrence Erlbaum.

Goldberg, A. (1983). Self psychology and alternative perspectives on internalization. In J. Lichtenberg & S. Kaplan (Eds.), *Reflections on self psychology* (pp. 297–312). Hillsdale, NJ: The Analytic Press.

Goldberg, S., Benoit, D., Blokland, K., & Madigan, S. (2003). Typical maternal behavior, maternal representations and infant disorganized attachment. *Development and Psycho-pathology, 15*, 239–257.

Gottlieb, G., Wahlsten, D., & Lickliter, R. (1998). The significance of biology for human development: A developmental psychobiological systems view. In W. Damon & R. Lerner (Eds.), *Handbook of child psychology*, Vol. 1 (5th ed., pp. 210–257). New York: Wiley.

Gottman, J., & Ringland, J. (1981). Analysis of dominance and bi-directionality in social development. *Child Development, 52*, 393–412.

Greenberg, J., & Mitchell, S. (1983). *Object relations in psychoanalytic theory*. Cambridge, MA: Harvard University Press.

Grigsby, J., & Hartlaub, G. (1994) Procedural learning and the development and stability of character. *Perceptual Motor Skills, 79*, 355–370.

Grossman, K. E., Grossmann, K., & Waters, E. (Eds.). (2005). *Attachment from infancy to adulthood: The major longitudinal studies*. New York: Guilford Press.

Grossmann, K. E., Grossmann, K., Winter, M., & Zimmermann, P. (2002). Attachment relationships and appraisal of partnership: From early experience of sensitive support to later relationship representation. In L. Pulkkinen & A. Caspi (Eds.), *Paths to successful development* (pp. 73–105). Cambridge: Cambridge University Press.

Hains, S., & Muir, D. (1996). Effects of stimulus contingency in infant-adult interactions. *Infant Behavior and Development, 19*, 49–61.

Haith, M., Hazan, C., & Goodman, G. (1988). Expectation and anticipation of dynamic visual events by 3.5 month old babies. *Child Development, 59*, 467–479.

Hane, A. A., Fox, N., Henderson, H., & Marshall, P. (2008). Behavioral reactivity and approach-withdrawal bias in infancy. *Developmental Psychology, 44*, 1491–1496.

Hatfield, E., Cacioppo, J., & Rapson, R. (1993). Emotional contagion. *Current Directions in Psychological Science, 2*, 96–99.

Hay, D. (1997). Postpartum depression and cognitive development. In L. Murray & P. Cooper (Eds.), *Postpartum depression and child development*. New York: Guilford Press.

Heller, M. (2012). *Body psychotherapy: History, concepts, and methods*. New York: W. W. Norton & Company.

Heller, M., & Haynal, V. (1997). A doctor's face: Mirror of his patient's suicidal projects. In J. Guimon (Ed.), *The body in psychotherapy*. Basel, Switzerland: Karger.

216

Hennelenlotter, A., Dresel, C., Castrop, F., Ceballos-Baumann, A., Wohlschlager, A., & Haslinger, B. (2008). The link between facial feedback and neural activity within central circuitries of emotion—New insights from botulinum toxin-induced denervation of frown muscles. *Cerebral Cortex, 19*(3), 537–542.

Hentel, A., Beebe, B., & Jaffe, J. (2000). Maternal depression at 6 weeks is associated with infant self-comfort at 4 months. International Conference on Infant Studies, Brighton, England, July.

Hodges, S., & Wegner, D. (1997). Automatic and controlled empathy. In W. Ickes (Ed.), *Empathic accuracy* (pp. 311–339). New York: Guilford Press.

Hoffman, I. (1998). *Ritual and spontaneity in the psychoanalytic process: A dialectical-constructivist view*. Hillsdale, NJ: The Analytic Press.

Holtz, P. (2004). The self- and interactive regulation and coordination of vocal rhythms, interpretive accuracy, and progress in brief psychodynamic psychotherapy. *Dissertation Abstracts International, 64*, 3526.

Hrdy, S. (2010). *Mothers and others, the evolutionary origins of mutual understanding*. Cambridge, MA: Belknap, Harvard University Press.

Jacobvitz, D., Hazen, N., & Riggs, S. (1997, April). Disorganized mental processes in mothers: Frightening/frightened caregiving and disoriented, disorganized behavior in infancy. Paper presented at the biennial meeting of the Society for Research in Child Development, Washington, DC.

Jaffe, J., Beebe, B., Feldstein, S., Crown, C., & Jasnow, M. (2001). Rhythms of dialogue in infancy. *Monographs of the Society for Research in Child Development, 66*(2, Serial No. 264), 1–132.

Jaffe, J., & Feldstein, S. (1970). *Rhythms of dialogue*. New York: Academic Press.

Kagan, J. (1997). Temperament and the reactions to unfamiliarity. *Child Development, 68*(1), 139–143.

Kendon, A. (1970). Movement coordination in social interaction: Some examples described. *ActaPsychologica, 32*, 101–125.

Knoblauch, S. (2000). *The musical edge of therapeutic dialogue*. Hillsdale, NJ: The Analytic Press.

Kohut, H. (1971). *The analysis of the self*. New York: International Universities Press.

Koos, O., & Gergely, G. (2001). A contingency-based approach to the etiology of "disorganized" attachment: The "flickering switch" hypothesis. *Bulletin of the Menninger Clinic, 65*, 397–410.

Kopp, C. (1989). Regulation of distress and negative emotions: A developmental view. *Developmental Psychology, 25*, 343–354.

Koulomzin, M., Beebe, B., Anderson, S., Jaffe, J., Feldstein, S., & Crown, C. (2002). Infant gaze, head, face, and self-touch at four months differentiate secure vs. avoidant attachment at one year: A microanalytic approach. *Attachment and Human Development. 4*, 3–24.

Kushnick, G. (2002). Maternal spatial intrusion patterns in mother–infant face-to-face play: Maternal dependency, depression, and mother–infant chase and dodge. Doctoral Dissertation, L. I. U., C. W. Post Campus, Brookville, NY.

Lachmann, F. (2000). *Transforming aggression: Psychotherapy with the difficult-to-treat patient*. Northvale, NJ: Jason Aronson.

Lachmann, F. (2008). *Transforming narcissism: Reflections on empathy, humor, and expectations*. New York: The Analytic Press.

Lachmann, F., & Beebe, B. (1996). Three principles of salience in the organization of the analyst–patient interaction. *Psychoanalytic Psychology, 13*, 1–22.

Levenson, R., Ekman, P., & Friesen, W. (1990). Voluntary facial action generates emotion-specific autonomic nervous system activity. *Psychophysiology, 27*, 363–384.

Lewis, M., Feiring, C., & Rosenthal, S. (2000). Attachment over time. *Child Development, 71*, 707–720.

Lewis, M., & Goldberg, S. (1969). Perceptual-cognitive development in infancy: A generalized expectancy model as a function of the mother–infant interaction. *Merrill Palmer Quarterly, 15*, 81–100.

Lewkowicz, D. (2000). The development of intersensory temporal perception: An epigenetic systems/limitations view. *Psychological Bulletin, 126*(2), 281–308.

Lickliter, R., & Bahrick, L. (2001). The salience of multimodal sensory stimulation in early development: Implications for the issue of ecological validity. *Infancy, 2*, 451–467.

Lieberman, J. (2000). *Body talk: Looking and being looked at in psychotherapy.* Northvale, NJ: Jason Aronson.

Liotti, G. (1992). Disorganized/disoriented attachment in the etiology of dissociative disorders. *Dissociation: Progress in the dissociative disorders, 5*(4), 196–204.

Llinas, R. (2001). *I of the vortex.* Cambridge, MA: MIT Press.

Loewald, H. (1962). Internalization, separation, mourning, and the superego. In *Papers in psychoanalysis* (pp. 257–276). New Haven: Yale University Press.

Lyons-Ruth, K. (1998a). Attachment disorganization: Unresolved loss, relational violence, and lapses in behavioral and attentional strategies. J. Cassidy & P. Shaver (Eds), *Handbook of attachment theory and research* (pp. 520–554). New York: Guilford Press.

Lyons-Ruth, K. (1998b). Implicit relational knowing: Its role in development and psychoanalytic treatment. *Infant Mental Health Journal, 19*, 282–291.

Lyons-Ruth, K. (1999). The two-person unconscious. *Psychoanalytic Inquiry, 19*, 576–617.

Lyons-Ruth, K. (2000). "I sense that you sense that I sense . . ." Sander's recognition process and the specificity of relational moves in the psychotherapeutic setting. *Infant Mental Health Journal, 21*, 85–98.

Lyons-Ruth, K. (2003). Dissociation and the parent–infant dialogue: A longitudinal perspective from attachment research. *Journal of the American Psychoanalytic Association, 51*(3), 883–911.

Lyons-Ruth, K. (2008). Contributions of the mother–infant relationship to dissociative, borderline, and conduct symptoms in young adulthood. *Infant Mental Health Journal, 29*(3), 203–218.

Lyons-Ruth, K., & Block, D. (1996). The disturbed caregiving system: Relations among childhood trauma, maternal caregiving, and infant affect and attachment. *Infant Mental Health Journal, 17*, 257–275.

Lyons-Ruth, K., Bronfman, E., & Parsons, E. (1999). Maternal disrupted affective communication, maternal frightened or frightening behavior, and disorganized infant attachment strategies. *Monographs of the Society for Research in Child Development, 64*(3, Serial No. 258).

Lyons-Ruth, K., Bureau, J., Holmes, B., Easterbrooks, M., & Henninghausen, K. (2011). Borderline features and suicidality/self-injury: Prospective and concurrent relationship correlates from infancy to young adulthood. Unpublished manuscript.

Lyons-Ruth, K., Dutra, L., Schuder, M., & Bianchi, I. (2006). From infant attachment disorganization to adult dissociation: Relational adaptations or traumatic experiences? *Psychiatric Clinics of North America, 29*, 63–86.

Lyons-Ruth, K., & Jacobvitz, D. (2008). Disorganized attachment: Genetic factors, parenting contexts, and developmental transformation from infancy to adulthood. In J. Cassidy

& P. Shaver (Eds.), *Handbook of attachment: Theory, research and clinical applications* (2nd ed., pp. 666–697). New York: Guilford Press.

Madigan, S., Bakermans-Kranenburg, M., van Ijzendoorn, M., Moran, G., Pederson, D., & Benoit, D. (2006). Unresolved states of mind anomalous parental behavior, and disorganized attachment: A review and meta-analysis of a transmission gap. *Attachment & Human Development, 8,* 89–111.

Main, M., & Hesse, E. (1990). Parents' unresolved traumatic experiences are related to infant disorganized attachment status: Is frightened and/or frightening parental behavior the linking mechanism? In M. Greenberg, D. Cicchetti, & E. Cummings (Eds.), *Attachment in the preschool years: Theory, research, and intervention* (pp. 161–182). Chicago: University of Chicago Press.

Main, M., Hesse, E., & Kaplan, N. (2005). Predictability of attachment behavior and representational processes at 1, 6, and 19 years of age. In K. E. Grossmann, K. Grosmann, & E. Waters (Eds.), *Attachment from infancy to adulthood: The major longitudinal studies.* New York, NY: Guilford Publications.

Main, M., Hesse, E., & Goldwyn, R. (2008). Studying differences in language usage in recounting attachment history: An introduction to the AAI. In H. Steele & M. Steele (Eds.), *Clinical application of the adult attachment interview* (pp. 31–68). New York: The Guilford Press.

Main, M., Kaplan, N., & Cassidy, J. (1985). Security in infancy, childhood, and adulthood: A move to the level of representation. In I. Bretherton & E. Waters (Eds.), Growing points in attachment theory and research. *Monographs of the Society for Research in Child Development, 50*(1–2, Serial No 209), 60–106.

Main, M., & Solomon, J. (1990). Procedures for identifying infants as disorganized/disoriented during the Ainsworth Strange Situation. In M. Greenberg, D. Cicchetti, & E. Cummings (Eds.), *Attachment in the preschool years* (pp. 121–160). Chicago: University of Chicago Press.

Malatesta, C., Culver, C., Tesman, J., & Shepard, B. (1989). The development of emotion expression during the first two years of life. *Monographs of the Society for Research in Child Development, 54*(1–2, Serial No. 219).

Mandler, J. (1988). How to build a baby: On the development of an accessible representation system. *Cognitive Development, 3,* 113–136.

Marquette, L. (1999). The relation of infants' and mothers' affective behavioral profiles to level of maternal depressive symptomatology. Doctoral Dissertation, New York University.

Meltzoff, A. (1985). The roots of social and cognitive development: Models of man's original nature. In T. Field & N. Fox (Eds.), *Social perception in infants* (pp. 1–30). Norwood, NJ: Ablex.

Meltzoff, A. (2007). Like me: A foundation for social cognition. *Developmental Science, 10*(1), 126–134.

Meltzoff, A., & Moore, M. (1998). Infant intersubjectivity: Broadening the dialogue to include imitation, identity and intention. In S. Braten (Ed.), *Intersubjective communication and emotion in early ontogeny* (pp. 47–62). Cambridge: Cambridge University Press.

Messinger, D. (2002). Positive and negative: Infant facial expressions and emotions. *Current Directions in Psychological Science, 11,* 1–6.

Messinger, D., Ruvolo, P., Ekas, N., & Fogel, A. (2010). Applying machine learning to infant interaction: The development is in the details. *Neural Networks, 23*(8–9), 1004–1016.

Miller, J. (1985). How Kohut actually worked. In A. Goldberg (Ed.), *Progress in self-psychology* (Vol. 1, p. 13–32). New York: Guilford Press.

Milner, M. (1952). The role of illusion in symbol formation. In M. Klein, P. Heinemann, & R. E. Money-Kyrie (Eds.), *New directions in psycho-analysis* (pp. 82–108). London: Tavistock.

Mitchell, S. (2000). *Relationality*, Hillsdale, NJ: The Analytic Press.

Murray, L., Fiori-Cowley, A., Hooper, R., & Cooper, P. (1996). The role of postnatal depression and associated adversity on early mother–infant interactions and later infant outcome. *Child Development, 67*, 2512–2526.

Murray, L., & Trevarthen, C. (1985). Emotional regulation of interactions between two-month- olds and their mothers. In T. Field & N. Fox (Eds.), *Social perception in infants* (pp. 177–197). Norwood, NJ: Ablex.

Nahum, J. (1994). New theoretical vistas in psychoanalysis: Louis Sander's theory of early development. *Psychoanalytic Psychology, 11*, 1–19.

Newtson, D. (1990). Alternatives to representation or alternative representations: Comments on the ecological approach. *Contemporary Social Psychology, 14*, 163–174.

Niedenthal, P., Mermillod, M., Maringer, M., & Hess, U. (2010). The Simulation of Smiles (SIMS) model: Embodied simulation and the meaning of facial expression. *Behavioral and Brain Sciences, 33*, 417–480.

Oberman, L., Winkielman, P., & Ramachandran, V. (2007). Face to face: Blocking facial mimicry can selectively impair recognition of emotional expressions. *Social Neuroscience, 2*(3–4), 167–178.

Ogawa, J., Sroufe, L., Weinfeld, N., Carlson, E., & Egeland, B. (1997). Development and the fragmented self: Longitudinal study of dissociative symptomatology in a nonclinical sample. *Development and Psychopathology, (9)*, 855–879.

Ogden, P., Minton, K. & Pain, C. (2006). *Trauma and the body: A sensorimotor approach to psychotherapy*. New York: Norton.

Ohman, A. (2002). Automaticity and the amygdala: Nonconscious responses to emotional faces. *Current Directions in Psychological Science, 11*, 62–66.

Ornstein, P. (1974) The dread to repeat and the new beginning: A contribution to the analysis of narcissistic personality disorders. *The annual of psychoanalysis*, Vol. 2 (pp. 231–248). New York: I. U. P.

Overton, W. F. (1994). Contexts of meaning: The computational and the embodied mind. In W. F. Overton & D. Palermo (Eds.), *The nature and ontogenesis of meaning* (pp. 1–18). Hillsdale, NJ: Erlbaum Associates.

Pally, R. (2000). *The mind–brain relationship*. London: Karnac Books.

Pally, R. (2005). A neuroscience perspective on *Forms of intersubjectivity in infant research and adult treatment.* In B. Beebe, S. Knoblauch, J. Rustin, & D. Sorter (Eds.), *Forms of intersubjectivity in infant research and adult treatment* (pp. 191–241). New York: Other Press.

Papousek, M. (1992). Early ontogeny of vocal communication in parent–infant interaction. In H. Papousek, U. Juergens, & M. Papousek (Eds.), *Nonverbal vocal communication* (pp. 230–261). New York: Cambridge University Press.

Peck, C. (2003). Measuring sensitivity moment-by-moment: A microanalytic look at the transmission of attachment. *Attachment and Human Development, 5*, 38–63.

Pederson, D., & Moran, G. (1996). Expressions of attachment relationship outside the strange situation. *Child Development, 67*, 915–927.

Pine, F. (1981). In the beginning: Contributions to a psychoanalytic developmental psychology. *International Review of Psychoanalysis, 8*, 15–33.

Porges, S. W., Doussard-Roosevelt, J. A., & Maiti, A. K. (1994). Vagal tone and the physiological regulation of emotion. *Monographs of the Society for Research in Child Development, 59*, 167–186.

Puig-Antich, J., & Chambers, W. (1978). *The schedule for affective disorders and schizophrenia for school-age children (Kiddie-SADS)*. New York: New York State Psychiatric Institute.

Rizzolatti, G., Fadiga, L., Fogassi, L., & Gallese, V. (1996). Premotor cortex and the recognition of motor actions. *Cognitive Brain Research, 3*, 131–141.

Ruesch, J., & Bateson, G. (1951). *Communication: The social matrix of psychiatry*. New York: Norton.

Rustin, J. (1997). Infancy, agency, and intersubjectivity. *Psychoanalytic Dialogues, 7*, 43–62.

Rustin, J. (2013). *Infant research and neuroscience at work in psychotherapy: Expanding the clinical repertoire*. New York: Norton.

Saffran, J., Aslin, R., & Newport, E. (1996). Statistical learning by 8-month-old infants. *Science, 274*, 1926–1928.

Sameroff, A. (1983). Developmental systems: Contexts and evolution. In W. Kessen (Ed.), *Mussen's handbook of child psychology*, Vol. 1 (pp. 237–294). New York: Wiley.

Sander, L. W. (1977). The regulation of exchange in the infant–caretaker system and some aspects of the context–content relationship. In M. Lewis & L. Rosenblum (Eds.), *Interaction, conversation, and the development of language* (pp. 133–156). New York: Wiley.

Sander, L. W. (1984). The Boston University Longitudinal Study—Prospect and retrospect after twenty five years. In J. Call, E. Galenson, & R. Tyson (Eds.), *Frontiers of infant psychiatry* (Vol. 2, pp. 137–145). New York: Basic Books.

Sander, L. W. (1995). Identity and the experience of specificity in a process of recognition. *Psychoanalytic Dialogues, 5*, 579–593.

Sander, L. W. (2002). Thinking differently: Principles of process in living systems and the specificity of being known. *Psychoanalytic Dialogues, 12*, 11–42.

Saunders, R., Jacobvitz, D., Zaccagnino, M., Beverung, L., & Hazen, N. (2011). Pathways to earned-security: The role of alternative support figures. *Attachment & Human Development, 13*:4, 403–420.

Schafer, R. (1968). *Aspects of internalization*. New York: International Universities Press.

Schore, A. (1994). *Affect regulation and the origin of the self: The neurobiology of emotional development*. Hillsdale, NJ: Lawrence Erlbaum Associates.

Schore, A. (2009). Attachment trauma and the developing right brain: Origins of pathological dissociation. In P. Dell & J. O'Neil (Eds.), *Dissociation and the dissociative disorders* (pp. 107–131). New York: Routledge.

Schore, A. (2011). Preface. In Bromberg, P., *The shadow of the tsunami and the growth of the relational mind* (p. ix – xxxvi). New York: Routledge.

Schuengel, C., Bakermans-Kranenburg, M., & van Ijzendoorn, M. (1999). Frightening maternal behavior linking unresolved loss and disorganized infant attachment. *Journal of Consulting and Clinical Psychology, 67*, 54–63.

Seligman, S. (2011). Review of Daniel Stern's "Forms of Vitality: Exploring Dynamic Experience in Psychology, the Arts, Psychotherapy, and Development." *Journal of the American Psychoanalytic Association. 59*(4), 859–868.

Seligman, S. (2012). The baby out of the bathwater: Microseconds, psychic structure, and psychotherapy. *Psychoanalytic Dialogues, 22*(4), 499–509.

Seligman, S. (in press). The experience of time: Trauma, non-responsive parenting and the vacuity of the future. *Psychoanalytic Dialogues.*

Seligman, S., & Harrison, A. (2011). Infant research and adult psychotherapy. In G. Gabbard, B. Litowitz, & P. Williams (Eds), *American Psychiatric Association textbook of psychoanalysis* (2nd ed., pp. 239–252). Washington, DC: American Psychiatric Publishing.

Shackman, J., & Pollak, S. (2005). Experiential influences on multimodal perception of emotion. *Child Development, 76,* 1116–1126.

Shi, Z., Bureau, J., Easterbrooks, M., Zhao, X., & Lyons-Ruth, K. (2012). Childhood maltreatment and prospectively observed quality of early care as predictors of antisocial personality disorder. *Infant Mental Health Journal, 33,* 1–14.

Shields, P., & Rovee-Collier, C. (1992). Long-term memory for context-specific category information at six months. *Child Development, 63,* 245–259.

Siegel, D. (1999). *The developing mind.* New York: The Guilford Press.

Siegel, D. (2012). *Pocket guide to interpersonal neurobiology.* New York: Norton.

Slade, A. (in press). Attachment, fear, and evolution: A paradigm shift for psychoanalysis. *Psychoanalytic Dialogues.*

Slavin, M. (2010). On recognizing the psychoanalytic perspective of the other: A discussion of "Recognition as: Intersubjective vulnerability in the psychoanalytic dialogue," by Donna Orange. *International Journal of Psychoanalytic Self Psychology, 5,* 274–292.

Slavin, M. (2011). Lullaby on the dark side: Existential anxiety, making meaning and the dialectic of self and other. In L. Aron & A. Harris (Eds.), *Relational psychoanalysis,* Vol. IV (pp. 391–413). New York: The Analytic Press.

Slavin, M. (2012). "Self as illusion—in patient and analyst: A discussion of Elizabeth Carr's 'You can call me Al.'" *International Conference on The Psychology of the Self,* Washington, DC, October 19, 2012.

Slavin, M., & Kriegman, D. (1992). *The adaptive design of the human psyche: Psychoanalysis, evolutionary biology, and the therapeutic process.* New York: Guilford Press.

Slavin, M., & Kriegman, D. (1998). Why the analyst needs to change: Toward a theory of conflict, negotiation and mutual influence in the therapeutic process. *Psychoanalytic Dialogues, 8*(2), 247–284.

Solomon, J., & George, C. (1999). The measurement of attachment security in infancy and childhood. In J. Cassidy & P. Shaver (Eds.), *Handbook of attachment: Theory, research and clinical applications* (pp. 287–316). New York: Guilford.

Sorter, D. (1996). Chase and dodge: An organization of experience. *Psychoanalysis and Psychotherapy, 13,* 68–75.

Spangler, G., & Grossman, K. (1993). Biobehavioral organization in securely and insecurely attached infants. *Child Development, 64,* 1439–1450.

Spiegel, D., & Cardeña, E. (1991). Disintegrated experience: The dissociative disorders revisited. *Journal of Abnormal Psychology, 100,* 366–378.

Spitz, R. (1963). The evolution of the dialogue. In M. Schur (Ed.), *Drives, affects and behavior,* Volume 2. New York: IUP.

Squire, L., & Cohen, N. (1985). Human memory and amnesia. In J. M. G. Lynch & N. Weinberger (Eds.), *Neurobiology of learning memory* (pp. 3–64). Guildford: New York.

Sroufe, L. A. (1983). Infant–caregiver attachment and patterns of adaptation in the preschool: The roots of maladaptation and competence. In M. Permutter, Ed., *Minnesota Symposia on Child Psychology* (pp. 41–79). Erlbaum Associates: Hillsdale, NJ.

Sroufe, L. A. (2005). Attachment and development: A prospective, longitudinal study from birth to adulthood. *Attachment and Human Development, 7*(4), 349–367.

Sroufe, L. A., Carlson, E., Levy, A., & Egeland, B. (1999). Implications of attachment theory for developmental psychopathology. *Development and Psychopathology, 11*, 1–13.

Sroufe, L. A., Egeland, B., Carlson, E., & Collins, W. (2005). Placing early attachment experiences in developmental context: The Minnesota Longitudinal Study. In K. Grossman, K. Grossmann, & E. Waters (Eds.), *Attachment from infancy to adulthood* (pp. 48–70). New York: Guilford Press.

Stack, D. (2001). The salience of touch and physical contact during infancy: Unraveling some of the mysteries of the somasthetic sense. In G. Bremner & A. Fogel (Eds.), *Blackwell handbook of infant development* (pp. 351–378). Malden, MA: Blackwell.

Steele, H., & Steele, M. (2008). Infant–mother attachment predicts accuracy in emotion judgments at 6 and 11 years. *Attachment and Human Development 10*, 379–394.

Stepakoff, S. (1999). Mother–infant tactile communication at four months: Infant gender, maternal ethnicity, and maternal depression, Doctoral Dissertation, St. Johns University.

Stepakoff, S., Beebe, B., & Jaffe, J. (2000). Mother–infant tactile communication at four months: Infant gender, maternal ethnicity, and maternal depression. International Conference on Infant Studies, Brighton, England, July.

Stern, D. (1971). A microanalysis of the mother–infant interaction. *Journal of the American Academy of Child Psychiatry, 10*, 501–507.

Stern, D. (1977). *The first relationship.* Cambridge, MA: Harvard University Press.

Stern, D. (1985). *The interpersonal world of the infant.* New York: Basic Books.

Stern, D. (1995). *The motherhood constellation.* New York: Basic Books.

Stern, D. (2010). *Forms of vitality: Exploring dynamic experience in psychology, the arts, psychotherapy and development.* Oxford and New York: Oxford University Press.

Stern, D., Hofer, L., Haft, W., & Dore, J. (1985). Affect attunement: The sharing of feeling states between mother and infant by means of intermodal fluency. In T. Field & N. Fox (Eds.), *Social perception in infants.* Norwood, NJ: Ablex.

Stern, D., Sander, L., Nahum, J., Harrison, A., Bruschweiler-Stern, N., & Tronick, E. (1998). Non-interpretative mechanisms in psychoanalytic therapy. *International Journal of Psychoanalysis, 79*, 903–921.

Stolorow, R. and Atwood, G. (1992). *Contexts of being.* Hillsdale, NJ: The Analytic Press.

Sullivan, H. (1940). *Conception of modern psychiatry.* New York: Norton.

Sullivan, H. (1953). *The interpersonal theory of psychiatry.* New York: Norton.

Sullivan, H. (1964). *The fusion of psychiatry and social science.* New York: Norton.

Tarabulsy, G., Tessier, R., & Kappas, A. (1996). Contingency detection and the contingent organization of behavior interactions: Implications for socioemotional development in infancy. *Psychological Bulletin, 120*, 25–41.

Taylor, C. (1991). *The ethics of authenticity.* Cambridge, MA: Harvard University Press.

Thelen, E., & Smith, L. (1994). *A dynamic systems approach to the development of cognition and action.* Cambridge, MA: MIT Press.

Thomas, E., & Malone, T. (1979). On the dynamics of two-person interactions. *Psychological Review, 86*, 331–360.

Thomas, E., & Martin, J. (1976). Analyses of parent–infant interaction. *Psychological Review, 83*(2), 141–155.

Tomlinson, M., Cooper, P., & Murray, L. (2005). The mother–infant relationship and infant attachment in a South African peri-urban settlement. *Child Development, 76*, 1044–1054.

Trevarthen, C. (1977). Descriptive analyses of infant communicative. In H. Schaffer (Ed.), *Studies in mother–infant interaction* (pp. 227–270). London: Academic Press.

Trevarthen, C. (1998). The concept and foundations of infant intersubjectivity. In S. Braten (Ed.), *Intersubjective communication and emotion in early ontogeny* (pp. 15–46). Cambridge, MA: Cambridge University Press.

Tronick, E. (1989). Emotions and emotional communication in infants. *American Psychologist, 44*, 112–119.

Tronick, E. (1998). Dyadically expanded states of consciousness and the process of theraputic change. *Infant Mental Health Journal, 19*(3), 290–299.

Tronick, E. (2007). *The neurobehavioral and social emotional development of infants and young children.* New York: Norton.

Tronick, E., & Weinberg, M. (1990). The infant regulatory scoring system. Unpublished manuscript, Children's Hospital, Harvard Medical School, Boston, MA.

vanIjzendoorn, M., Goldberg, S., Kroonenberg, P., & Frenkel, O. (1992). The relative effects of maternal and child problems on the quality of attachment: A meta-analysis of attachment in clinical samples. *Child Development, 63*, 840–858.

vanIjzendoorn, M., Schuengel, C., & Bakerman-Kranenburg, M. (1999). Disorganized attachment in early childhood: Meta-analysis of precursors, concomitants and sequelae. *Development and Psychopathology, 11*, 225–250.

Warner, R. (1992). Cyclicity of vocal activity increases during conversation: Support for a nonlinear systems model of dyadic social interaction. *Behavioral Science, 37*, 128–138.

Waters, E., Merrick, S., Treboux, D., Crowell, J., & Albersheim, L. (2000). Attachment security in infancy and early adulthood: A twenty-year longitudinal study. *Child Development, 7*, 684–689.

Watson, J. (1985). Contingency perception in early social development. In T. Field & N. Fox (Eds.), *Social perception in infants* (pp. 157–176). Norwood, NJ: Ablex.

Watzlawick, P., Beavin, J., & Jackson, D. (1967). Some tentative axioms of communication. In *Pragmatics of human communication: A study of interactional patterns, pathologies and paradoxes* (pp. 48–71). New York, NY: W. W. Norton & Company.

Weinberg, M. K., & Tronick, E. (1994). Beyond the face: An empirical study of infant affective configurations of facial, vocal, gestural, and regulatory behaviors. *Child Development, 65*, 1503–1515.

Weinberg, M. K. (1992). Sex differences in emotional expression and affective regulation in 6-month-old infants. *Pediatric Research, 32*(4), Part 2, 15A.

Weinberg, M. K., Tronick, E., Cohn, J., & Olson, K. (1999). Gender differences in emotional expressivity and self-regulation during early infancy. *Developmental Psychology, 35*, 175–188.

Weinfield, N., Whaley, G., & Egeland, B. (2004). Continuity, discontinuity, and coherence in attachment from infancy to late adolescence: Sequelae of organization and disorganization. *Attachment & Human Development, 6*(1), 2007.

Weiss, P. (1970). Whither life or science? *American Scientist, 8*, 156–163.

Werner, H. (1948). *The comparative psychology of mental development.* New York: International Universities Press.

White, R. (1959). Motivation reconsidered: The concept of effectance. *Psychological Review, 66*, 297–323.

Whitmer, G. (2001). On the nature of dissociation. *Psychoanalytic Quarterly, 70*, 807–837.

REFERENCES

Winnicott, D. (1965). *The maturational processes and the facilitating environment.* New York: International Universities Press.

Winnicott, D. W. (1960). The theory of the parent–infant relationship. In: *The Maturational Processes and the Facilitating Environment.* NY: IUP, pp. 37–55.

Wolf, N., Gales, M., Shane, E., & Shane, M. (2001). The development trajectory from a modal perception to empathy and communication: The role of mirror neurons in this process. *Psychoanalytic Inquiry, 21,* 94–112.

INDEX

action knowledge 139, 143, 147–8, 153–4
action–dialogues 3, 21, 30, 32, 70, 71, 83–4
Adult Attachment Interview 110
adult treatment 70–93; affect regulation in 78–9, 80–3, 191; dissociation in 67–9; distressed states 151–5; implicit, procedural communication in 143, 144, 147–9; knowing and being known 78–80, 169–71, 172–6; nonconscious procedural dimension of face-to-face communication 70–4; relational patterns of origins of disorganized attachment 77–80, 169–71, 172–6; self- and interactive contingency in face-to-face communication 74–7, 141–4; video feedback consultations 83–92; *see also* case vignettes; psychotherapy
affect: discrepant affect 53, 121, 122, 145–6, 155; dyadic affective conflict 38, 122–6, 160–2, 167–8; embodied simulation 72–3, 129, 153–4; heightened affective moments 38, 121, 122; interactive contingency of 51–2, 100; maternal emotional sensitivity 6, 7, 144–5; *see also* facial affect; sensing the state of the other; vocal affect
affect attunement 28, 35
affect contagion 29
affect regulation 147, 195; in adult treatment 78–9, 80–3, 191; infant dysregulation 55, 117–18, 177; maternal dysregulation 55–6, 118, 124–6, 166–7
agency *see* expectancies
Ainsworth, M. *et al. see* Strange Situation
alarm, infant signs of 155
approach–avoid pattern *see* chase and dodge

attention: coding 43; contingency of 100; in depression 51; in future disorganized dyads 55, 116–17, 122–3; in future resistant dyads 105; in future secure dyads 100; joint attention 76, 91; regulation in adult treatment 78
Atwood, G. 29

Badalamenti, A. 75
Balint, M. 29
Bateson, G. *et al.* 161
Beebe, B. *et al.* 34, 44, 49, 75, 110, 142, 154, 165, 166, 174, 190, 192, 194, 205
behavioral qualities 40, 96–7; coding of ordinalized behavioral scales 52, 197–9; definitions of behavioral extremes 209–10; of future disorganized dyads 124–5, 133–4; of future resistant dyads 105, 124–5; measures of 43, 52–3, 96; self-regulation 50
Benjamin, J. 26, 69
Berlin, L. 104, 106, 108, 110
Bernstein, E. 62
Bloom, L. xviii
Bowlby, J. 29, 35, 166
Bretherton, I. 107
Bromberg, P. 69
Bucci, W. 3, 24, 69, 73, 75, 148

Cardeña, E. 63
Carlson, E. 65–6
case vignettes 80, 92–3; 80 year old man 80–3, 148; Chloe 177–87; Daniel 154; Dolores 83–7, 142–3, 148, 154; Noah 164–5, 166, 167–8; Oliver 172–6; Paulina 151–2; Sandra 79, 88–92, 148
Cassidy, J. 104, 106, 108, 110

226